PRECARITY IN CONTEMPORARY LITERATURE AND CULTURE

PRECARITY IN CONTEMPORARY LITERATURE AND CULTURE

Edited by
Emily J. Hogg and Peter Simonsen

BLOOMSBURY ACADEMIC
LONDON • NEW YORK • OXFORD • NEW DELHI • SYDNEY

BLOOMSBURY ACADEMIC
Bloomsbury Publishing Plc
50 Bedford Square, London, WC1B 3DP, UK
1385 Broadway, New York, NY 10018, USA
29 Earlsfort Terrace, Dublin 2, Ireland

BLOOMSBURY, BLOOMSBURY ACADEMIC and the Diana logo are trademarks of
Bloomsbury Publishing Plc

First published in Great Britain 2021
Paperback edition published 2023

Copyright © Emily J. Hogg and Peter Simonsen and Contributors, 2021

Emily J. Hogg and Peter Simonsen and Contributors have asserted their right under the
Copyright, Designs and Patents Act, 1988, to be identified as Authors of this work.

For legal purposes the Acknowledgements on p. x–xi constitute an extension
of this copyright page.

Cover design by Jade Barnett
Cover image © David Wall / Getty Images

All rights reserved. No part of this publication may be reproduced or transmitted
in any form or by any means, electronic or mechanical, including photocopying,
recording, or any information storage or retrieval system, without prior
permission in writing from the publishers.

Bloomsbury Publishing Plc does not have any control over, or responsibility for, any
third-party websites referred to or in this book. All internet addresses given in this
book were correct at the time of going to press. The author and publisher regret
any inconvenience caused if addresses have changed or sites have ceased
to exist, but can accept no responsibility for any such changes.

A catalogue record for this book is available from the British Library.

A catalog record for this book is available from the Library of Congress.

ISBN: HB: 978-1-3501-6670-7
PB: 978-1-3502-3531-1
ePDF: 978-1-3501-6671-4
eBook: 978-1-3501-6672-1

Typeset by Deanta Global Publishing Services, Chennai, India

To find out more about our authors and books visit www.bloomsbury.com and
sign up for our newsletters.

CONTENTS

List of figures	vii
List of contributors	viii
Acknowledgements	x

INTRODUCTION   1
Emily J. Hogg

Part One
FEELING

Chapter 1
ANXIOUS READING: THE PRECARITY NOVEL AND THE
AFFECTIVE CLASS   27
   Liam Connell

Chapter 2
ANXIETY IN THE PRECARIAT: THE AFFECTS OF CLASS IN JAMES
KELMAN'S FICTION   42
   Mathies G. Aarhus

Chapter 3
PERFORMING PRECARITY: THREATENING THE AUDIENCE IN GARY
OWEN'S *IPHIGENIA IN SPLOTT*   56
   Peter Simonsen

Part Two
BODIES

Chapter 4
IMAGINED SOVEREIGNTY: MAPPING AND RESISTING PRECARITY IN
INDIRA ALLEGRA'S *WOVEN ACCOUNT*   75
   Marianne Kongerslev

Chapter 5
PRECARIOUS BODIES ON THE MOVE, PRECARIOUS BODIES UNDER
ATTACK   91
   Katharina Pewny and Tessa Vannieuwenhuyze

Chapter 6
DEATH KNELLS AND DEAD ENDS: LATENT FUTURITY IN MASANDE NTSHANGA'S *THE REACTIVE* AND MOHALE MASHIGO'S 'GHOST STRAIN N'   109
    Sophy Kohler

Part Three
TIME

Chapter 7
PERIODIZATION AND PRECARIOUS LABOUR: THE WORK OF GENRE IN *LA LA LAND* AND *SORRY TO BOTHER YOU*   127
    Alissa G. Karl

Chapter 8
SUBSTANCELESS SUBJECTIVITY: FROM PROLETARIANIZATION TO PRECARIZATION IN BRITISH EXPERIMENTAL FICTION   143
    Benjamin Kohlmann

Chapter 9
THE FUTURE IS A GHOST: PRECARITY, ANTICIPATION AND RETROSPECTION IN ANNELIESE MACKINTOSH'S 'LIMITED DREAMERS' AND LEE ROURKE'S *VULGAR THINGS*   160
    Emily J. Hogg

Chapter 10
MAKE IT NOW: POETRY, PRECARITY AND SECURITY IN JORIE GRAHAM AND GHAYATH ALMADHOUN   176
    Walt Hunter

Chapter 11
FINDING TIME IN COMMON: SPECULATIVE FICTION AND THE PRECARIAT IN ROBINSON'S *NEW YORK 2140*   189
    Bryan Yazell

Index   203

FIGURES

5.1 *Misplaced Women?* Project (2009–20). Dedicated to the missing and murdered indigenous women in Canada. Performed by Tanja Ostojić   96
5.2 *Misplaced Women?* Project (2009–20). 'Which Colonial Comfort Would You Like to Consume Today?' Performed by Rhea Ramjohn   99
7.1 Cash in his cubicle in *Sorry to Bother You*, directed by Boots Riley   128
7.2 Overpass choreography in 'Another Day of Sun,' in *La La Land*, directed by Damien Chazelle   128

CONTRIBUTORS

Mathies G. Aarhus is a postdoc in literature at the University of Southern Denmark. His research interests include affect theory, social class and gender in British, American and Scandinavian literature.

Liam Connell teaches literature at the University of Brighton. He is the author of *Precarious Labour and the Contemporary Novel* (2017) and the editor of *Literature and Globalization: A Reader* (2010).

Emily J. Hogg is Associate Professor of contemporary anglophone literature in the Department for the Study of Culture, University of Southern Denmark. Her research focuses on contemporary literature's social uses in relation to human rights, gender inequality, alcohol and precarity, and has appeared or is forthcoming in *English Studies, Textual Practice* and *Criticism*, among other venues.

Walt Hunter is Associate Professor of world literature at Clemson University. He is the author of *Forms of a World: Contemporary Poetry and the Making of Globalization* (2019) and the co-translator, with Lindsay Turner, of Frédéric Neyrat's *Atopias: Manifesto for a Radical Existentialism* (2017).

Alissa G. Karl is Associate Professor of English at the State University of New York, Brockport. She is the author of *Modernism and the Marketplace* (2009) and co-editor of *Neoliberalism and the Novel* (2015), and her work has appeared in venues including *Novel, American Literature, Textual Practice* and *Modern Fiction Studies*. Her research investigates the relationships between economics, labour and cultural and literary forms in the twentieth and twenty-first centuries.

Sophy Kohler is a PhD student in the Department for the Study of Culture at the University of Southern Denmark, where she is part of a research group formed around Rita Felski's *Uses of Literature*. She has an MA in literature and modernity from the University of Cape Town.

Benjamin Kohlmann teaches English literature at the University of Regensburg, Germany. He is the author of two monographs, *Committed Styles: Modernism, Politics, and Left-Wing Literature in the 1930s* (2014) and *Speculative States: British Literature, Institutionality, and the Idea of the State* (forthcoming). His most recent articles on the intersections between literature and politics have been published in *ELH*, *PMLA* and *NOVEL*. With Matthew Taunton he has recently co-edited *A History of 1930s British Literature* (2019).

Marianne Kongerslev is Assistant Professor of US literature and cultural studies at Aalborg University, Denmark. She has carried out research on Native American literature, US popular culture, feminisms/gender studies and critical race studies. In 2018, she started researching spite and precarity in US literatures and culture, in a project funded by the Carlsberg Foundation.

Katharina Pewny is a Berlin-based yoga teacher with a specialization in inclusive and accessible practice. From 2009 to 2019 she served as Professor of Performance Studies at Ghent University. Her current research interests are the ethics of spirituality and/in movement studies. With Yana Meerzon she edited the collection *Dramaturgy of Migration: Staging Multicultural Encounters in Contemporary Theatre* (2020). Her anthology on 'the drama of the precarious' (*Das Drama des Prekären*) (2011) was the first study on precarity in theatre and performance within the German-speaking contexts.

Peter Simonsen is Professor of European literature at the Department for the Study of Culture, University of Southern Denmark. He has researched, published, taught and disseminated widely in fields such as Wordsworth studies, British romanticism, book history, literary and cultural gerontology, Scandinavian literatures and the welfare state as well as literary studies in the precariat.

Tessa Vannieuwenhuyze is a doctoral researcher with a specific interest in the theatrical presence of music performers. Currently she is preparing PhD research on how these musical personae interact with dimensions of precarious identity within our contemporary context of social media performance and new technologies. After studying art history, musicology and theatre studies at Ghent University and the Free University of Berlin, she obtained an advanced master's degree in literature studies from KU Leuven. She also dramaturgically assists the contemporary operatic performances of multidisciplinary arts company OYSTER and writes for several cultural platforms.

Bryan Yazell is an Assistant Professor in the Department for the Study of Culture and the Danish Institute for Advanced Study at the University of Southern Denmark. With assistance from the Danish National Research Foundation (grant no. DNRF127), his research focuses on the various ways that literary sources inform public debates regarding social welfare and migration in the United States. Examples of this work appear in *Modern Fiction Studies*, *The Journal of Transnational American Studies* and *Configurations*.

ACKNOWLEDGEMENTS

The editing of this book, the workshop at which it originated, our work package focused on class and precarity, and the writing of Chapters 2, 3, 6, 9 and 11 were all generously funded by the Danish National Research Foundation, grant number DNRF127.

For their intellectual engagement and practical support, we are grateful to all of our colleagues in the Uses of Literature project at the University of Southern Denmark, especially Rita Felski, Anne-Marie Mai, Klaus Petersen and Pernille Hasselsteen.

Particular thanks are due to members of the social class and precarity work package, past and present, particularly Jon Helt Haarder, Camilla Schwartz, Patrick Fessenbecker and the book's contributors Bryan Yazell, Sophy Kohler and Mathies G. Aarhus, for productive discussions about precarity and contemporary literature, and for practical help with the editing of early versions of the chapters included here.

We also thank all of our colleagues in the Department for the Study of Culture at the University of Southern Denmark for providing a supportive and stimulating environment for this research.

Precarity in Contemporary Literature and Culture began with a workshop called 'The Precariat in Art and Culture' at the University of Southern Denmark in September 2018, and we are grateful to all the participants at that workshop for their contributions and for deepening and extending our understanding of precarity. In the subsequent development of the book manuscript, we have been greatly helped by Bloomsbury Academic, and we thank Lucy Brown for her enthusiasm and interest in the project, and for ensuring such a smooth and efficient publication process. The perceptive and encouraging feedback of the book's anonymous reviewers has also been of significant help to us and has strengthened the book considerably. We thank them for their work. Finally, we would like to express our thanks to the book's contributors for the commitment and energy they have brought to this collaborative project: it has been a pleasure to work with and learn from them.

Sections from the Introduction were originally published in Emily J. Hogg and Peter Simonsen, 'The potential of precarity? Imagining vulnerable connection in Chris Dunkley's *The Precariat* and Amy Liptrot's *The Outrun.*' *Criticism: a Quarterly for Literature and the Arts*, vol. 62, no. 1, 2020, pp. 1–28. Sections from Chapter 5 ('Precarious Bodies on the Move, Precarious Bodies Under Attack') were published in an earlier version in Katharina Pewny, 'Performing the Precarious:

Economic Crisis in European and Japanese theatre.' *Forum Modernes Theater*, vol. 26, no. 1–2, 2011, pp. 43–52. Sections from Chapter 8 ('Substanceless Subjectivity: From Proletarianization to Precarization in British Experimental Fiction') were originally published in Benjamin Kohlmann, 'Sounding the Present: Crisis and Collective Voice in David Peace's *GB84*', *English Literary History*, vol. 87, no. 3, 2020, pp. 829–54.

INTRODUCTION

Emily J. Hogg

From temporary work contracts to imminent environmental catastrophe, from state violence to pervasive anxiety, in recent years a diverse range of experiences and affects have been analysed using the cluster of related terms 'precarity', 'precariousness' and 'the precariat'. These terms have moved flexibly across activist, media and academic discourses, and, perhaps unsurprisingly, in making these moves they have transformed, taking on new meanings and shedding others. For the economist Guy Standing, a new social class – the precariat – is emerging today, composed of workers who lack the multiple forms of employment security won by twentieth-century labour movements. For philosopher Judith Butler, precarity is the inescapable vulnerability of social being as it is organized, distributed and hierarchized by contemporary neoliberal capitalism. Meanwhile, anthropologist Maribel Casas-Cortés argues that it was the very adaptability of the term 'precarity' that enabled it to become central to EuroMayDay – the flowering of protests against insecure work and securitized borders that began in Italy and spread throughout Europe and to Canada and Japan in the early 2000s. She describes precarity as a 'toolbox concept': not a 'perfect analytical description of current transformations', but rather a 'point of departure' – something that is currently available to be taken up and used (221). In her view, the term's descriptive precision – the extent to which it explains actually existing social reality – is less important than the way it is put to work by individuals and groups in order to contribute to the reshaping of those social realities.

Despite this emphasis on adaptability, however, the usefulness and relevance of precarity and its related concepts have been widely questioned.[1] Especially persuasive critiques ask whether there is anything *new* about experiences of insecurity and instability produced by capitalism. 'Precarity' may only seem like a distinctively contemporary phenomenon for those in the Global North privileged enough to have become accustomed to the so-called standard employment relationship during the relatively brief, and historically exceptional, period of the post-war consensus. Has the flurry of attention associated with the concept of precarity tended to obscure long, entrenched global histories of poverty and exclusion, disguising inequality and hierarchy through claims of shared, universal vulnerability? Should we distinguish precarity from broader and more fundamental notions of vulnerability – and if so, how? Are we all precarious – and what are the risks of making such universalizing gestures?

In this book, precarity, precariousness and the precariat are – in Casas-Cortés' words – theoretical departure points for the contributors, who align themselves with different conceptual approaches and define the key terms in different ways. Some chapters, such as Chapter 8, 'Substanceless subjectivity: From proletarianization to precarization in British experimental fiction', by Benjamin Kohlmann, and Chapter 7, 'Periodization and precarious labour: The work of genre in *La La Land* and *Sorry to Bother You*', by Alissa G. Karl, employ textual readings to robustly interrogate prominent theorizations of precarity. Others, like Chapter 11, 'Finding time in common: Speculative fiction and the precariat in Robinson's *New York 2140*', by Bryan Yazell, argue that examining cultural texts can help to illustrate prevailing discussions of precarization, providing insights that strengthen and extend current theoretical accounts. The book therefore represents a critical examination of the various dimensions of precarity theory; the cluster of related terms are variously clarified, expanded, critiqued and rethought in the chapters that follow, as the contributors consider the extent to which notions of precarity help to explain and describe the contemporary moment, and weigh up competing conceptualizations of precarious life.

As a whole, the book argues that vulnerability and insecurity, as they are experienced at work, in lack of access to state benefits and healthcare, in housing crisis, and in brutal anti-migrant policies, are central topics in the contemporary moment, and require urgent investigation. Secondly, it proposes that literary, cultural and artistic texts can be a crucial resource for thinking through these issues. The chapters reveal that a diverse range of recent cultural texts – from Hollywood films to experimental performance pieces, from realist novels to science fiction, from poetry to plays – can help to negotiate the ongoing debates over precarity, precariousness and the precariat and contribute to the critical examination of the concepts' relevance and significance. At the same time, the contributors show how thinking with notions of precarity can also illuminate the texts they explore. Bringing various precarity theories to bear on these diverse cultural forms produces new interpretations, allowing a variety of texts in different genres and produced in different geographical contexts to be placed into dialogue.

Precarity in Contemporary Literature and Culture, therefore, tracks some of the multiple ways that contemporary culture and the precarity concept can elucidate each other, proposing that reading notions of precarity through and with contemporary cultural forms can generate new insights into both. The book aims, in particular, to describe the points of connection between theories of precarity and modes of literary and cultural expression in relation to three key, interrelated themes: feeling, bodies and time. It makes the case that these three themes are crucial to the theorization of precarity, and shows that literary and cultural texts, by virtue of their ability to represent and reconfigure feeling, bodily experience and temporality, are ideally situated to explore these themes. In this introduction, I set the scene for the chapters that follow by providing an overview of the contours of the debate on precarity as it has played out to date. I highlight some of the main definitions of the key terms while also identifying some of the limitations of current theoretical discussions, and I show how this book seeks to intervene in these ongoing debates. I describe how the themes of feelings, bodies and time emerge from contemporary theorizations of precarity, show why they are significant to the ongoing attempt to work out what precarity is and why the concept matters, and indicate the approaches the chapters take to address these central themes.

Defining precarity, the precariat and precariousness

The root of the connected words 'precarity', 'precariat' and 'precariousness' is, as Katharina Pewny and Tessa Vannieuwenhuyze point out in this volume, the Latin verb 'precare', meaning 'to beg' (91). According to the *Oxford English Dictionary*, the Latin '*precārius*' indicates something 'given as a favour' or 'depending on the favour of another' ('Precarious, Adj.'). Liam Connell notes in this book that the word 'precarious' was first used in English in the seventeenth century and tended to refer to insecure tenancy rights ('Anxious Reading,' 27). In France, sociologists have been using the word 'prècaritè' since the 1970s to describe the effect of new employment conditions, but the topic received particular attention in the work of Robert Castel and Pierre Bourdieu in the late 1990s. Bourdieu highlights the rise of job insecurity, characterized by increasing numbers of 'temporary, part-time and casual positions' (82) and the high rate of unemployment. From changes to the way work is organized, Bourdieu traces a series of accumulating and increasingly drastic effects. The key issue he draws attention to is the effect of insecure employment on individual subjectivity and on the possibility of collective action: the issue is not simply casualization itself, but the unsettling and disorienting effect that casualization has, which spreads out far beyond the labour situation. Casualization, he writes, 'profoundly affects the person who suffers it' (82). In particular, 'by making the whole future uncertain, it prevents all rational anticipation'. This produces 'the destructuring of existence', and the 'deterioration of the whole relationship to the world, time and space' (82).[2] Moreover, these effects do not only relate to the casualized employee herself, but also percolate out through society. 'Objective insecurity gives rise to a generalized subjective insecurity which is now affecting all workers in our highly developed economy' (83); 'the awareness of it never goes away: it is present at every moment in everyone's mind [. . .] It pervades both the conscious and the unconscious mind' (82).

For Bourdieu, then, 'prècaritè' denotes the radical disorientation, uncertainty and loss of meaning that is caused by the new forms of flexible, casualized labour associated with neoliberalism: it is viewed as an inherently and overwhelmingly negative subjective experience of future loss and confusion produced directly by changing patterns of employment. In his account, precarity operates as 'mode of domination' (85): a means of control and expression of power that systematically undermines workers' capacity to rebel. However, many more recent accounts of precarity have also attempted to identify its potentials and possibilities, while consistently critiquing the harm it causes. One source of inspiration for this turn to guarded optimism – referenced by numerous theorists with various conceptual orientations, including Lauren Berlant, Guy Standing and Isabell Lorey – is the EuroMayDay movement: an innovative and transnational form of collective action in the early 2000s which centrally employed the concept of precarity. EuroMayDay was significant because it demonstrated the purchase that the concept of precarity could have on actual political life – not as a speculation, nor as a possible opening for the future, but in dynamic, actual, grassroots protest.

From its origins in Italy in 2001, the EuroMayDay movement staged protests against precarity in European cities including Milan, Barcelona, Hamburg, Copenhagen, Paris and Seville-Málaga (Marchart). The movement was engaged in processes of redefinition on multiple fronts. It tried to create forms of European political community that could serve as alternatives to the often bureaucratic and undemocratic institutions of the European Union, and which would welcome migration and oppose the anti-migrant politics associated with the protection of 'Fortress Europe' – the heavy securitization of the EU's external borders (Doerr and Mattoni). In one EuroMayDay poster, two statements appeared in parallel at the top left and right corners: 'no borders' and 'no precarity' (EuroMayDay Poster – Tactical Media Files). At the same time, staging its protests on May Day, EuroMayDay also sought to challenge and refigure understandings of labour prevalent in the labour movement itself. It reacted against the perceived inability of traditional unions to come to terms with the changing conditions of work in the twenty-first century, especially what Casas-Cortés describes as the unions' 'nostalgic position, [. . .] mired in a mythical labour stability the young had never experienced' (209). As it protested the exploitation associated with the neoliberal doctrine of flexibilization, it was also opposed to uncritical valorizations of security, noting the way that ideals of protection could be invoked to support nationalist, anti-migrant politics and reinforce normative conceptions of wage labour. The 2010 'Middlesex Declaration of the European Precariat' called for 'angry temps, disgruntled part-timers and union activists to mobilize against precarity and inequality to reclaim flexibility from managers and bureaucrats, thus securing flexicurity against flexploitation' (n.p.). It was not flexibility itself that EuroMayDay critiqued – instead, it sought to reclaim the promise and progressive potential of the concept from its capture by regimes of neoliberal labour.

EuroMayDay was a very short-lived phenomenon; as Neilson and Rossiter note, it began in 2001 and 'had entered a crisis by 2006' (53). At this point, the academic dissection of the movement has been a much lengthier phenomenon than the movement itself; in fact, they argue, 'the emergence of precarity as an object of academic analysis corresponds with its decline as a political concept motivating social movement activity' (53). However, in conceptual terms, Casas-Cortés writes, EuroMayDay was significant because it 'contributed [. . .] to shifting [precarity's] meaning toward a certain ambiguity, denouncing its consequences but also showing many of its potentialities' (210). In *The New Spirit of Capitalism*, Luc Boltanski and Eve Chiapello show that capitalism endures by transforming itself, especially in response to those who critique it. Neoliberal flexibility is, in their account, a response to critiques of work made in the counterculture of the 1960s and 1970s, when prevailing patterns of employment were often derided as conformist, mind-numbingly dull and deathly to independence and creativity. What neoliberal work offers, in theory, is greater freedom (the freedom to take on different temp contracts or work flexibly in the gig economy without being tied down to a fixed schedule) and opportunity for creativity (as demonstrated by the rise of immaterial labour, and the rise in the proportion of the workforce whose roles require communication and independent, original thought). EuroMayDay, in its call to reclaim 'flexicurity' from 'flexploitation' ('The Middlesex Declaration of the European Precariat' n.p.) attempted to make a critique of precarity that nonetheless recognized the real needs and desires that this neoliberal ideology of flexibility appealed to. Precarity thus emerged as an ambivalent experience – one to be protested against at the same time as it held the potential for reclaiming a degree of freedom.

This sense that new political potential inheres within the crisis of precarious living is something that runs through much of the theoretical work that has followed. In his 2011 book *The Precariat: The New Dangerous Class*, Guy Standing argues that the precariat might turn to nativism and anger in order to express its discontent but might also become a radical political subject with the ability to secure progressive change. For him, the precariat as a class includes the temporary workers Bourdieu and other French sociologists refer to, but it is also a broader category. Standing argues workers from across the globe are part of the precariat if they lack seven specific forms of labour security, which were – he argues – guaranteed to workers during the labour-capital compromise associated with industrial capitalism. This group can be understood as a *class* in his account because of its distinctive relations of production (in particular, the precariat experiences insecure and temporary employment), relations of distribution (because its members are highly reliant on money wages rather than employment-related benefits) and relations with the state (because its members lack many welfare state protections, such as the labour rights associated with unionized industry). In addition, Standing states that the precariat has 'a peculiar *status* position, in not mapping neatly on to high status professional or middle-status craft occupations' (14). Despite these shared interests, Standing argues that the precariat is not yet conscious of itself as a class, though it is this class-consciousness that is essential to producing social change. There is no guarantee that it will develop; members of the precariat might eschew class solidarity for more divisive forms of political commitment, such as racist and anti-immigrant politics.

The idea that the precariat constitutes a new class has been widely criticized. Ronaldo Munck points out that Standing's definitions of the precariat's class status tend to be negative; that is, Standing describes the precariat in terms of 'what it is not – a mythical, stable working class with full social and political rights – and by its vague feelings of anomie and distance from the orthodox labour movement' (752). The question that remains under-examined in this tendency towards negative definition, according to Standing's critics, is whether the precariat's experience of insecure labour means that it has relations of production that are so different from those of other classes that it possesses antagonistic interests and a distinctive role in the reproduction of the social system. Francesco Di Bernado maintains that it is 'conceptually misguided to define precarity as a new condition characterizing a new social class', because 'precariousness is instead quite simply the condition of the working class under capitalism. It always has been, and it always will be' (np). Indeed, even on Standing's own account, the precariat's class identity is still rather more potential than real. Consequently, one of the questions this book explores is what kind of collective subject the precariat is, or might be: What are the conditions for its emergence *as a group*? In Chapter 1, Liam Connell shows how literature can help produce an affective class, as Lauren Berlant describes this notion, while Chapter 2, by Mathies G. Aarhus, uses a close reading of James Kelman's novel *You Have to Be Careful in the Land of the Free* (2004) to caution that the differential distribution of anxiety stymies working-class solidarity.

What links Bourdieu and Standing, despite the latter's emphasis on the precariat as a distinct social class, is that – as Kathleen Millar notes – they both 'place labor at the center of their conceptualization of precarity' (4). Yet a number of critics have questioned the way that theorizations of precarity tend to focus on the relationship between capital and labour as the primary site for the emergence of new political subjectivities. Angela McRobbie argues that theorizations of immaterial labour and precarity focus on the workplace in a way that erases the more multidimensional views of politics, struggle and identity that have developed from gender and race studies over the past thirty years. Centring class identity and the site of the workplace as the foundations of a new radical politics, she argues, indicates a nostalgia for older forms of masculinized industry and obscures other locations for the development of political consciousness and collective struggle which might be more relevant for women, such as 'schooling for their children, nursery provision, health provision, care for the elderly, crime, improvements in social housing, breast cancer awareness, environment, pressure group politics etc' (69). Silvia Federici, similarly, suggests that there is a tendency in recent theorizations of precarious affective and immaterial work to focus on wage labour in a way that ignores a central feminist insight: that the work of social reproduction is unwaged and yet absolutely central to capitalism.

An alternative approach to the notion of precarity, grounded in feminist politics, can be found in Judith Butler's post-9/11 writings. Butler began to use the term 'precariousness' to refer to unavoidable vulnerability of social existence – 'the fact that one's life is always in some sense in the hands of the other', as she puts it (*Frames* 14). Precariousness in this sense names an understanding of the body and human social relations that is opposed to the 'dominant ontological understanding of the embodied subject' – a 'masculinist' one in which dependence on others is disavowed and unacknowledged ('Rethinking' 21). This is a fantasy in which 'nothing acts on me against my will or without my advanced knowledge', a 'posture of control over the property that I have and that I am' ('Rethinking' 24). To think of the embodied subject as sovereign and separate in this way is, Butler maintains, a profound mistake. She states that 'part of what a body is [...] is its dependency on other bodies and networks of support' ('Bodily Vulnerability' 103).

The entangled dependence which conventional masculinist accounts of the body have refused to recognize is something that feminist thought, by contrast, is able to articulate. As Jacqueline Rose writes, feminism can and ought to be 'the place in our culture which asks everyone, women and men, to recognize the failure of the present dispensation – its stiff-backed control, its ruthless belief in its own mastery, its doomed attempt to bring the uncertainty of the world to heel' (259). Butler, in a related vein, insists that to live in a world with others always means that complete security is impossible; existing with others is to exist in a state of vulnerability to the interventions *of* others. Events are unpredictable; the future can never be entirely controlled, and inevitably holds the possibility of surprise, for good or ill. She therefore 'exposes the disavowed dependency at the heart of the masculinist idea of the body' ('Rethinking' 21) by showing that vulnerability is 'not just a trait or an episodic disposition of a discrete body, but is, rather, a mode of relationality that time and again calls some aspect of that discreteness into question' ('Bodily Vulnerability' 103). There is no bodily existence which does not depend on other bodies, and which is not made vulnerable and insecure by this exposure. If the problem with 'the liberal privileging of mind and anxiety about embodiment', as Elizabeth Anker puts it, is that it 'can work to minimize forms of suffering that are a ubiquitous reality of all lived experience', (22) then Butler employs her notion of precariousness to outline a new bodily ontology founded on interconnection and dependence – and the unavoidable uncertainty and need for one another they imply – that contrasts with the dominant masculinist fantasy of control.

This concept of precariousness is not without risks. Rose argues, for example, that there is already an association between women and vulnerability to harm that serves particular social functions: 'If women are always or always potentially frightened', she writes, 'then the illusion can be nurtured that no one else ever has to be' (10). Thus – as Butler acknowledges – growing attention to precariousness, especially when it originates in feminist, anti-racist or queer thought, might work to strengthen and naturalize the connection between oppressed or marginalized groups and heightened exposure to harm, as if there were something natural or inevitable about it. In addition, Butler notes that there are 'justified political objections to the fact that dominant groups can use the discourse of "vulnerability" to shore up their own privilege' ('Rethinking' 23). As I discuss in more detail later in this Introduction, vulnerability can be put to progressive political use – but this is not inevitable, and claims to vulnerability can be made in profoundly damaging ways; one can think here, for example, of the long history of white women asserting fear and vulnerability in order to put black men in danger of violent harm and death.[3] As Mari Ruti therefore writes, Butler's insistence on shared and unavoidable vulnerability could flatten out differences and inequalities; it could, for example, 'function as a way for relatively privileged Western intellectuals to imply that we are all equally vulnerable, oppressed, deprived and harassed' (96–7). In a social world of intersecting axes of oppression, in which – inter alia – racialization, norms of gender and sexuality, class positions and citizenship statuses produce intricate and shifting hierarchies of security, protection and privilege, it is clear that if precariousness is shared, it is not something we all experience to the same extent or in the same way.

It is here that the notion of 'precarity' becomes useful. In *Frames of War*, Butler used the concept of precarity to supplement her earlier accounts of precariousness, while Isabell Lorey has also offered a thorough and detailed account of Butlerian precariousness in relation to the obviously disparate experiences of social vulnerability in the world today. For Butler and for Lorey, 'precarity' refers to the way that precariousness becomes organized in social situations, so that it is heightened for some subjects and minimized for others. It is the basic vulnerability and instability that is held in common by all living things – human and non-human – as it is conditioned, intensified and managed by political structures. Precarity is, Lorey writes, 'the striation and distribution of precariousness' (12) – the 'hierarchized difference in insecurity [which] arises from the segmentation, the categorization, of shared precariousness' (21). The value, interest and complexity of the term derives from its harnessing together of these two quite different aspects of experience: it encompasses the risk, insecurity and instability that are intrinsic to sociality, but draws attention to the mutable and historically variable practices that intensify the experience of vulnerability in particular times and places and allow certain individuals and groups to evade reckoning with their dependence on others.

Neoliberal economic ideology, which has become so globally dominant since the 1970s, is one such mode of organizing and hierarchizing precariousness. As Lauren Berlant argues, 'capitalist activity always induces destabilizing scenes of productive destruction – of resources and of lives being made and unmade according to the dictates and whims of the market' (192). Nonetheless, according to Berlant, 'neoliberal economic practices mobilize [...] instability in unprecedented ways' (ibid.). Lorey employs the term 'precarization' to describe the distinctive way that precarity is being mobilized in neoliberalism. Drawing on Foucault's notion of governmentality as the imbrication of individual self-government with the government of nation states, Lorey proposes that precarization is a 'technique of governing that is in the process of being normalized' in the present (66). If precarity feels new (despite its historical pervasiveness), it might be because governmental precarization contrasts markedly with post-war modes of governmentality in Europe and North America.

During the Keynesian-Fordist consensus, the governmental paradigm was protectionist. Nation states in Europe and North America promised security in exchange for labour: the 'safety net' of the welfare state was an inducement, Lorey suggests, for workers to be productive, reliable and hard-working. In the context of contemporary insecurity, it is tempting to look back on this period with longing and nostalgia: ideals such as the state's cradle-to-grave provision can seem nearly utopian in the United Kingdom and the United States, for example, today. However, Lorey argues that the Keynesian-Fordist situation was not one in which precarity was absent. For her, the difference between the contemporary period and the period of Keynesian-Fordist consensus is not a difference between precarity and security, but rather a matter of different distributions of precarity. In fact, she argues, social democratic welfare state capitalism itself was 'based on multiple forms of precarity as inequality through *othering*':

on the one hand, on the unpaid labour of women in the reproduction area of the private sphere; on the other hand, on the precarity of all those excluded from the nation-state compromise between capital and labour – whether as abnormal, foreign or poor – as well as those living under extreme conditions of exploitation in the colonies. (36)

In welfare state capitalism, security and protection were promised to a particular type of normative worker, and not to those understood as 'other'. The promise of security became appealing on the ideological level through the invocation of the threatening margin of others. A 'normal', 'productive', 'functioning' member of a liberal society could expect to be protected both from the threat of the deviant other and from the threat of *becoming* deviant and other. This mode of governmentality therefore relied on strong distinctions between the protected centre and the insecure margins, and these distinctions were typically maintained through categories of gender and race. In post-Fordism, such distinctions are no longer so important to governmentality, though of course they have not disappeared. Post-Fordism no longer promises much protection at all. If the family wage, for example, once promised a degree of security to (some) men as workers and (some) women as wives, Lorey argues that today governmentality operates by maximizing precariousness as far as possible for everyone without producing a breakdown in the social order.

Central to second-wave feminism was the demand that women should receive equal pay and have equal opportunities for employment in all sectors of the economy, and the second half of the twentieth century saw a gradual shifting of gendered norms around work, such that paid employment became normalized and, indeed, eventually, expected for middle-class women (as it had long been for working-class women). However, as women 'poured into labour markets around the globe' (Fraser 110), those labour markets themselves changed. Nancy Fraser argues that neoliberalism was able to resignify feminist claims about female economic independence, so that regressive working conditions – 'depressed wage levels, decreased job security, declining living standards, a steep rise in the number of hours worked for wages per household' – were justified or disguised by the 'new romance of female advancement and gender justice', as if performing paid work itself (no matter its conditions) were a symbol of women's empowerment (110). So if many women under mid-twentieth-century welfare state capitalism experienced 'precarity as inequality through *othering*' due to their 'unpaid labour [. . .] in the reproduction area of the private sphere' (Lorey 36), paid labour under the neoliberal regime does not necessarily provide an escape from, but often rather a new version of, precarity: a disproportionate degree of responsibility for reproductive labour continues, but is accompanied by insecure and poorly paid work that is presented as empowering and a source of independence.

Meanwhile, the increasing global economic importance of the service sector means that the forms of emotional labour that, as Arlie Russell Hochschild shows, have traditionally been disproportionately performed by women, are now central to the contemporary labour market. Kathi Weeks writes that to 'the extent that the flexible, caring, emotional, cooperative, and communicative model of femininity has come to represent the ideal worker, women's work under Fordism has arguably become the template for, rather than merely ancillary to, post-Fordist capitalist economies' (38). For men, this can mean working in areas long considered 'feminine', and in labour conditions that women have historically experienced, such as part-time work, and work without clearly demarcated working hours or defined workplaces. In their study of the effects of the decline of iron and steel production in a South Wales community, Walkerdine and Jimenez argue that a particular type of 'proud, hard and dirty masculinity' developed to deal with the difficulties and dangers of industrial labour (95), and that the loss of the possibility of embodying such a masculinity was experienced as 'frightening and painful' (103). To reimagine masculine identity while undertaking 'feminine' work, like care work, was destabilizing to the men they interviewed, and the loss of the individual and collective masculine identities constructed through hundreds of years of labour tradition was 'catastrophic', seeming 'to bring death' (95). Under neoliberalism, then, Fordism's normative worker – the white, male, citizen of a nation state – often finds himself in the position of precarity that was once reserved for 'others'. The 'others' become able to access the labour market on more equal terms – but the labour market no longer promises access to the stable benefits and forms of protection it once did.

As difficult and painful as many of these changes have been, Lorey also argues that they should not be understood only as negative. Because she understands precarization as governmentality in Foucauldian terms, it is for Lorey an essentially ambivalent process. On the one hand, governmentality means that the individual makes herself subject *to* power; she subjects herself. On the other hand, the individual becomes a subject – in the sense of a reflective entity. The modern individual is both acting and being acted upon. Agency and domination cannot be picked apart, and nor do they present themselves in straightforward opposition. Therefore, 'modes of self-governing do not only serve to make oneself and others governable. At the same time, the potential emerges in them to no longer be governed in existing ways and even to be ever less governed' (4). Thus, as the forms of self-government required by the economic system shift, they open up new possibilities for resistance and hope, as well as new ways of becoming subject to power.[4] Today, Lorey argues, 'modes of production and living are based on political virtuosity – on the art of the possible and dealing with the unforeseen, with insecurity and risk' (87), and this is a source of fear and insecurity, as well as a source of potential.

One such potential is the possibility that, through precarization, formerly protected subjects are forced to confront their unavoidable fragility and insecurity – the precariousness which other recent modes of governmentality enabled them to deny or evade, but which is actually an irresistible fact of social being. Such recognition of the inevitable and shared nature of precariousness might show that the construction and maintenance of more robust networks of social support is essential, so that vulnerability is minimized where possible. Butler argues that by coming to recognize the mutual dependency of bodies, we can come to recognize that precariousness is not something to be fled from in horror, or something that can be evaded, but rather the basic condition of existence. If interdependence is recognized, we are more likely to focus on developing hospitable, fair and just political and social conditions, she argues; conditions which might tackle the grave inequalities in security and protection which exist today. Those who recognize that others' bodily existence is the precondition for their own are more likely to think seriously about the political and social structures that are necessarily to support and sustain life and ensure that vulnerability is not heightened beyond what can be borne.

For many people around the world, close encounters with the fragility of life are hardly a new phenomenon. Benjamin Bateman writes, for example, that 'queerness is always under threat and that its survival cannot be taken for granted', highlighting the homophobic and heteropatriachal social practices ('harassment or forcible medical intervention, queer sensibilities derided as dangerous or immature, or queer intimacies denied respect and legitimacy') that have produced a 'close companionship between queerness and precariousness' (1). However, as Amber Jamilla Musser explains in reference to the work of José Esteban Muñoz, precarity has also functioned as the 'precondition' for a 'mode of theorization', in which queerness functions as 'a repository for an alternate politics' and 'opens into alternate models of envisioning agency, life, and creativity' (247). If precarization means the encroachment of insecurity into the lives of those accustomed to feeling secure, then those who have the tools to navigate the uncertainty of the present are likely to be those whose continuing precarity has long provided intimate understanding of vulnerability. Erinn Gilson argues that vulnerability is not only exposure to harm, but also a 'condition of openness, openness to being affected and affecting in turn', that makes it possible to 'fall in love, to learn, to take pleasure and find comfort in the presence of others' (310). Yet this often fails to be recognized, because of the 'ignorance of vulnerability', that is, according to Gilson, a pervasive form of ignorance that underlies other oppressive types of ignorance' (309). Precarization might therefore be hopeful to the extent that the increasingly obvious failures of conventional bodily ontology could make these alternative accounts of interdependence, support and collectivity central to the task of imagining a more just and equitable future.

Such a prospect is, of course, utopian and deeply uncertain. The experience of vulnerability can provoke violence and the attempt to displace insecurity and project it on to others instead of reflection on the conditions that support existence. But it is this ambivalence – the extent to which precarity is associated with deep insecurity and fear at the same time as it may hold the potential to reshape social structures in more equitable ways – that makes precarity such an interesting and potentially fruitful area of discussion, and forms a major focal point in this book.

Cultures of precarity

Literary and cultural forms have an important role to play in representing, illuminating and explaining the contemporary ambivalent condition of precarity: the potentials and possibilities which inhere even within its difficulties and exploitations.

Moreover, for many theorists, artistic works and cultural products possess the potential to change or intervene in the precarious present, in addition to depicting it. Jennifer Lawn, for example, argues that the literature of precarity must have some feasible connection with social change. She responds to Butler's argument about precarity's possible ability to instigate new forms of collectivity – new structures of social belonging that encompass individuals from disparate class and geographical and wealth positions and are developed on the basis of the mutual apprehension of unavoidable insecurity. Lawn argues that if this potential is to be realized, it requires the development of a particular sensibility – an ability to perceive vulnerability as shared – and she argues that literary reading, although of course unable to accomplish this entirely, or on its own, can make a contribution to the development of such a sensibility.

Artistic works deal with – and seek to challenge – contemporary insecurity in both thematic and formal ways; they engage with precarious life in terms of the topics they represent (migration, housing insecurity, unemployment, for example) and the ideas they directly express about contemporary vulnerability, as well as in the techniques and strategies they employ. This distinction between precarity dealt with at the level of form and at the level of content is made by a number of scholars. In *Poverty, Inequality and Precarity in Contemporary American Culture*, for example, Sieglinde Lemke outlines a definition of a 'precarious text', in which the aim of producing social change is married to particular thematic and formal features. 'Instead of just presenting' the experience of precarity, the precarious text 'begs, implicitly or explicitly, to reform the precarious conditions (outside the text) it describes' (18–19). Because, she argues, people from different classes in the United States rarely encounter one another in a substantial or meaningful way outside of cultural and media representations, such representations play an important role in producing dominant ideas about what poverty and wealth look like and consist of. Thus, the content of the precarious text must include an accurate representation of precarious life, showing others what it is like to inhabit a marginalized and insecure existence. At the same time, a precarious text must employ a 'textual mode' that is 'fragmented' and 'jagged' (19), and which can produce for the reader or viewer an 'unsettling effect' (18).

Like Lemke, Marc Botha also distinguishes texts' content from the way they are written. He takes 'fragility' – the difficult to define, yet pervasive experience of contingency – as his central term, and argues that literature is 'uniquely positioned', to both present and represent it (4). First, literary texts might take fragility as an explicit subject that they seek to depict. Second, they might enact fragility in formal terms, through 'the strategic deployment of certain poetic, plot and intertextual devices' (4). In this way, they are 'intensifying at a formal level the fragility that pervades the text at the level of representation' (4). Botha goes on to extend this argument beyond the aesthetic to the materiality of texts. He argues that literature might engage with contingency by exhibiting and experimenting with the fragility integral to its own materiality: language is unstable, paper decays and the digital world changes constantly. Texts can thus explore fragility by embarking on 'a search not only for the appropriate words, but also the appropriate medium or combination of media to convey the intensity of experience which pervades our experience of the contingency of all things' (5). In these three ways – content, form and materiality – he argues, literature has a singular ability to show precarity to its readers.

For Lemke, it is the interaction of literary content and formal destabilization which is crucial, while Botha suggests that precarity can be engaged with at thematic, formal and/or material levels. Other critics tend to prioritize the formal, arguing that literary and cultural texts' potential to create social and political change is related, first and foremost, to their aesthetic strategies. In this sense, what matters about artistic texts is not primarily what they say about precarity, but rather the way they forge new ways of seeing and describing, new possibilities for perception and novel styles of representation, in order to disrupt some of the stagnant political formations and taken-for-granted narratives of the contemporary moment. In the introduction to their edited collection *Poetics and Precarity*, Myung Mi Kim and Cristanne Miller argue that language has become blunted and static in the political arena – emptied out of its liveliness. They write that in the early twenty-first century, 'Isolationism, misogyny, and ethnic divisiveness have been given distinctively more powerful voice in public discourse than in the late twentieth century. At times, language seems to fail, to have failed' (xv). In such a context, they argue, poetry has a crucial role. It 'can create a proliferative mode of communicating', and, in so doing, it 'pluralizes paradigms for meaning-making, contributing to new configurations of affiliation, both local and global' (xvii). Here it is poetry's commitment to the multiplicity, perhaps even undecidability, of meaning that allows it to open up new ways of thinking, something which is desperately needed, especially in relation to the seeming intractability of precarity today.

Similarly, in the introduction to a special focus section of the *Minnesota Review* on 'Emergent Precarities and Lateral Aesthetics', Elizabeth Adan and Benjamin Bateman use the term 'drift' to describe the way that 'postwar and contemporary cultural production spreads out across various forms and practices, shifts between different states of material existence, and emerges among myriad modes of distribution and display' (109). This 'drift' means that it can be difficult to situate such cultural texts – to decide, once and for all, if they are emancipatory or hopelessly complicit with power structures. However, the impossibility of pinning such texts down, of figuring out their aims and intentions definitively, is not necessarily a problem. If traditionally conceived political art makes its intentions clear, contemporary texts with the potential to engage with the conditions of the neoliberal present do so through their 'indeterminacy', which causes 'sensation and perception' to 'drift from their otherwise preconceived meanings and effects and emerge unfettered by familiar, canonical, or otherwise dominant suppositions' (110). Here it is formal and aesthetic undecidability, the resistance to conventional categories, that allows artistic work to challenge established norms. Moreover, Adan and Bateman suggest that, for the contributors to their special issue, 'art should not simply show precarity but should simultaneously make manifest its failure to do so fully, thereby performing its own precarity as well' (111). In response to the radical uncertainty and felt contingency of the present, it makes sense that artistic texts find their forms and representational capacities themselves rendered uncertain and tentative.

Despite Adan and Bateman's emphasis on drift and generic boundary-crossing, many accounts of the points of connection between precarity and the cultural sphere focus on the distinctive aesthetic characteristics of one literary genre, and its resulting special ability to deal with precarity. Most commonly, it is the genres of performance and narrative fiction, especially the novel, that have been widely identified as the forms of cultural production most likely to produce new insight into the experience of precariousness. Katharina Pewny, co-author of Chapter 5 in this volume, uses the work of Emmanuel Lévinas to describe a genre of theatrical performance which produces moments of encounter in which the audience can see, acknowledge and realize the precarious vulnerability of the other. Quite differently, Nicholas Ridout and Rebecca Schneider point out that in the shift to neoliberal capitalism, affective and immaterial forms of labour have displaced the production of commodities as the central engine of profit-making. If the 'manipulation of affect is stock-in-trade for theatrical performance labour', they argue, then theatrical performance labour might be able to reflect and, crucially, reflect *on*, the broader conditions of work today (6).

Similarly, a number of critics have argued that the representational strategies and generic characteristics of the novel are useful for illuminating precarity. In his book *Precarious Labour and the Contemporary Novel*, Liam Connell (the author of Chapter 1 in this volume) argues that the novel is able to explore two of the pressures exerted simultaneously by precarious labour; first, the pressure on individuals to take control of their own life narrative – for example, by 'selling themselves' in their CVs, or sustaining a sense of individual development without the conventional markers of career identity and progress – and secondly, the anxiety, uncertainty and instability precariousness entails. The Bildungsroman, the novel of individual development, can track the way individuals try to construct their own life narratives, while the novel's emphasis on interiority allows it to 'explore the affective encounter with the regimes of flexible labour' (Connell, *Precarious Labour and the Contemporary Novel* 5). Simon During uses Amit Chaudhuri's 2009 novel *The Immortals* to argue that 'the literary' has a special capacity to know the condition of precarity. He maps this novel's distance from conventional realist, modernist *and* and postmodernist representational strategies on to a new conception of class hierarchy, in which intellectual elites have greater personal experience of economic insecurity, as 'relatively geographically and culturally stable relations of dominance and subordination are being replaced by relatively unstable and dispersed conditions of deprivation and insecurity' (During 19).

Precarity in Contemporary Literature and Culture seeks to build on and develop these existing accounts. Many of the chapters show how a particular genre of cultural production (speculative fiction, for example, in Chapter 11 by Bryan Yazell, or lyric poetry, in Walt Hunter's Chapter 10) can, by virtue of their specific aesthetic affordances, provide distinctive insight into precarity. At the same time, by bringing together chapters on a diverse range of genres and texts (from performance to Hollywood film, from realist novels to a hybrid artwork incorporating a woven blanket), the book enables readers to develop an overview of the way different types of text deal with contemporary insecurity, and to draw comparisons. It thus provides a broad picture of the energy and inventiveness with which different cultural forms respond to precarious conditions and shows how different aspects of precarious life are brought to light through diverse generic strategies of representation and thematization. When these varied texts are placed in dialogue, moreover, three cross-cutting themes emerge: feeling, bodies and time. *Precarity in Contemporary Literature and Culture* therefore develops the current discussion of cultural responses to precarity in a new direction by arguing that the interrelated topics of feeling, the body and time are crucial to the theorization of precarity, and that these are topics which diverse literary and cultural texts can productively explore.

Structure of this book: Feeling, bodies and time

This book takes up three main themes that emerge from current theorizations of precarity, are explored through literary and cultural texts, and which, we argue, require further discussion: feeling, bodies and time. These are not separate, discrete concepts, but are rather inherently entangled. Ann Cvetkovich notes that the word 'feeling' in everyday usage is interestingly ambiguous, suggesting both 'feelings as psychic or cognitive experiences' and 'feelings as embodied sensations' (4). It thus 'indicates, perhaps only intuitively but nonetheless significantly, a conception of mind and body as integrated' (4). Accordingly, while the first part of the book focuses on feeling in the sense of the 'psychic or cognitive' experiences related to precarious living, the chapters also emphasize the embodied nature of such experiences. Similarly, the second part of the book lays primary emphasis on the way the physical body is implicated in processes of precarization, while also investigating the affective experiences of, and investments in, the body that are an integral part of these processes.

Temporality – the theme of the third part of the book – is also impossible to disentangle from affect and embodiment. Ben Anderson, for example, argues that 'what defines the affective quality of precarity' is a specific kind of temporal experience: 'it is not only that the present is saturated with a sort of restlessness, but also that the future is made uncertain and becomes difficult or impossible to predict' (129). Moreover, neoliberalism organizes time in ways that produce distinctive ways of relating to the body. In *24/7*, Jonathan Crary shows how the market's demand for ceaseless, endlessly productive labour is inspiring the creation of products to reduce the human need for sleep. Donna McCormack and Suvi Salmenniemi, meanwhile, use the notion of the 'biopolitics of precarity' to argue that the temporal uncertainties of precarious living incline individuals towards participating in intensive processes of monitoring and maintaining their bodies and selves, 'a series of self-regulatory processes that are supposed to enable the prospect (and fantasy) of one day not being vulnerable' (8). Therefore, the three parts of the book are closely connected, and reading across the book provides a multidimensional view of precarity; an exploration of the thick texture of contemporary capitalism's lifeworld.

In Part One, the contributors show how literature and theatre can register and represent precarity's characteristic affects, while also producing affective responses in readers and audiences that might hold political potential. If, as Kit Dobson writes, under capitalism 'bodies are reduced [...] to machines designed to reproduce capital' and the 'neoliberal turn signals a retrenchment and resurgence of such reduced visions of the body's potential' (262), Part Two of the book focuses on performances and artworks in which performers literally embody challenges to this reduction, while also opposing the bodily violence of bordering processes and racist exclusion. In Part Three, the multiple ways in which different genres of cultural production seek to represent and manipulate experiences of time provide tools for reflecting on the temporal disorientations of precarity.

Feeling

When Munck argues that, for Standing, the precariat is united by 'its vague feelings of anomie and distance from the orthodox labour movement', he intends it as a criticism (752). But he also identifies something important about Standing's argument, which this book seeks to investigate further: its frequent use of the language of feeling and emotion. Standing writes, for example, that 'The precariatised mind is fed by fear and is motivated by fear' (35), and describes the precariat's 'passivity born of despair' and the way it 'lives with anxiety' (34). Lauren Berlant builds on this, arguing that if the precariat is to emerge as a new class – something she thinks is not at all certain or realized in the present – then it must be understood as an *affective* class. This is because, she argues, insecurity is saturating the experience of increasing numbers of people across the globe today, without dissolving established inequalities; all the older hierarchies, forms of differentiation and sites of oppression remain in place, even as instability seems to expand. Neoliberalism, she writes, is characterized by its 'efficiency at distributing and shaping the experience of insecurity throughout the class structure and across the globe' (193). Here contemporary insecurity is not reshaping the class structure (or producing a new class as Standing proposes), but rather pervading the class hierarchy more intensively and extensively. In this context, if there is to be a coherent precariat group, it is most likely to share affective experience – 'a *sense* of precarity' – rather distinctive relations of production (195).

The first part of this book therefore explores the affective quality of precarity through contemporary literary and theatrical texts, asking whether there are certain affects which are associated with precarious living, and – if so – how we might characterize them. One prominent strand in affect theory, associated particularly with Brian Massumi, distinguishes it analytically from emotion. As Callard and Papoulias put it, affect in this more restricted definition 'refers to an amorphous, diffuse, and bodily "experience" of stimulation impinging upon and altering the body's physiology' while 'emotions are the various structured, qualified, and recognizable experiential states of anger, joy, sadness, and so on, into which such amorphous experience is translated' (247). Affect has also been distinguished from emotion on the grounds that it is not personal or individual. According to Lisa Blackman, 'Affect refers to those registers of experience which cannot be easily seen, and which might variously be described as non-cognitive, trans-subjective, non-conscious, non-representational, incorporeal and immaterial' (4). Similarly, Elisha Cohn writes that affective states are 'Fugitive and impersonal', and 'circulate outside of the individual, irreducible to the more conceptual thoughts or even emotions an individual might have about them' (563).

Because precarity has often been understood as a potential site for collective politics, the emphasis such definitions place on the impersonality and trans-subjective nature of affect is important. However, in this book we take a broader and more general approach, following Ann Cvetkovich, who uses the term 'affect' to name 'a category that encompasses affect, emotion, and feeling, and that includes impulses, desires, and feelings that get historically constructed in a range of ways (whether as distinct specific emotions of as a generic category often contrasted with reason)' (4). The advantage of this approach is that it allows connections to be drawn *between* personal feelings and impersonal, trans-subjective affects, rather than bracketing them off from one another. As Kathleen Stewart has suggested, this broader approach allows us to get closer to the messy and entangled experience of everyday life – an argument she has made specifically in the context of attempting to understand the insecurity of contemporary capitalism. Stewart argues that 'the terms neoliberalism, advanced capitalism, and globalization [. . .] and the five or seven or ten characteristics used to summarize and define it in shorthand, do not in themselves begin to describe the situation we find ourselves in' (1). Instead of such shorthand, she uses the term 'ordinary affects' to name the traffic between the personal and the impersonal as it is manifested in a specific historical conjuncture. 'Ordinary affects', she writes, 'are public feelings that begin and end in broad circulation, but they're also the stuff that seemingly intimate lives are made of '(2). Stewart proposes that it is through the careful study of ordinary affects that we can begin to describe our current situation.

The chapters in the first part of the book therefore examine the way that novels and plays communicate, express and change the affective states associated with precarity. Liam Connell develops Berlant's argument on affective class, arguing that class politics and collective consciousness can be developed through shared affective experience. He makes this case through attention to the way that readers respond to literary texts, focusing in particular on the experience of anxiety induced by reading a novel such as Matt Thorne's *Eight Minutes Idle* (1999). Connell's emphasis on anxiety develops a long-standing association between precariousness and anxious feelings. The Institute for Precarious Consciousness (a radical research collective based in the United Kingdom) has, for example, argued that each stage in the development of capitalism has a dominant affect and that today's dominant affect is anxiety. In Chapter 2, Mathies G. Aarhus therefore also focuses on anxiety, but he draws our attention to the differential distribution of this affect through class hierarchies. If, for The Institute for Precarious Consciousness, 'we are all very anxious', Aarhus instead argues that anxiety is stratified, and that some of us deal with much more of it than others. He reads James Kelman's novel *You Have to Be Careful in the Land of the Free* (2004) as working-class speculative fiction: a depiction of a worryingly familiar near future, in which the hierarchization of anxiety has been formalized and is thus rendered more visible to us as readers. Chapter 3, by Peter Simonsen, focuses on another feeling: anger. He argues that, over the course of Gary Owen's play *Iphigenia in Splott* (2015) we find the main character's aggressive fury transformed into principled anger at austerity conditions. The play begins with a direct and furious speech aimed directly at the audience, and Simonsen argues that this direct address is characteristic of a new theatrical genre that eschews both conventional realism and Brechtian alienation in its aesthetic politics, and which here works to encourage the audience to assume responsibility for the precarious conditions the play describes.

Bodies

As I have already argued, the body – or, more precisely, the need to think the body differently – is central to Judith Butler's account of precariousness. To say that life is precarious, she writes, 'is to say that the possibility of being sustained relies fundamentally on social and political conditions, and not only on a postulated internal drive to live' (*Frames* 14). Yet the recognition of this shared precariousness is hindered by dominant 'masculinist' conceptions of embodiment, which picture 'individual bodies as completely distinct from one another' ('Rethinking' 16). When bodies are imagined as controllable and self-contained, vulnerability and interconnectedness can only be perceived as frightening, seeming to threaten the very dissolution of the subject. Thus, the recognition of precariousness as a shared and irresistible fact of social being (rather than a threat that needs to be eliminated wherever possible) can only occur once the conventional view of the body as individual and completely distinct from others is replaced by a distinctly different perception of embodied existence: the acknowledgement that 'the body, despite its clear boundaries, or perhaps precisely by virtue of those very boundaries, is defined by the relations that makes its own life and action possible' ('Bodily Vulnerability' 103).

Drawing directly from Butler's argument on this point, in Chapter 4 Marianne Kongerslev explores a complex artistic text: *Woven Account* (2014) by Indira Allegra, which comprises a blanket and a filmed performance. Kongerslev argues that the artist's representation of her own physical embodiment becomes a form of what she calls 'imagined sovereignty' – an insistence on the full humanity of precaritized Others, in particular women, Native Americans, African Americans and LGBTQI2S+ people, in the context of violent and traumatic histories of erasure, and the ongoing legacies of racist and colonial exploitation which have rendered them precariously vulnerable to bodily injury and death. In Chapter 5, Katharina Pewny and Tessa Vannieuwenhuyze explore other contexts in which artists' bodies in space become crucial: the performance piece *Misplaced Women* by Tania Ostojić and Yael Ronen's play *The Situation*. Both texts identify migration as a cause of precarity, and yet both texts also find in the experience of precarity a form of new connection and connectivity which is expressed through the inhabiting of physical, shared space by performers, characters and audiences. At the same time, Pewny and Vannieuwenhuyze also show the real physical dangers that are associated with this bodily vulnerability.

In Chapter 6, Sophy Kohler examines two contemporary South African texts: Masande Ntshanga's novel *The Reactive* and Mohale Mashigo's short story 'Ghost Strain N'. While the extent to which countries in the Global South can be usefully described using precarity theory has been widely debated, Kohler shows how illness and infection function in these texts as metonyms for precarity that imaginatively connect South Africa's post-apartheid social stagnancy with theorizations of the delayed and unrealized futurity associated with precarity on a global level.

Time

Precarious work organizes time in ways that are often experienced as disorienting and anxiety provoking – take, for example, zero-hour contracts, a form of employment in which workers have no guarantee that they will be required to work any hours at all in a given month. But if expecting a full-time, permanent life-long career no longer seems realistic or imaginable or – in some, though not all, cases – desirable for many people, due to the rise of portfolio careers, temporary contracts and the gig economy, this does not necessarily lead to a reduction in time spent working. In *Non-Stop Inertia*, his book about his own experiences of precarious work, Ivor Southwood writes that he and his partner wonder, 'In the manner of a couple imagining some gleaming Utopia' what it would be like 'to reclaim the hours filled by commuting and job applications' (77). Here it is not work itself that takes up too much time, but its subsidiary tasks – the tasks upon which work depends, but which workers cannot expect to be paid for. Unpaid labour – which once tended to be the particular domain of women, for example through housework and care work – is increasingly expected of everyone, and often functions as an accepted and normal adjunct to paid work. Claiming benefits requires intensive bureaucratic work; applying for jobs means endlessly reworking and perfecting your CV; trying to remain employable necessitates taking extra training courses.

On a more abstract level, as we have seen, one of the key debates in theorizations of precarity relates to its *newness*. For Standing, the precariat is emerging as a distinctively new phenomenon, while for Lorey it is not the experience of precarity itself which is new, but rather the extent to which it has become central to contemporary modes of governmentality. On the other hand, di Bernado argues that it is counterproductive to emphasize the novelty of precarity, because doing so obscures the historical continuities between labour in different periods and the historical pervasiveness of precarious work. This discussion of the place of contemporary employment practices in a longer arc is often connected with a consideration of the way time is organized in contemporary capitalism on a more mundane everyday level. For example, Dieter Lesage argues that the 'relative "advantage"' of the 'regime of strict control of working hours' which characterized work in the mid-twentieth century was that 'at some point, even if very late, the work day would be over' (19). Today, however, '"Time doesn't matter". What matters is the output, or the impact. The 40-hour work-week is a fiction, and everybody seems to have interiorized that, of course, nobody with a 40-hour work-week is supposed to work just forty hours a week' (19). For Lesage, the contemporary organization of workers' time is not only potentially unsettling and exploitative in itself. It also constitutes a backward step, erasing the gains of twentieth-century labour movements, as if they had never happened: it means that, despite 'many years of workers' contestations fighting for a reduced work week, today, the capitalist gets 50 per cent of labour for free' (19).

Conceptualizing precarious labour in this longer historical context is difficult, however, in part because of the outsized influence of Fordist labour on contemporary ideas about what work should be, despite the brief and fleeting nature of its actual existence. As part of his 1998 discussion of work, *The Corrosion of Character*, Richard Sennett reflects on his earlier study of blue-collar workers in the 1970s and is struck 'by how linear time was in their lives' (15). They experienced 'year after year of working in jobs which seldom varied from day to day. And along that line of time, achievement was cumulative' (15–16). This ordered, structured life was – as Boltanski and Chiapello also argue – often criticized for being boring and predictable, and challenged by the neoliberal ideology of creativity and flexibility. As Sennett points out, the new, flexible regime presented itself as rebellion against repetitive and stultifying patterns of work that were presented as long-standing, historically established and therefore in need of a radical overhaul. Yet, as Sennett points out, the '"long-term" order' against which the freer, flexible future was defined, 'was itself short-lived – the decades spanning the mid-twentieth century. This span of thirty or so years defines the "stable past" now challenged by a new regime' (23). Labour in industrial capitalism has, somehow, come to seem the paradigmatic experience of labour as such, even though – in quantifiable, historical terms – it was not a long-term phenomenon. Thus, thinking about the history of precarious labour requires dealing with a series of emotional, affective, shared ideas about the past, which may bear little relation to the past as it can be more objectively described.

The chapters in this part of the book show how the temporal effects of various genres and types of cultural production work to mediate, respond to or challenge the difficulties associated with time in precarity. Alissa G. Karl, Benjamin Kohlmann and I all examine the problem of the past for precarity theory. How should we conceptualize the past, especially the past of Fordist labour, and how does precarity fit with the longer arc of capitalism and opposition to it? Karl's chapter is a critique of what she describes as the 'deindustrialization thesis': the idea that we can draw hard boundaries between a stable, Fordist post-war past and a precarious neoliberal present. She uses analysis of two contemporary films – the 2016 blockbuster *La La Land* and the 2018 low-budget critical success *Sorry to Bother You* – to reveal the unsustainability of this thesis. Contrasting *La La Land*'s use of the generic codes of the conventional Hollywood musical with *Sorry to Bother You*'s absurdist elements reveals two quite different pictures of the history of wage labour, with the latter film better able to articulate the insecurity that is, and always has been, integral to capitalism.

Kohlmann reads David Peace's novel *GB84* (2004), about the British miners' strike, with an earlier strike novel: John Sommerfield's *May Day* (1936). He describes both texts as examples of 'proletarian modernism' – an aesthetic tradition which has been largely ignored, but which imagines insecurity very differently to Butler's model of ontological precariousness and which offers resources for imagining a radical collectivist politics. My chapter describes a structure of feeling which I claim is characteristic of precarity: the melancholic sense that the present has not realized the hopes and dreams for the future that existed in the past – especially the ambitious dreams of industrial capitalism and the post-war welfare state. Through close readings of two contemporary British fictions (the short story 'Limited Dreamers' by Anneliese Mackintosh and the novel *Vulgar Things* by Lee Rourke) and drawing on Ricouer's notion of refiguration, I argue that literature can mediate the anxiety about the past's relationship with the present that is characteristic of precarious life.

Walt Hunter focuses on the present. He suggests that, in contrast to the futile attempt to cling to security embodied by white nationalism and bordering processes, the distinctive nature of poetry can help readers come to terms with the fragile, fleeting and precarious now. Drawing together poems by the American poet Jorie Graham and the Palestinian-Syrian-Swedish poet Ghayath Almadhoun, Hunter shows how poetic image and poetic line allow the value of the present, despite its inevitable passing away, to be perceived by the reader. In this way, Hunter argues that poetry can help readers reconsider the fear and anxiety often produced by the inevitable precariousness and insecurity of the present. In the book's final chapter, Bryan Yazell turns to the future, reading Kim Stanley Robinson's science fiction novel *New York 2140* (2017) alongside Guy Standing's account of precariat solidarity. Yazell's close readings of the novel highlight the contrast between, on the one hand, the general recognizability and familiarity of its speculative future, and on the other the success of its anti-precarity social collectives, which form a progressive political movement that goes well beyond anything currently existing. Bringing these close readings into dialogue with an under-discussed part of Standing's discussion of precarity which concerns time, Yazell reveals the significance of shared temporal experience in creating the foundation for solidarity and collective political action in conditions of precarity.

Precarity in Contemporary Literature and Culture therefore critically explores the use of the term 'precarity' as it relates to urgent contemporary crises, including forced displacement, illness, unemployment and austerity politics. Drawing different types of literary and cultural production together, placing texts from different geographical and generic contexts into dialogue, the collection argues for the centrality of feeling, bodies and time to the theorization of precarity, and shows why turning to literature and culture can help to explore these complex topics. In the following pages, innovative readings of novels, performances, poems, films, objects, short stories and plays are used to shed new light on the intersecting vulnerabilities of the contemporary moment, to ask new questions of precarity theory, and thus to situate literary and cultural texts in relation to some of the urgent political crises of our time.

Notes

1 See for example Breman, Munck, Di Bernardo, Federici and Frase.
2 See my own chapter in this volume, Chapter 9, for further discussion of Bourdieu's account of time and precarity.
3 See for example Blow, Edwards, Patton and Snyder-Yuly and De Welde.
4 For a detailed examination of the possibility that precarity might be, in some senses, considered hopeful, see Hogg and Simonsen.

Works cited

Adan, Elizabeth, and Benjamin Bateman. 'Emergent Precarities and Lateral Aesthetics: An Introduction'. *Minnesota Review*, vol. 2015, no. 85, 2015, pp. 107–18.

Anderson, Ben. *Encountering Affect: Capacities, Apparatuses, Conditions*. Ashgate, 2014.

Anker, Elizabeth. *Fictions of Dignity: Embodying Human Rights in World Literature*. Cornell University Press, 2012.

Bateman, Benjamin. *The Modernist Art of Queer Survival*. Oxford University Press, 2017.

Berlant, Lauren. *Cruel Optimism*. Duke University Press, 2011.

Blackman, Lisa. *Immaterial Bodies: Affect, Embodiment, Mediation*. Sage, 2012.

Blow, Charles M. 'How White Women Use Themselves as Instruments of Terror'. *The New York Times*, 27 May 2020, https://www.nytimes.com/2020/05/27/opinion/racism-white-women.html

Boltanski, Luc, and Eve Chiapello. *The New Spirit of Capitalism*. Translated by Gregory Elliott. Verso, 2007.

Botha, Marc. 'Precarious Present, Fragile Futures: Literature and Uncertainty in the Early Twenty-First Century'. *English Academy Review*, vol. 31, no. 2, 2014, pp. 1–19, doi:10.1080/10131752.2014.965411.

Bourdieu, Pierre. *Acts of Resistance: Against the New Myths of Our Time*. Translated by Richard Nice. Polity, 1998.

Breman, Jan. 'A Bogus Concept?'. *New Left Review* 84, November/December 2013, https://newleftreview.org/issues/II84/articles/jan-breman-a-bogus-concept

Butler, Judith. *Frames of War: When Is Life Grievable?* Verso, 2009.

Butler, Judith. 'Bodily Vulnerability, Coalitions, and Street Politics'. *Critical Studies*, vol. 37, 2014, pp. 99–119.

Butler, Judith. 'Rethinking Vulnerability and Resistance'. *Vulnerability in Resistance*, edited by Judith Butler, Zeynep Gambetti and Leticia Sabsay. Duke University Press, 2016, pp. 1–27.

Callard, Felicity, and Constantina Papoulias. 'Affect and Embodiment'. *Memory: Histories, Theories, Debates*, edited by Susannah Radstone and Bill Schwarz. Fordham University Press, 2010, pp. 246–62.

Casas-Cortés, Maribel. 'A Genealogy of Precarity: A Toolbox for Rearticulating Fragmented Social Realities in and out of the Workplace'. *Rethinking Marxism*, vol. 26, no. 2, 2014, pp. 206–26, doi:10.1080/08935696.2014.888849.

Cohn, Elisha. 'Affect'. *Victorian Literature and Culture*, vol. 46, no. 3–4, 2018, pp. 563–67, doi:10.1017/S1060150318000244.

Connell, Liam. *Precarious Labour and the Contemporary Novel*. Palgrave, 2017.

Connell, Liam. 'Anxious Reading: The Precarity Novel and the Affective Class'. *Precarity in Contemporary Literature and Culture*, edited by Emily J. Hogg and Peter Simonsen. Bloomsbury, 2021, pp. 27–41.

Crary, Jonathan. *24/7: Late Capitalism and the Ends of Sleep*. Verso, 2013.

Cvetkovich, Ann. *Depression: A Public Feeling*. Duke University Press, 2012.

De Welde, Kristine. 'White Women Beware!: Whiteness, Fear of Crime, and Self-Defense'. *Race, Gender and Class*, vol. 10, no. 4, 2003, pp. 75–91.

Di Bernardo, Francesco. 'The Impossibility of Precarity'. *Radical Philosophy*, vol. 198, July–August 2016, www.radicalphilosophy.com/commentary/the-impossibility-of-precarity. Accessed 28 January 2020.

Dobson, Kit. 'Neoliberalism and the Limits of the Human: Rawi Hage's *Cockroach*'. *Textual Practice*, vol. 29, no. 2, 2015, pp. 255–71, doi:10.1080/0950236X.2014.993519.

Doerr, Nicole and Alice Mattoni. 'Public Spaces and Alternative Media Practices in Europe: The Case of the EuroMayDay Parade Against Precarity'. *Media and Revolt: Strategies and Performances from the 1960s to the Present*, edited by Kathrin Fahlenbrach, Erling Sivertsen and Rolf Werenskjold. Berghahn Books, 2014, pp. 386–405.

During, Simon. 'Choosing Precarity'. *South Asia: Journal of South Asian Studies*, vol. 38, no. 1, 2015, pp. 19–38, doi:10.1080/00856401.2014.975901.

Edwards, Rebecca. *Angels in the Machinery: Gender in American Party Politics from the Civil War to the Progressive Era*. Oxford University Press, 1997.

'EuroMayDay Poster'. *Tactical Media Files*, www.tacticalmediafiles.net/picture?pic=1576. Accessed 28 January 2020.

Federici, Silvia. 'Precarious Labour: A Feminist Viewpoint'. *In the Middle of the Whirlwind*, inthemiddleofthewhirlwind.wordpress.com/precarious-labor-a-feminist-viewpoint/. Accessed 28 January 2020.

Frase, Peter. 'The Precariat: A Class or a Condition?' *New Labor Forum*, vol. 22, no. 2, 2013, pp. 11–14.

Fraser, Nancy. 'Feminism, Capitalism and the Cunning of History'. *New Left Review*, no. 56, 2009, pp. 97–117.

Gilson, Erinn. 'Vulnerability, Ignorance, and Oppression'. *Hypatia*, vol. 26, no. 2, 2011, pp. 308–32.

Hogg, Emily J., and Peter Simonsen. 'The Potential of Precarity? Imagining Vulnerable Connection in Chris Dunkley's *The Precariat* and Amy Liptrot's *The Outrun*'. *Criticism*, vol. 62, no. 1, 2020, pp.1–28.

Hochschild, Arlie Russell. *The Managed Heart: Commercialization of Human Feeling*. 3rd edition. University of California Press, 2012.

Institute for Precarious Consciousness. 'We Are All Very Anxious'. *We Are Plan C*, 4 April 2014, www.weareplanc.org/blog/we-are-all-very-anxious/.

Kim, Myung Mi, and Christanne Miller. 'Introduction'. *Poetics and Precarity*, edited by Myung Mi Kim and Christanne Miller. SUNY Press, 2018.

Lawn, Jennifer. 'Precarity: A Short Literary History, from Colonial Slum to Cosmopolitan Precariat'. *Interventions*, vol. 19, no. 7, 2017, pp. 1026–40, doi:10.1080/13698 01X.2017.1401944.

Lemke, Sieglinde. *Inequality, Poverty and Precarity in Contemporary American Culture*. Palgrave, 2016.

Lesage, Dieter. 'Permanent Performance'. *Performance Research*, vol. 17, no. 6, 2012, pp. 14–21, doi:10.1080/13528165.2013.775752.

Lorey, Isabell. *State of Insecurity: Government of the Precarious*. Translated by Aileen Derieg. Verso, 2015.

Marchart, Oliver. 'EuroMayDay'. *Encyclopedia of Social Movement Media*, edited by John D. H. Downing. SAGE, 2011, pp. 180–2.

McCormack, Donna, and Suvi Salmenniemi. 'The Biopolitics of Precarity and the Self'. *European Journal of Cultural Studies*, vol. 19, no. 1, 2016, pp. 3–15.

McRobbie, Angela. 'Reflections on Feminism, Immaterial Labour and the Post-Fordist Regime'. *New Formations*, vol. 70, 2011, pp. 60–76, doi:10.3898/NEWF.70.04.2010.

Millar, Kathleen. 'Towards a Critical Politics of Precarity'. *Sociology Compass*, vol. 11, no. 6, 2017, doi:10.1111/soc4.12483

Munck, Ronaldo. 'The Precariat: A View from the South'. *Third World Quarterly*, vol. 34, no. 5, 2013, pp. 747–62, doi:10.1080/01436597.2013.800751.

Musser, Amber Jamilla. 'Gender and Queer Theory'. *A Companion to Critical and Cultural Theory*, edited by Imre Szeman, Sarah Blacker, and Justin Sully. John Wiley, 2017, pp. 243–54.

Neilson, Brett, and Ned Rossiter. 'Precarity as a Political Concept, or, Fordism as Exception'. *Theory, Culture & Society*, vol. 25, no. 7–8, 2008, pp. 51–72, doi:10.1177/0263276408097796.

Patton, Tracey Owens, and Julie Snyder-Yuly. 'Any Four Black Men Will Do: Rape, Race, and the Ultimate Scapegoat'. *Journal of Black Studies*, vol. 37, no. 6, 2007, pp. 859–95. JSTOR, www.jstor.org/stable/40034959.

Pewny, Katharina. 'The Ethics of Encounter in Contemporary Theater Performances'. *Journal of Literary Theory*, vol. 6, no. 1, 2012, doi:10.1515/jlt-2011-0017.

Pewny, Katharina, and Tessa Vannieuwenhuyze. 'Precarious Bodies on the Move, Precarious Bodies Under Attack'. *Precarity in Contemporary Literature and Culture*, edited by Emily J. Hogg and Peter Simonsen. Bloomsbury, 2021, pp. 91–108.

'Precarious, Adj'. OED Online, Oxford University Press, December 2019, www.oed.com/view/Entry/149548. Accessed 28 January 2020.

Ridout, Nicholas, and Rebecca Schneider. 'Precarity and Performance: An Introduction'. *TDR/The Drama Review*, vol. 56, no. 4, 2012, pp. 5–9, doi:10.1162/DRAM_a_00210.

Rose, Jacqueline. *Women in Dark Times*. Bloomsbury, 2014.

Ruti, Mari. 'The Ethics of Precarity: Judith Butler's Reluctant Universalism'. *Remains of the Social: Desiring the Post-Apartheid*, edited by Maurits van Bever Donker, Russ Truscott, Gary Minkley and Premesh Lalu. Wits University Press, 2017.

Sennett, Richard. *The Corrosion of Character: The Personal Consequences of Work in the New Capitalism*. Norton, 1998.

Southwood, Ivor. *Non-Stop Inertia*. Zero Books, 2011.

Standing, Guy. *The Precariat: The New Dangerous Class*. Bloomsbury, 2014.

Stewart, Kathleen. *Ordinary Affects*. Duke University Press, 2007.

'The Middlesex Declaration of the European Precariat'. *Tactical Media Files*, 13 April 2010, www.tacticalmediafiles.net/articles/3340/The-Middlesex-Declaration-of-the-European-Precariat. Accessed 28 January 2020.

Walkerdine, Valerie, and Luis Jimenez. *Gender, Work and Community after De-Industrialisation. A Psychosocial Approach to Affect*. Palgrave, 2012.

Weeks, Kathi. 'Down with Love: Feminist Critique and the New Ideologies of Work'. *Women's Studies Quarterly*, vol. 45, no. 3, 2017, pp. 37–58.

Part One

FEELING

Chapter 1

ANXIOUS READING

THE PRECARITY NOVEL AND THE AFFECTIVE CLASS

Liam Connell

As Emily J. Hogg illustrates in the introduction to this collection, recent interest in the terms 'precariousness' and 'precarity' has produced a vigorous debate about contemporary forms of economic uncertainty. This debate appears to gather energy from the perception that new forms of capitalist practice have stripped away the benefits of social capitalism as it was constituted in the Global North during the immediate post-war period. This perception seems to be widespread and to be crucial for explaining the current vogue for the language of precariousness, at least in academic study. The word 'precarious' entered the English language in the seventeenth century and seems to have been widely used during the 1700s before falling into less frequent use. In recent years, the word has been revived in academic writing with the word 'precarious' being widely used to frame discussion of labour practices, social exclusion and a friable social contract. One measure of the new popularity for the term can be seen from examining the holdings of the British Library. Looking across the collection at books that contain the word precarious in their title, more than two-thirds were published this century, and more than half were published in the last decade. What is more, the proportion of these books that focus on work or labour practices has increased steadily from a quarter of titles published between 2000 and 2009, to over 40 per cent of the titles published since 2014. Whether or not the conditions for workers under capitalism are much changed, there appears to have been a substantial increase in the attempts to describe these conditions using the language of precariousness.

How to explain this shift? One way to answer this question would be to point to the growing prominence of finance capital since the end of the twentieth century. The earliest uses of precariousness related to the rights to tenancy in which a tenant was vulnerable to the will of another. The centrality of tenancy to this definition might hint towards the dominance of rentier capitalism for the eighteenth-century economy prior to the industrial revolution. In this context, the current vogue for the word may be indicative of Thomas Piketty's claim that the financialized economy of the neoliberal era has re-centred the rentier in contemporary capitalism (Piketty). In line with such a suggestion it is telling how prominent questions of housing have become to debates about precarious lives. For instance, Mike Savage extrapolates from Piketty's data to argue that the 'significance of housing as a source of wealth' means that 'the key economic division' in the twenty-first century is between those who have access to housing wealth and 'the "precariat" at the bottom of the scale, whose paucity of economic capital and their frequent reliance on rented housing is a defining feature of their insecurity' (Savage et al. 77–8). In line with this analysis, the increasing recourse to the language of precarity may be indicative of a return to forms of capitalism that involve the structural vulnerability of uninvested citizens.

A second way to respond to my question is to suggest that the shift in language indicates a cultural change rather than an economic one. In this view the change is not so much in the character of contemporary capitalism but rather in the ways that this is understood. As I have argued in my book *Precarious Labour and the Contemporary Novel*, the contemporary period is characterized not by the levels of insecurity that attend upon it but rather by 'an accompanying sense of loss for socialized forms of security that are recent in the memory but that no longer apply' (Connell 4). Although for some commentators the period of socialized capitalism represented what Max Haiven has called an 'illusion of non-precarity' (Haiven 44), the surrendering of this illusion appears to have traumatic consequences. Even for those too young to recall a period of Keynesian consensus-politics the myth of the benefits that have been lost is a ready symbol of structural economic change. For many, one of the key features of contemporary society appears to be a generational reversal of the gains of the post war democratic settlement, whereby younger citizens can no longer hope to obtain the advantages enjoyed by their parents and grandparents before them. The function of the welfare state in such a narrative is clearly synecdochic but it points to the significance of cultural representation.

To answer my question then, the increasing use of the term 'precariousness' might follow from structural changes in the nature of capitalism or, equally, from a growing belief in such a change that stands upon a narrative of growing insecurity. Most likely it is a combination of both, which immediately invites further questions about the relation between the objective character of economic vulnerability and its subjective experience. How far is a narrative of precariousness the product of new forms of insecurity, and how far might this narrative allow subjects to explain and act upon their own experiences of precarity? These questions are at the heart of this chapter, which concentrates on a genre of contemporary writing that I call the precarity novel. I try to think about what kind of responses readers might typically have to depictions of characters' precarity in such novels and to consider how the form of this representation of precarity might prompt readers to think about their own experiences through a lens of precariousness. The precarity novel is a species of contemporary fiction, predominantly realist, that depicts vulnerable subjects in the grip of escalating crises resulting from an endemic uncertainty that is a condition of contemporary capitalism. The crises in these novels are marked by a particular narrative dynamic in which the worsening of the character's fate is never met by a culminating catastrophe. The characteristic form of such writing is a novel that presents a seemingly permanent condition of anticipation of unrealized crisis.[1]

In thinking about how readers respond to this kind of narrative text, I propose that readers are likely to be unsettled by narrative depictions of crises and that the ways that they understand this depiction will likely determine the meaning that they attach to such texts. While there are likely to be many different kinds of responses to such novels, I want to suggest two broad ways that it is possible to imagine reading narratives about economically vulnerable subjects. The first response to the text is one that I suggest is broadly affective in that it depends upon feelings of unease which are not immediately cognitive.[2] However, the degree to which the reader is able to make sense of these feelings depends upon a second kind of response which Rita Felski has called recognition and which depends upon an alignment between self-identification and collective identities (Felski 29–30). Whether the reader is likely to be irritated by or sympathetic towards the characters in such texts may depend upon the level of identification between the reader and the character. However, it will also depend upon an ideological positioning which informs the reader's attitude about an individual's relation to their social environment. Crudely, do readers believe that individuals are to blame for the crises that they face in their lives or do they believe that individuals are subject to social forces that propel them towards crises that they cannot control? Such calculations are not wholly or immediately cognitive, but they do channel an initial somatic experience of the text towards conscious or calculating readings. One such reading of the precarity novel is a form of political reading in which the reader's affective anxiety opens up forms of solidarity that are constitutive of the precariat as an affective class. As I suggest in the following text, the reader's initial unease in response to narrative crises depends upon a subsequent sense of equivalence. The affect of crisis moves out from the narrative and is felt as a kind of reading experience. In this way the reader is able to image lines of affinity that are capable of extending the connection between the reader and the character to precarious subjects beyond the textual encounter.

Theoretically, the kind of reading that I propose here echoes a number of traditions of critical thought. My emphasis on the reader's capacity to make the narrative meaningful resembles the claims of reader-response theory, especially where such theory builds upon the earlier observations of formalist criticism (Davis and Womack). While I argue that meaning-making of this kind is modulated by a reader's experience beyond the text, I also argue that it depends upon textual cues, in particular the narrative staging of a particular kind of escalating crisis. Such a reading is not especially far from the modes of transactional reading proposed by Louise Rosenblatt in *The Reader, the Text, the Poem*, in which she argues:

> The reader's attention to the text activates certain elements in his [sic] past experience [. . .] that have become linked with the verbal symbols. Meaning will emerge from a network of relationships among the things symbolized *as he senses them*. The symbols point to these sensations, images, objects, ideas, relationships, with the particular association or feeling-tones created by his past experiences with them in actual life or in literature. (Rosenblatt 11)

Rosenblatt's notion of 'relationships' here is most immediately a reference to the associations built up between signs and feelings or, in her word, 'sensations'.

However, just as strong is her emphasis on past experience which cannot be reserved to the textual. The second occurrence of the word 'relationships' seems to point out from the text into the social meaning of this word and to imply, at least, the connection between the reader and other subjects. Rosenblatt's emphasis on feelings or sensation might also be relevant to the present discussion. While her language may owe a good deal to a Romantic tradition, it also appears to anticipate a more recent interest in affect that is rooted in contemporary cognitive sciences. Brian Massumi's writing on the autonomy of affect, for instance, signals a gap between the somatic affect and the cognitive indexing of meaning in response to narrative texts (Massumi). Although the language of affect theory differs from the classic terms of reader-response theory, Massumi's distinction between effect and signification, being the 'socio-linguistic qualification' (84) of effect as content, seems to differ little from Rosenblatt's terminology of sense and association.

In trying to trace how an initial affective response is translated into a secondary, cognitive, reading experience, I want to return to the idea of relationships that Rosenblatt associates with the reader's capacity to build meaning on the foundations of an initial sense of the text. In doing so I want to insist upon a precisely historicist reading, which rests upon the capacity of readers to interpret unease through the kind of contemporary narratives of precariousness that I have set out above. This would correspond to what Rosenblatt calls 'past experience' but which a later generation of critics might call discourse. In line with a long tradition of cultural materialist criticism, I want to propose that the readerly anxiety which is produced by depictions of crises becomes sensible in the context of particular stories about precariousness which are, now, regularly deployed to describe the present. However, in tracing this possibility, I want to propose a terminological distinction of my own, distinguishing the language of 'precariousness' from the language of 'precarity'. Whereas the former term can be interpreted as a vernacular description of the conditions of uncertainty that are endemic to contemporary capitalism, the latter is a more immediately political concept that signals both the conditions of uncertainty and a subjective *consciousness* of these conditions that can be actuated as a site for politics. It is in this site of politics that it might be possible to imagine intersubjective relationships that are organized around 'precarity' as an operative term.

The distinction between precariousness and precarity helps to shift a debate away from a purely descriptive account of social conditions towards a consideration of the space that these social conditions open up for forms of action. My thinking here is indebted to a language of 'precarity' that emerges out of an Italian tradition of autonomist Marxism, where the term was used to signal both forms of contingency and forms of opposition to the institutionalized relationships between labour and capitalism in the post-war settlement. Within the context of Italian industrial relations, the autonomists argued that organized labour had become a functionary of capitalism and, as a result, had become increasingly incapable of resisting capitalist appropriation. As a consequence, they sought to identify sites of opposition beyond the factory and looked increasingly to irregular workers as the locus of political opposition (Wright). These origins offered the term 'precarity' a dual meaning with negative and positive connotations. On the one hand, as patterns of irregular work came to be increasingly normalized, the term 'precarity' seemed to define forms of labour where the risks of market uncertainty were passed from the employer to disenfranchised workers. In line with this tendency, Franco Beradi defines the term 'precarity' as synonymous with 'labor precariousness' in a moment where flexible labour has become 'the black heart [. . .] of global capitalist production' (Beradi 148). At the same time, however, it is important also to note the centrality of political action within an autonomist tradition. In these terms, the word 'precarity' seems to speak of a kind of coalitional politics that is formed out of a shared condition of dispossession. Unlike precariousness, which signals only the objective conditions of uncertainty, precarity speaks of a political condition that seeks to repurpose systematic uncertainty in order to develop subject positions or alliances that are framed by precariousness.

This aspiration seems most obviously present in the definition of a third term, the neologism 'the precariat'. In seeking to define the precariat, Guy Standing has identified the complexities that arise from the heterogeneous nature of its constituents. Precarious work is so commonplace that it becomes hard to classify the characteristics of the precarious worker. Partly as a result of this heterogeneity, Standing's definition of the precariat lacks any clear or succinct description of its objective character (Standing, *The Precariat* 7–16). The key to his definition is what the precariat lacks. It lacks institutional security in its relations to labour, its relations to status and its relations to the state (Standing, *The Precariat Charter* 16–26). More immediately Standing claims that the precariat is 'a *class in-the-making*, if not yet a *class-for-itself*, in the Marxian sense of that term' (Standing, *The Precariat* 7). The first phrase in this quotation is often cited but the debt to Marxism is less often quoted and bears some unpacking. In particular, the phrase 'a class-for-itself' might want some kind of gloss. A class for itself is usually understood to mean a class in possession of class-consciousness (Ollman 579) or a class that is 'characterized by organization and consciousness of solidarity' (Przeworski 348).[3] In other words, Standing's sense of the precariat is that it is not yet capable of mobilizing against capitalism, albeit that it is 'in-the-making', that is to say that it is in the process of coming to consciousness and organising for its class interest. However accurate this may be as a prediction, it signals that the precariat should be seen less in terms of the objective criteria that define its relations and more in terms of its potential for mobilizing class interests against capital. This idea of consciousness, in both a colloquial and in its Marxist sense, is key to the modes of reading which I think are triggered by the precarity novel. In other words, when readers translate the experience of unease into a cognitive response to the genre they are propelled towards forms of meaning that operate around social relationships that originate in a shared precariousness.

Anxious reading

My interest in affect as the origins of this reading owes a considerable debt to Lauren Berlant's 2011 book, *Cruel Optimism*. In this work, Berlant argues that, because of its heterogeneity at an objective level, the precariat is best understood to be an 'affective class' that is bound together by 'a *sense* of precarity' (Berlant 195). The idea that the precariat is bound together by feelings of precariousness does not in itself lead to a moment of action. Indeed, to the contrary, Berlant argues that one of the conditions of 'the historical present' is what she refers to as the 'impasse, a thick moment of ongoingness' that is characterized by the recurrence of 'enduring and collectively binding loss' (200). This condition of ongoingness might skew Standing's belief in the imminent potential of the precariat, suggesting that its process of 'making' is perpetually deferred. Nevertheless, by focusing on the affective experience of precariousness rather than its objective condition, Berlant suggests the potential of the idea of precarity as a condition of action. Though grounded in affect, precarity offers the possibility that the experence of precariousness can crystalize as an identity with political significance. Potentially, felt insecurity offers a route towards an occupiable collectivity, which may further represent a space for action in the face of the radically dislocating individualism of contemporary captialism.

For Berlant this potential is narrated by what she calls the Cinema of Precarity, a genre that

> attends to the proprioceptive [. . .] to investigate new potential conditions of solidarity emerging from subjects not with similar historical identities or social locations but with similar adjustment styles to the pressures of the emergent new ordinariness. (201–2)

Films that depict the bodily inhabitation of the contemporary dramatize the possibilities for alliances between vulnerable subjects whose different material engagements with precariousness can constellate into precarity, as a form of lived collectivity. Such alliances offer a space for the kind of organizing realization that would constitute class-consciousness. But what is not clear is how a Cinema of Precarity might contribute to the formation of these kinds of alliances beyond the scope of the text itself. While mindful of the way that cinema can structure audiences' reactions to the films that they watch, Berlant's discussion of viewers' responses to the films that she analyses is mostly implicit. In trying to extrapolate Berlant's analysis to consider the precarity novel, I want to attend to this question: How, I ask, do readers respond to an initial experience of anxiety in ways that are capable of locating the reader within a social class that is marked by the 'adjustment styles' that it adopts in the face of contemporary precariousness?

To pursue this line of questioning, I want to refer to a touchstone example of the precarity novel, Matt Thorne's *Eight Minutes Idle* (1999). Thorne's novel tells the story of Dan Thomas, a call centre temp offering customer services to a range of client companies, whose meagre wages must cover his living expenses and also service a range of debts and fines. As a result of accidental misfortune, his father, who is also his housemate, is hospitalized and Dan finds himself unable to make the weekly payments on his flat. To defray this new crisis, Dan decides to leave his flat and attempts to spend his nights sleeping at work. It is not long before Dan's manager discovers him asleep in the office, and this forms one of a sequence of episodes in which Dan images that he might be fired. He spends the whole novel, in fact, considering the possibility that he will lose his job. This is never represented as cataclysmic: losing his job would not, one feels, be the end for Dan. He works and has worked as a temp and work is represented as a succession of impermanent appointments. Nonetheless, the threat of losing his job is expressed as an ongoing anxiety.

Though not cataclysmic, across the novel, Dan's situation does become incrementally worse. At the end of the book, Dan remains in his job, still on a temporary contract, and still with insufficient income to meet his regular outgoings. However, this apparent stasis masks his worsening situation whereby a series of short-term solutions to his indebtedness result in further decline. A third of the way through the novel he borrows a £1000 from a co-worker. This loan comes with interest so, immediately, Dan needs to pay back 'a thousand and five to [his] one' (Thorne 140). Anxious about carrying a large amount of cash, Dan puts the loan into his bank knowing that this will reduce the sum by £200 to clear arrears on his existing debts. While initially he intends to eke out the money, he quickly starts to spend it – eventually taking out the remaining balance of £200 before it is eaten up by the regular instalments on his debt. When Dan becomes embroiled with his manager through an opportunistic sexual relationship that he initiates after she catches him sleeping in the office, he takes out another loan from her to refinance his debt to his friend (284), though this money, too, he carelessly fritters away.

This last phrase feels judgemental, and it is noteworthy how quickly the moral language of prudence and responsibility creeps into my summary of the text. This response chimes with the dominant culture of individualism that requires the vulnerable subject to bear responsibility for the conditions of precariousness under which they live. This might be seen as an obvious and potentially common reading of the text. Certainly, most readers should be able to see the mistakes that Dan is making and to see that he is putting himself into a situation from which it will be difficult for him to extricate himself. Although the novel adopts a first-person narration through which Dan frames the events of the text, he is aware of, and candid enough about, the consequences of his actions. Indeed, a large share of the novel comprises his calculations about making ends meet and his behaviour in spending the money is in direct contradiction to his openly expressed best intentions. However, significantly and, I would suggest, characteristically, the novel offers no routes out of this situation. It is clear to the reader that Dan makes bad decisions and the self-justifying logic that frames these decisions does little to disguise this fact. However, what is equally clear is that there is no point in the novel where a different choice would remove the hardship under which Dan lives. While he may exacerbate this hardship there is no path that would lead him out of it. The novel makes clear that Dan is making life hard for himself but equally it does not shy away from showing the reader that life *is* hard and that Dan's choices are not the origins of that hardship. The novel represents Dan's actions as contributing to his own insecurity but nonetheless depicts his insecurity as systemic and as a product of conditions that are plainly beyond his control.

In the context of such a depiction, what really interests me about my response to Thorne's novel is how stressful I find reading the text. While it is reasonable to rationally imagine that Dan should make different choices, the fact that he does not do so generates feelings of stress or anxiety. It seems likely that these feelings are a key part of the experience of reading this novel in the way that I have proposed earlier. As I have suggested already, it is entirely possible to conceive of a conservative reader who is judgemental about Dan's choices and who is irritated by his refusal to take responsibility for his actions. Nonetheless, it seems equally plausible that this reader will similarly be made anxious by Dan's mounting precariousness. Indeed, the very conflict between a rational set of choices and the apparent irrational choices that are played out in the text is itself contributory to such feelings. This is likely heightened by the narration, which includes Dan's repeated declarations of his own anxiety. This narrative element seems, necessarily, to unsettle the reading experience and produce the kind of primary affective response that I am calling an *anxious reading*.

This kind of affective experience clearly isn't limited to precarity novels. For instance, the pleasures of the horror or thriller genres arguably reside in the somatic effects of unease: adrenalin and an accelerated heart rate in the reader are necessary components in successful examples of these textual forms.[4] However, what distinguishes the experience of reading the precarity novel from the thriller or the horror genre is its relation to realism. If there is horror here, it emanates from facing the social and human conditions that assail the characters. Unlike the horror genre, the anxiety of the precarity novel emanates from the ordinary rather than from the supernatural or the ordinary made strange. Unlike the thriller, the anxiety of the precarity novel emanates from a fear of the known rather than the unknown. This distinction is actually made quite apparent in *Eight Minutes Idle*, which includes elements that gesture towards the horror/thriller genres (it includes two unsolved deaths and Dan spends much of the novel imagining plots against him) but pushes these elements to the edges of the narrative focusing instead on the more real and ever-present fear of not having enough.

Realism and class affect

In trying to think about how this initial affective response is transformed in the kind of political engagement which I associate with precarity, it is worth noting that political solidarity is rarely depicted in the novels themselves. Precisely because the forms of contemporary precariousness constitute the subject as an individual and demand that accountability for circumstances reside in individuality, novels that depict these circumstances rarely include moments of political organization. This alters a tradition of early twentieth-century working-class fiction, such as Walter Greenwood's *Love on the Dole* that deals directly with the potential for, and frustrations of, organized class-consciousness among industrial workers. The precarity novel also differs from consciously activist contemporary fiction such as Robert Newman's *The Fountain at the Centre of the World*, which stages coalitional solidarity by blending a network of stories about economic dispossession with reportage of the 1999 World Trade Organization protests in Seattle. Likewise, Matthew Lee's polemical novel *Predatory Blender* draws together accounts of families in the grip of the subprime lending market and stages a kind of wildcat activism that draws together disgruntled former employees, liberal campaigners and low-wage debtors. In contrast, the precarity novel's depiction of immanent but unfulfilled crises forgoes the possibility of political organization because its generic convention is one of stasis.[5] In place of any fictional solidarity within the precarity novel, it may be possible to see the affective origin of an anxious reading opening up a different form of solidarity between the vulnerable subjects depicted in the text and the vulnerable reader who consumes that fiction. Which is to say that the feelings of anxiety which the reader experiences are the mirror to the depicted insecurity. This is not to say that the reader shares the historical identity and social location of the character. However, it is to propose that the affective content of the reading experience is sufficiently similar to the mode of experiencing the pressures of contemporary insecurity that the text represents. This similarity may, then, rehearse the conditions for solidarity.

Arguably, the realism of the precarity novel is key to its capacity to rehearse moments of solidarity, in particular because of the generic conventions of the realist novel that require the plot to adhere to events that marry with the reader's expectation of what is believable. An anxious reading operates between the readers' desire for the amelioration of crisis on the one hand and their expectations of what is likely on the other. Terms of critical opprobrium like *deus ex machina* demonstrate that readers of realist novels are suspicious of the improbable and that they require the fictional world to match their own experiences of the world beyond the text. These normative expectations clearly attach to genre, and while other styles of writing might be more open to less probable outcomes, the realist text is formally resistant to such devices. This is neatly illustrated by comparing Thorne's novel with its film adaptation (Hewis), which repackages the story as a romantic comedy. Although, in this version, Dan's precariousness remains an important element in the text, it is suppressed in favour of the generic requirement of romantic fulfilment. At the end of the film, for instance, Dan rescues his co-worker, Teri, from homelessness and recreates her bedroom in the office space (now vacated by QuickCalls which has gone into receivership). In the final scene, Dan tries to tell Teri that he only has the lease for three months, hinting at their continuing and future insecurity. She, however, is enchanted by his romantic gesture and cannot hear him, leading Dan to give up his attempt in preference for a starry-eyed embrace. While such an ending retains a degree of ambivalence, the capacity of the romantic comedy to dissipate or repress the anxious charge that accompanies the depiction of precariousness helps to underline the force of the realist novel. The comparison may be usefully contained within Fredric Jameson's discussion of the difference between the *récit* and the *roman* as one between the preterite of the tale and the temporality of past-present-future of the novel (Jameson *Antinomies*). Whereas the romantic comedy is structured around the necessity for closure, the realist novel leaves open the 'eternal present', a fact that is visible in one of the most enduring complaints against realism, that being the reader's tendency to imagine the realist character beyond the confines of the narrated text. In the realist text, the attempt to repress the conditions of precariousness activates an alternate set of conventions in which the reader's certain knowledge that these conditions prevail would manufacture further anxiety rather than see it dispelled.

This emphasis on realism's believability, and on its conjoining of the textual world with the 'real' world, might appear blind to the numerous criticisms of realism, not least the caution that if we turn to realism for 'social truth or knowledge [. . .] we will soon find that what we get is ideology' (Jameson *Antinomies*). Other kinds of texts might be equally adept at triggering and sustaining anxiety, and the lack of closure is perhaps more readily associated with modernist aesthetic experimentation than the realist novel in its classic form. There are two observations to make about the precarity novel in this context. First, the status of modernist aesthetics has changed since the early twentieth century to the extent that 'modernism and its accompanying techniques of estrangement have become the dominant style' (Jameson, 'Reflections' 211). Consequently, the contemporary realist novel has absorbed elements of modernism and utilises its techniques even while it continues to represent in a primarily realist mode.[6] Second, there is no pristine state beyond ideology and all writing reflects the structures of authority governing its composition. The precarity novel will stage notions of individuality and of social relations that are shaped by dominant social narratives but it is not realism, alone, that facilitates this. Certainly, a reading that interprets these fictions as a transparent rendering of social relations may be more susceptible to the ideological force that narrative fiction encodes.[7] Nevertheless, the capacity of readers to transform their affective anxiety into a mode of solidarity may be a form of oppositional reading that is able to read in the interstices of realism's 'ontological commitment to the status quo' (Jameson *Antinomies*). Unlike the genre of the *bildungsroman*, for instance, which operates upon an opposition of narrative and crisis (Moretti 12, 54) and which depicts the everyday as a kind of individual fulfilment, the precarity novel constitutes crisis as the ongoing and ordinary condition of narrative itself. In this way, the precarity novel would seem to invite critique even without staging this critique at the level of the plot.

In order to account for this apparent contradiction, I want to propose a reading of the precarity novel as a kind of historical novel. In doing so, it seems natural to turn to the work of Georg Lukács, whose aesthetic writing most famously defined the historical novel and defended realism as a literary mode capable of rendering social relations visible through a depiction of the social totality. Lukács has not fared well in the development of 'literary theory' during the latter part of the twentieth century, and his disagreement with Theodor Adorno on the relative virtues of realism and modernism has led him to be associated with a naive form of 'content-analysis' (Jameson, 'Reflections' 203).[8] However, my turn to Lukács, here, seeks to recognize two aspects of his work: first, his insistence that the realist novel is always historical and, second, the centrality of affect (or in his terms 'feelings') to his account of this genre. These two ideas come together in *The Historical Novel* when Lukács declares that what matters for the genre

> is not the re-telling of great historical events, but the poetic awakening of the people who figured in those events. What matters is that we should re-experience the social and human motives which led men to think, feel and act just as they did in historical reality. (Lukács 44)

This passage clearly contains within it a conception of expressive realism that has irked so many of Lukács' critics, and it may appear to rest upon a universal humanism with all the blindness to gender that later theory has productively unpacked. Lukács' claim is partly that the historical novel reproduces the historical individual as a universal figure who acted in his time much as the contemporary reader would act were he (or she?) facing similar circumstances. Hence the concentration on the 'more or less mediocre, average English gentleman' (32) rather that the 'important personalities' of history (38). Yet, from here also comes the habit of the historical novel to reduce grand historical events to minor existential details; the illustrative example of this is the way that Tolstoy turns the *mass experience* (20) of the Napoleonic War into selected episodes from the conflict that can express 'the entire mood of the Russian army and through them of the Russian people' (45). For my purposes, the crucial phrase in the aforementioned passage is the idea that the reader will *re-experience* (my emphasis) the motives, feelings and actions of the historical figure. Historical fiction doesn't aim to re-create the historical figure but to produce, through fiction, the lived experience of history in the reader. As such, the notion of re-experiencing seems to capture the claims that I am making for an anxious reading insofar as the feeling of the character finds some resemblance in the experience of reading.

The version of Lukács that I am trying to identify here is one that Lauren Berlant sets out in an attempt to adumbrate a tradition of cultural Marxism, one which 'foregrounds affect [. . .] as the very material of historical embeddedness'(Berlant 66). In this version of Lukács, the historical novel is 'the aesthetic expression of an affective epistemology, an encounter with the historical present via the intensities of its tone.' Lukács, Berlant concludes, 'constantly refers to the "feeling" and the aesthetic "tone" that gets at the heart of the *experiential shape* of a historical period'(64–5, my emphasis). In Berlant's account of Lukács, the 'historical novel' does not name a species of realism set in a distant period but rather it names a mode of realism that draws together the fictional account of affect with the affective response of the reader. This would seem to account for the type of anxious reading that I have been proposing, where the form of the precarity novel provokes affective feelings of anxiety which are then registered as a mirror of the character's experience of precariousness as set out at a narrative level.

Nonetheless, it still seems necessary to think about how this experience becomes *historical* in the sense that Lukács describes. One way that these novels achieve this is by creating a sense of the generational nature of contemporary experience which is not represented as the open-ended experience of a disinterested everyday present. Often, this takes the form of a contrast between the life of the central character and the relative comfort of an older generation. In Halle Butler's *The New Me* (2019), for instance, the central character is insulated from the crises of temporary work by the resources of her middle-class parents. Although reviewers have often criticized the novel for this depiction (Bloom; Tolentino), this contrast between generations is typical of the precarity novel. Even in *Eight Minutes Idle*, where Dan's father finds himself in similar straightened circumstances to his son, his backstory implies that he had previously shared in the benefits of post-war capitalism typically associated with social mobility of the Keynesian interregnum. In this sense, then, contemporary capitalism is represented not as an immovable or naturally occurring circumstance but rather as conditions that have become demonstrably worse. Even if this only opens up a reformist agenda, in keeping with the kinds of socialized capitalism that represent the post-war settlement, it does invite the reader to imagine the conditions of positive change.

Additionally, the precarity novel can be thought of as a genre of the mundane. This may, indeed, be a feature of realism in general but what is striking about the precarity novel is the degree to which plot is subordinated to the description of unexceptional events. In Thorne's novel, this is borne out by the teasing evocation of genre fiction which, as I noted earlier, is dispelled. In the place of genre fiction's melodramatic mode, *Eight Minutes Idle* spends considerable passages discussing Dan's eating habits, his taste in books or his choice of television viewing. Admittedly, Dan's preferences are eccentric but the attention to the mundane in Thorne's novel seems to epitomize a genre. Again, *The New Me* is illustrative of this tendency: the novel moves from episode to episode with little obvious story arc; in place of incident, the novel records passages of internet shopping, television watching, uneventful social (and antisocial) drinking; Millie's dismissal from her job as a temp arises from no significant incident and is prompted merely by her supervisor's capricious feelings; the potential staging of a dramatic climax is hinted at, repeatedly, but is never fulfilled, and even the loss of her job dissipates into a strange coda to the novel where Millie is transformed into an abject figure, 'a cautionary thing' (Butler 189) warning future temps of the perils of staying too long.

Thinking again of Lukács, it is possible to see in this form a version of what Jameson has called the 'deterioration of protagonicity', which involves nineteenth-century realism's move away from 'putative heroes and heroines' in favour of 'minor or secondary characters'. Although, for Jameson, the key figure here is the Spanish novelist Benito Pérez Galdós, he compares Galdós to Lukács' analysis of the world historical figures which I cited earlier. For Lukács, the minor character is crucial to the form of the historical novel and becomes the 'typical' figure, which Jameson asserts is to be distinguished from 'the merely stereoptypical' being instead, a means of registering the 'subterranean movements of History itself' (Jameson *Antinomies*). Mundanity registers the ordinariness of the characters being depicted. They are not protagonists, the subjects of history, but rather they are characters, subject to it. The key to the historical character of the precarity novel, however, is the potential that the reader may recognize this ordinariness as a social relation. Again, the implied equivalence of the anxious reading is key. I've suggested that the anxiety that is produced by reading echoes or mirrors the character's anxiety that is expressed by the narrative. The suggestion here is not that the readers recognize the character's life as their own but rather that they recognize an experience that feels alike with the feelings that are expressed by the text: resemblance operates at the level of affect rather than, precisely, at the level of representation. The ordinariness of the character contributes to this anxiety because it suggests that the character is not in a position to alter the totality of social relations. In terms of resemblance, the character is unable to defray the feelings of anxiety that are produced by these social relations and, consequently, the feelings of anxiety that are produced by reading. This, then, opens the door to precarity as a mode of solidarity because it crystallizes the common source of the character and readers' anxiety even while their encounter with the forces of history may not be identical. In the context of an anxious reading, readers have only two means to alleviate their anxiety: either they turn to modes of action that might address the sources of characters' anxiety as they are narrated within the text or they stop reading.

Notes

1   I offer a more sustained analysis of this genre in Connell 57–89.
2   My use of 'affect' to mean a somatic response in opposition to a conscious state broadly follows Fredric Jameson, who distinguishes affect from 'named emotion' (Jameson *Antinomies*). But it also corresponds with the definition of affect supplied by Gregory Seigworth and Melissa Gregg, who define affect as 'visceral forces beneath, alongside, or generally *other than* conscious knowing' (Seigworth and Gregg 1).
3   For an alternative view, see (Andrew).
4   For instance, reviewing a range of writing on the affective content of horror, Brigid Cherry concludes that 'the genre is named for the emotional or psychological response it is expected to produce' (Cherry 46) and suggests that emotional responses combine with adrenalin or 'shiver sensation' to produce this affect (53).
5   This is not to ignore the cyclical nature of Greenwood's novel, which begins and ends with a description of morning in the Salford streets. While this suggests that nothing has changed for the community that the novel depicts, this cannot wipe away the possibilities for political organization that the novel stages through the figure of its doomed hero Larry Meath.
6   There are, of course, contemporary novels that correspond more closely to the model of classic nineteenth-century realism and, often, indulge in a conscious imitation of the form. A good example of this kind of text would be John Lanchester's *Capital* (2012), which approaches the idea of a contemporary crisis-capitalism through a concentration on plot in a series of entwined story arcs that are all neatly resolved.
7   Once again, the act of reading becomes important here, and, as species of reader-response theory, I find it useful to recall the early work of British Cultural Studies, which insisted that readers could decode texts in ways that opposed the hegemonic message that the text transmits (Hall). The shift from ideology to hegemony may be an important one here. Although Althusser was influenced by Gramsci, the notion of

ideology that emerges from his writings is often assumed to be much less fluid than the idea of hegemony with its emphasis on coalitions of power.
8   For a recent account and revaluation of this dispute, see Warwick Research Collective 57–61.

Works cited

Althusser, Louis. *Lenin and Philosophy and Other Essays*. Translated by Ben Brewster. NLB, 1971.
Andrew, Edward. 'Class in Itself and Class against Capital: Karl Marx and His Classifiers'. *Canadian Journal of Political Science/Revue canadienne de science politique*, vol. 16, no. 3, 1983, pp. 577–84.
Beradi, Franco. 'Bifo'. *Precarious Rhapsody: Semiocapitalism and the Pathologies of the Post-Alpha Generation*. Minor Compositions, n.d.
Berlant, Lauren. *Cruel Optimism*. Duke University Press, 2011.
Bloom, Katie. 'All Precarity, No Pathos: Halle Butler's the New Me and Other Millennial Workplace Novels Use Tropes as Shortcuts to Generational Fatigue'. https://www.thenation.com/article/archive/halle-butler-new-me-book-review-millennial-fiction-temp-work/. Accessed 11 February 2020.
Butler, Halle. *The New Me*. Widenfield & Nicholson, 2019.
Cherry, Brigid. *Horror*. Routledge, 2009.
Connell, Liam. *Precarious Labour and the Contemporary Novel*. Palgrave, 2017.
Davis, Todd F. and Kenneth Womack. *Formalist Criticism and Reader-Response Theory*. Palgrave, 2002.
Felski, Rita. *Uses of Literature*. Blackwell, 2008.
Gramsci, Antonio. *Selections from the Prison Notebooks of Antonio Gramsci*. Translated by Quintin Hoare and Geoffrey Nowell Smith. Lawrence and Wishart, 1971.
Greenwood, Walter. *Love on the Dole*. Penguin, 1969.
Haiven, Max. *Cultures of Financialization: Fictitious Capital in Popular Culture and Everyday Life*. Palgrave Macmillan, 2014.
Hall, Stuart. 'Encoding/Decoding'. *Culture, Media, Language: Working Papers in Cultural Studies, 1972–79*, edited by Stuart Hall, et al. Hutchinson, 1980, pp. 128–38.
Hewis, Mark Simon. '8 Minutes Idle'. Content Film, 2014.
Jameson, Fredric. 'Reflections in Conclusion'. *Aesthetics and Politics*, edited by Ronald Taylor. Verso, 1980 [1977], pp. 196–213.
Jameson, Fredric. *The Antinomies of Realism*. Verso, 2013. Kindle edition.
Lanchester, John. *Capital*. Faber, 2012.
Lee, Matthew. *Predatory Bender: America in the Aughts, a Story of Subprime Finance: With a Non-Fiction Advocates' Afterword; Predatory Lending: Toxic Credit in the Global Inner City: An Afterword to Predatory Bender, a Story of Subprime Finance*. Inner City Press, 2004.
Lukács, Georg. *The Historical Novel*. Translated by Hannah Mitchell and Stanley Mitchell. Penguin Book, 1962.
Massumi, Brian. 'The Autonomy of Affect'. *Cultural Critique*, no. 31, 1995, pp. 83–109, JSTOR, doi:10.2307/1354446.
Moretti, Franco. *The Way of the World: The Bildungsroman in European Culture*. Verso, 1987.

Newman, Robert. *The Fountain at the Centre of the World*. Verso, 2003.
Ollman, Bertell. 'Marx's Use of "Class"'. *American Journal of Sociology*, vol. 73, no. 5, 1968, pp. 573–80.
Piketty, Thomas. *Capital in the Twenty-First Century*. Translated by Arthur Goldhammer. Harvard University Press, 2017.
Przeworski, Adam. 'Proletariat into a Class: The Process of Class Formation from Karl Kautsky's the Class Struggle to Recent Controversies'. *Politics & Society*, vol. 7, no. 4, 1977, pp. 343–401.
Rosenblatt, Louise M. *The Reader, the Text, the Poem: The Transactional Theory of the Literary Work*. Southern Illinois University Press, 1978.
Savage, Mike et al. *Social Class in the 21st Century*. Penguin Books, 2015.
Seigworth, Gregory J. and Melissa Gregg. 'An Inventory of Shimmers'. *The Affect Theory Reader*, edited by Melissa Gregg and Gregory J. Seigworth. Duke University Press, 2010, pp. 1–25.
Standing, Guy. *The Precariat: The New Dangerous Class*. Bloomsbury, 2011.
Standing, Guy. *The Precariat Charter: From Denizens to Citizens*. Bloomsbury, 2014.
Thorne, Matt. *Eight Minutes Idle*. Sceptre, 1999.
Tolentino, Jia. 'Halle Butler's "the New Me" Is an Office Novel for a Precarious Age: The Story of a Temp Worker in Chicago Feels Like a Definitive Work of Millennial Literature'. *New Yorker*. Condé Naste 8 April, https://www.newyorker.com/magazine/2019/04/15/halle-butlers-the-new-me-is-an-office-novel-for-a-precarious-age.
Warwick Research Collective. *Combined and Uneven Development: Towards a New Theory of World-Literature*. Liverpool University Press, 2015. *Postcolonialism across the Disciplines*, Graham Huggan and Andrew Thompson.
Wright, Steve. *Storming Heaven: Class Composition and Struggle in Italian Autonomist Marxism*. Pluto Press, 2002.

Chapter 2

ANXIETY IN THE PRECARIAT

THE AFFECTS OF CLASS IN JAMES KELMAN'S FICTION

Mathies G. Aarhus

Precarity and anxiety are closely related concepts that are often treated either as synonyms or as if one is a symptom of the other. Guy Standing, for instance, describes anxiety as a *symptom* of precarious labour when he speculates about the four a's (anxiety, anger, anomie and alienation) that dominate the precariat's emotional disposition (Standing, *The Precariat* 19–24). Similarly, in the activist manifesto 'We are all very anxious' by the anonymous, 'militant research collective' named the Institute for Precarious Consciousness, anxiety is considered to be today's dominant emotional disposition, or the 'reactive affect [. . .] which holds [contemporary capitalism] together' (The Institute for Precarious Consciousness).[1] An obvious problem with many of these diagnoses of our age as a new 'age of anxiety' is that they tend to conflate the psychological pathologies of anxiety, stress and precarity and fail to offer a very nuanced interpretation of anxiety's continuing role in working-class life.[2] The claim that anxiety is a particularly neoliberal emotion caused by our precarious labour markets is doubtful, because, clearly, anxiety is not new and our age is not the first self-proclaimed 'age of anxiety' – as Kierkegaard's 1844 philosophical treaty *The Concept of Anxiety* and W. H. Auden's 1947 poem *Age of Anxiety* indicate. Further, the credo that today 'We are all very anxious' universalizes anxiety and does not account for the fact that some people are more anxious than others. Nevertheless, the attempt to *historicize* the affective present in conjunction with our changing labour conditions is important, because it can add to an at-times stagnant mapping of feelings performed by more traditional Marxists.[3]

With this chapter, I want to consider the classed dimensions of contemporary anxiety. If the precariat is one way of describing the modification of the traditional working class that has taken place over the last thirty years, then how do affect and emotion fit in this transmutation? What would it mean to think of neoliberalism as not only a project of economic redistribution but also a project of affective redistribution?

Many sociologists of emotion argue that emotions can serve as commodities and be subject to speculation and unequal distribution on a similar level as other resources.[4] The potentially commodified nature of certain emotions is the central reason that emotional life can become a domain of inequality and stratification. As Hochschild points out, marketing and speculation in emotions often happen through the service industry, where workers are expected to perform various forms of emotional labour in order to 'sell' emotional states to customers who are, implicitly or explicitly, paying for these pleasant feelings (Hochschild). The increasingly commoditized nature of certain pleasurable emotions, in turn, is the reason for the flourishing of materially non-productive industries in contemporary capitalism, like the 'security enterprise' or the 'wellness industry', where workers are employed for the primary purpose of making the customers *feel* secure and content.[5] In cynical terms, these industries offer the upper classes the pleasure of escaping their anxiety, stress or discomfort, for a moment at least, but in a process of emotional exchange where the unpleasant feeling is transferred onto the worker in a form of transaction. This transmission of feeling can be structured into particular flows that systematically transfer certain feelings downward by shielding those with economic resources from 'bad' feelings while putting the emotional baggage on the backs of workers. One can take this analysis even further and argue that the distribution of anxiety is one of the central arenas where class stratification is played out today.[6]

While a society organized around the systematic distribution of unpleasant feelings to the lower classes and the poor sounds rather dystopian, or like something from the sci-fi show *Black Mirror*, this nightmarish scenario is perhaps creeping ever closer today. The Scottish author James Kelman offers a literary example of a kind of speculative working-class fiction, in which he turns up the knob on certain present-day developments in terms of precarization and the unequal distribution of affect. In particular, Kelman's novel *You Have to Be Careful in the Land of the Free* (2004) points to valuable insights about how anxiety and exposure to risk have come to function as forms of class power in our times. In this chapter, I argue that Kelman's novel exposes us to a not-too-distant class society in which status anxiety and a slighting of dignity have become formalized in order to ensure worker productivity and consent. In Kelman's fiction, the only form of escape from this psychologically binding class system is to embrace a form of extreme precarity, often through gambling, where one wilfully puts one's fate 'in the hands of others' as an act of defiance.

Anxiety as an affect of class

Before turning to literature, however, it seems necessary to dwell for a bit on the phenomenology of anxiety to explain exactly what it means to be anxious rather than, say, scared, nervous or stressed out. Whereas some psychoanalytic traditions have tried to universalize anxiety (often following Lacan's example (Salecl)), some aspects of anxiety clearly relate to social hierarchy, status and loss of face. It is these classed dimensions of the feeling that are of particular interest to us here.

In its broadest form, anxiety can be defined as an emotional reaction to the perception of being in danger from something not fully conceivable (May). Four traits thus seem central to the definition of anxiety in sociological and philosophical theories: threat, vagueness, futurity and loss. First, from a biological perspective, anxiety is always, in however obscure a way, connected to our universal pursuit of self-preservation (Nussbaum). However, compared to the more directly conceivable threat of fear, anxiety is characterized by vagueness and a relative lack of prospects for agency (Wilkinson; May). Further, anxiety necessarily relates to a vague sense of the future and an expectation of a coming loss. In Sianne Ngai's words, it is a 'future-oriented' affect (Ngai 209). Finally, anxiety always involves a sense of a *loss* of something important to the self's identity or sense of meaning in the world (May).

However, there is also a less immediate side to anxiety that does not revolve around covering basic physiological needs, namely the feeling sometimes known as 'status anxiety'. Status anxiety can broadly be defined as a fear of a loss of social status in the eyes of others. As opposed to anxiety over self-preservation, status anxiety has to do with less immediate needs for respect, prestige, honour or recognition that nevertheless can be seen as universal human aspirations. Indeed, following Cobb and Sennett's account of status anxiety, the fundamental *threat* of status anxiety can be defined as a threat to dignity. In *The Hidden Injuries of Class*, Cobb and Sennett revealed an emotional class system based on the *slighting of dignity* that keeps the working classes in America subdued and in check:

> The burden of class today is thus a strange phenomenon: social inequality is maintained by creating a morality of anxiety, and this discontent is hard to organize by the Left because the logic of discontent leads people to turn on each other rather than on the 'system'. (Cobb and Sennett 173)

A central characteristic of this 'system' is indeed that it remains vague or, in Cobb and Sennett's words, 'hidden'. Thus, the *vagueness* that is a central feature of anxiety also finds its way into status anxiety, as a feeling of social injustice is coupled with a lack of a fixed object for this injustice. According to Cobb and Sennett, the efficiency of the class system is founded on a very intricate form of authority where institutional structures award certain people with 'badges of ability' to uphold the status anxiety felt by both the upwardly mobile and those 'left behind'. The working class, then, lose connection and solidarity with the upwardly mobile, who are considered more dignified or above them, in addition to the less privileged or the unemployed who are considered unwilling to make the same sacrifices that they themselves make. Working-class subjects do injury to each other not because they want to, but because their location in the system leaves them unable to understand the reciprocally produced status anxiety which fuels the system on a psychological level.

Cobb and Sennett further analyse several psychological defence mechanisms that the working classes use in the face of this class system; most interestingly for us, 'sacrificing' oneself for future generations. Rather than confronting the lack of dignity in one's own life and work, working-class parents had a tendency to sacrifice their wellbeing for their kids, by taking the indignity of their current situation upon themselves and working tirelessly for their family. The lack of dignity that parents felt was thus appeased by projecting onto the future a better life for their children: 'Sacrifice, as we have seen, makes men future-oriented' (Cobb and Sennett 201). Thus, in addition to being characterized by *threat* and *vagueness*, status anxiety also seems to imply a dimension of *futurity*. As with existential anxiety, it does not make much sense to call status anxiety atemporal or only related to the immediate present. Our worries about a lack of status and dignity are always related to our sense of being selves in a larger continuum. In the case of the working people Cobb and Sennett interviewed, this was expressed in their hopes and vague anxieties for the fate of future generations.

Lastly, to complete the connection between existential anxiety and status anxiety, we can speculate about the potential *loss* implied by status anxiety. Cobb and Sennett's work seems to suggest that status anxiety fundamentally revolves around a fear of a loss of dignity both from the community and from ourselves. Of course, even though the upwardly mobile can feel anxious or that they have lost dignity by abandoning their class belonging, clearly – and especially in times of increasing precarization and austerity politics – what most people are anxious about is downward mobility.[7] Whereas existential anxiety is always derived from self-preservation or a threat to one's life, status anxiety's endgame seems to be social exclusion or 'social death'.[8]

Working-class speculative fiction

As wealth and mobility are distributed unequally in capitalism, so are safety and security. Rich people, generally speaking, are safer than poor people, because they are relatively shielded from poverty, unemployment or physical threats, but this does not necessarily entail *feeling* less anxious or vulnerable. Whether rich people or poor people feel more anxious by default is beside the point of this chapter – rather, what I am interested in here is the preventive measures taken to redistribute painful feelings like anxiety from one class to another. To explore this dynamic and see how it affects contemporary class relations, it is valuable to turn to contemporary literature and the emotional depths fiction allows us access to.

In this endeavour, the Scottish novelist and short story writer James Kelman is a particularly interesting author to explore, because of his lasting interest in the psychological and emotional affects of social class. Throughout his over forty-year writing career, Kelman's work has revolved around characters suffering from the psychological injuries caused by various variants of social exclusion. As the title indicates, the novel *You Have to Be Careful in the Land of the Free* (2004) contributes to this oeuvre by exploring the themes of suspicion, safety and insecurity. On a personal, psychological level, these themes pervade the protagonist Jeremiah's thinking and his – at times rebellious, at times paranoid – outlook on life. On a broader, societal level, insecurity and suspicion pervade the anxious social universe that the novel inhabits, including the post-9/11 US security state's actions and the social encounters that Jeremiah has.

In the novel, we follow Jeremiah, a Scottish-born immigrant, who has lived in the United States for the past decade working a variety of small jobs and gigs like bartending, waiting tables, standing guard at art galleries and being a security operative in airports. In his own words, the only constant in Jeremiah's life is failure: 'failed security operative [. . .] add to that failed husband and failed parent, failed father, general fucking no hoper. And now I was gaun hame, gaun hame! I was a failed fucking immigrant!' (Kelman, *You Have to Be Careful in the Land of the Free* 20). In the beginning of the novel, Jeremiah finds himself unemployed, he has blown his chances with his wife and he has decided to finally return 'hame' to Scotland. The novel unfolds over the last night before Jeremiah's flight when he frequents a number of bars in the vicinity of his airport motel and reminisces about his time spent in the United States while he continually questions whether he really will get on that plane the next day.

Due to his immigrant status and lack of basic employment security and citizenship rights, Jeremiah belongs to what Guy Standing calls the precariat. In terms of Standing's theory, Jeremiah's relations of production are precarious because he is on the margins of the job market, having to work as a contingent labourer in a wide variety of 'bullshit jobs' (Graeber). As Standing points out in relation to the precariat, Jeremiah's line of no-future jobs leaves him *alienated* from the job market and his own career: 'Nay dreams. Reality. I had a job that took me nowhere, that became more difficult by the night. It was like I was separated from things' (297). Even though Jeremiah is thirty-four and thus well into his working life, he still does not really know what he wants to do in his career. He knows that his dream is not to be a security guard in an airport, and he therefore tries his luck with writing crime novels, while he maintains a part-time occupation as a gambler on the side. Jeremiah's relations of production are also particularly precarious because he receives his relatively low pay in money wages and thus is forced to live on a month-to-month basis: 'for the crucial work we do here the wages are, I would say, fairly low, mair akin to the wage of an adolescent' (160). When work is scarce, Jeremiah goes into debt, and because he is only in the United States on a temporary work visa, he is forced to constantly take up new small gigs if he does not want to be deported on the grounds of unemployment. Finally, in Standing's terms, what makes Jeremiah belong to the global precariat are his antagonistic *relations to the state*. Because of Jeremiah's employment status as a migrant labourer, his rights are restricted and he is treated with suspicion by the state and its governing bodies.

In many ways, the novel is Kelman's version of a piece of speculative fiction, as it is cast in a near future when the US state has intensified several of the policies modern states already use for population control and stratification based on citizenship. Thus, the state has introduced a 'card system' where people's individual rights are determined by the status of one's ID card. One's card is affected by one's descendance, national citizenship, political allegiances and, even more subtly, selected character traits such as religion and skin colour. Jeremiah is a Class III Red Card, and his card indicates that he is an 'atheist and a socialist', which implies that he has to deposit his money in an official state-savings account and is prohibited from having a credit card and getting permanent residency. One of Jeremiah's hopes is that he will one day move into the ranks of green cards, or the promised land of the even more prestigious 'blue cards', as this would allow him to reside in the country more permanently and would take away some of his precarious working conditions.

One can only guess as to why the US state in *Careful* has found it necessary to implement the discriminatory, human rights violating and deeply classist 'card system', but the policies of the state in *Careful* of course imitate many of the policies that nation states are already implementing today to confront the 'threat' of a globalized labour force. States are already implementing a somewhat discriminatory green card system where the right to work is only available to certain income groups or nationalities – along with tight restrictions on the mobility of low-income labour, travel bans, demonization of immigrants, sometimes ethnic discrimination and so on. From the perspective of capital, the incentive for the card system seems to be to ensure productivity while at the same time keeping up a strict system of citizenship distinctions. By limiting certain migrant labourers' rights, the state ensures that labourers are productive because they are forced to work to stay in the country.

A characteristic of the way class operates in the novel is that people are given different rights and privileges based on a combination of different axes of stratification: from ethnicity and nationality to political affiliation. A further characteristic is the unequal distribution of insecurity on the basis of card status, as Red Card immigrant workers like Jeremiah really 'have to be careful in the land of the free', and generally more so than others. The card system maintains a fundamental system of distinctions between people while allowing them to live side by side. In the globalized labour market of *Careful*, inequality and class exclusion seem only to have increased while nationalism and racism continue unhindered. As Berthold Schoene has pointed out, the novel can thus be understood as a nightmarish vision of globalization where strict borders for the movement of labour and services have been erased, while the world still clings to the worst traits of sectarianism and racial conflict.[9] The fact that the 'segregated, fiercely competitive factions' (Schoene 93) now live closer to each other has not changed the fundamental logic of class conflict which has simply found new means (the card system) and a new arena (security) through which to express itself.

The hidden injuries of class anxiety

One of the main interests of the novel is to investigate the social dynamics that come to pass in a society where security and status are distributed unequally. As already mentioned, the social universe that *Careful* imagines is one in which status has been formalized and structured into a rigid card system where people from different classes with differing descendance, ethnicity and social standing are divided into strict, measurable and easily governable groups. Consequently, people from higher-card classes are often free to treat the lower-status groups like lesser beings which is an issue that Jeremiah runs into on a daily basis. Thus, whenever Jeremiah enters a bar – and he enters quite a few in this barfly novel – he is asked to show his ID card, which displays his Class III Red Card status. Here, for instance, is a typical encounter Jeremiah has with a bartender:

> I returned to the bar and passed him the documentation. The shotguns were out of sight. Oh, says he, you got a Red Card?
> Aye, says I, surprised?
> He smiled, took it from me and studied it. He nodded, pursing his lips.
> So ye interested in politics? I says.
> He looked at me.
> Politics is an interesting subject. I know quite a few jokes about politics.
> You do?
> Yeh.
> He smiled to me and returned my ID. Nothing poisonal. [. . .]
> But it made me smile. Did they no know it was always goddam poisonal. Did they no know that was precisely what it was, what it all was, them and their fucking armoury man, so why did they continue to lie and fuck knows what dissembling hypocritical bastarn. (179–80)

This scene is an intricate portrayal of the emotional injuries of status anxiety. As earlier mentioned with reference to Cobb and Sennett, status anxiety fundamentally concerns a lack of dignity at the hands of others and is thus a feeling that is deeply related to one's personal (or 'poisonal') sense of oneself. In the quote, the status denial that Jeremiah suffers at the hands of the bartender is felt as an indictment of his personhood, exactly because the card system is built on judging character traits like politics, religion, descendance and so on. The underlying status anxiety implied in Jeremiah's encounter with the bartender feels so deeply personal because it is based on the denial of dignity and whatever makes him feel valued as a member of society.

Naturally, as in the aforementioned quote, status anxiety and status denial in the novel are often followed by anger or resentment towards the card system and the dominant classes with higher-card statuses, who Jeremiah refers to as the 'right-wing fascist fuckers ye sometimes see creeping out from behind the middens' (98). In Jeremiah, signs of class solidarity emerge among the precarious and vulnerable of society. However, because of affective patterns that force the precarious and lower classes to turn their disaffection and discontent inwards, the novel never moves to outward class antagonism. These forces are on display in a scene where a snobby, self-entitled couple steals Jeremiah's chair after he goes to get a drink at the bar:

> Amigo, I said, why don't ye just fucking apologize, save all this hassle. You ess in the wrong for taking my chair.
> Hey can you leave now? said the lassie.

Ye talking to me or him?

I'm talking to you.

Okay, snap yer fingers I'm about to vanish. I gied the two a salute and walked on outa there. While in earshot I distinguished the terms 'power' and 'humiliation'. Aint it amazing how strangers reach to the root of one's veriest deep-down innermost essence. Fuck them.

No, it was me, it was me to blame.

Madness is a short step from the deathwish. It is my opinion that the progression from madness leads to the selfsame point as when the world takes on a clarity such that no sane person would desire an escape. I rejoined the smokers. [. . .]

I was of no service to her. I was a fucking dumpling. (295)

In this quote, Jeremiah very quickly goes from demanding respect and an apology from the couple, to blaming himself and telling himself that his wife is better off without him. The encounter follows a familiar emotional pattern of Jeremiah's: Jeremiah is robbed of dignity → Jeremiah becomes angry and defiant → Jeremiah turns anger inwards into feelings of self-blame and a lack of self-esteem. For all his anarchist defiance, Jeremiah's rebelliousness is often subdued and pacified – in part, of course, because he is on the lower steps of the social and status ladder and therefore easy for people to step on. His lack of respect and recognition, symbolized by his Class III Red Card, leaves him unable to fully break out of the injury to his dignity that his encounters with disrespectful strangers confront him with.

As Jeremiah mentions in the above quote, 'strangers reach to the root of one's veriest deep-down innermost essence', exactly because they challenge his inner sense of himself as a valuable member of the community. Much like the system designed for the slighting of injury that Cobb and Sennett analysed in working-class life in the 1970s, Jeremiah is kept in check by a system that grants him submissive status as a Red Card. However, as opposed to a system of 'hidden injuries', the slighting of dignity in *Careful* is formalized and made explicit through ID cards. *Careful*, thus, depicts a semi-dystopian world where the class injuries that used to be 'hidden' and not fully legitimate in the public sphere have become intimately integrated into people's everyday social interactions. The consistent status denial of certain 'unwanted' people, like Jeremiah, which the card system allows for, thus heightens the social gap between people and prevents communal bonds from emerging between status groups.

Gambling and precarity

In this way, throughout the novel, anxiety and other injuries of class prevent a shared precarious voice from emerging as they keep the system of social distinctions in place. This form of emotional class warfare seems invulnerable, because it takes aim at the innermost, hidden depths of people's lives. A few openings, however, are hinted at throughout the novel, that point to possible ways to struggle against contemporary anxiety, including gambling, and solidarity around a more egalitarian distribution of precarity.

James Kelman's interest in gambling goes back to his earliest written novel, *A Chancer*, a novel about a twenty-year-old compulsive gambler which was put in print in 1985 following the success of *Busconductor Hines* (1984). Throughout Kelman's novels, the gambling motif has played at least two significant symbolic purposes; on the one hand, standing in place for everyday working-class life and the contingency this necessarily involves; and, on the other hand, symbolizing an economic system where, at the end of the day, 'the house always wins'. In Kelman's later fiction, the gambling motif has increasingly been tied to this second symbolism as is the case in the novel *Mo Said She Was Quirky* (2012), in which the heroine Helen is treated with arrogance and sexism by the financial elite in a London casino where she works as a croupier. Kelman's newer fiction is clearly interested in the new inequalities caused by globalized, financial capitalism where certain people are awarded for their capacities for 'risk taking', while that risk always ends up hurting someone else on the other side of the fence.

In the case of *Careful*, at various times Jeremiah speculates and philosophizes about the meaning of his gambling as it relates to his own classed experience. In the novel, gambling thus attains at least two symbolic meanings: (1) as a metaphor for precarity, or having your fate in the hands of others, and (2) as a means for agency. In the first sense, Jeremiah's membership of the precariat ensures that his fate is in the hands of others, in a similar sense that one's fate is in the hands of others when rolling the dice or playing the roulette. Thus, Jeremiah is both precariously employed and a gambler who continually and throughout the novel blames his bad luck on 'the fates' or what he sometimes refers to as 'auld Zeus' or 'these ancient Greek dramatist fuckers':

> It is a peculiar thing to say, and I'm beginning to see this mair, speaking as somebody who likes to gamble, but I've aye been an unlucky body. Incredibly so. It isnay that my opponents carry good luck man it is me that carries bad. All my life I've been battling against the odds and the worst and most prolonged struggle has been against the fates. (364)

In this quote, gambling is theorized as something that is out of the hands of Jeremiah, because he has been predetermined by 'the fates' to be a man who carries bad luck. When this understanding of gambling dominates in the novel, Jeremiah seems to enjoy gambling because it implies 'passivity' and acceptance of his fate as an inevitable loser ('There is a passivity about gambling' (107)). Gambling paradoxically serves as a break from the anxious existence that Jeremiah otherwise suffers under, because in this domain he *willingly* puts his fortune in the hands of higher powers.

In this way, gambling momentarily distracts from the anxious experience of life, but it does so in a contradictory and ultimately unsustainable manner because the very essence of gambling implies precariousness. The word for precarious originates in prex (prayer) and, in the Renaissance, the word became a legal term implying that one possessed something 'through the favour of another'. The precarious experience of being at the mercy of higher powers is expressed equally in gambling and in contingent labour. As a result, whether or not Jeremiah chooses to gamble really does not make a big difference: 'It doesnay matter what ye bet ye are fukt. Even if ye dont bet' (78). Gambling is seen as a symbolic extension of Jeremiah's fate as an immigrant contingent worker who depends on the will of both employers and an American state which, most graciously, lets him stay and work. Thus, even though this understanding of gambling as passivity, for Jeremiah, can serve to numb his anxiety, it really does not change the fundamental pattern that structures his life, because as a member of the precariat he is always already gambling or in the hands of higher powers.

The second meaning of gambling in the novel, which of course initially seems to be at odds with the first, is based on the idea of gambling as a form of agency or power. When this understanding of gambling dominates in the novel, 'the fates' do not seem to have a significant role to play in gambling at all, but gambling on the contrary seems controlled by will and a proud insistence on agency: 'I wouldnay blame the fates; if ye get dealt a hand ye play it, ye play it to its proper value' (143). At these times, gambling almost takes on a redemptive force as more or less the only form of power that the precarious and the disenfranchised have: 'The thing with gambling, there was aye that wee chance like ye could do something, change something, just fucking if ye got in front man, just a wee bit' (129). At least with gambling, the precarious *choose* to put their wills in the hands of others and thus assert a minimum of autonomy and self-determinacy in an existence that is otherwise characterized by a lack of freedom. Thus, gambling comes to represent a potential for autonomy and self-will, both in the sense that the gambler could actually win and break free from his precarious dependency on others and in the sense that the very act of gambling counts as a form of agency in itself. With gambling, Jeremiah takes back parts of his control over his life, or at least he chooses to live precariously as an act of will.

The gambling symbolism, that runs through the entirety of the novel and alternates between signifying precarity and agency, gets its most absurd culmination in what in the novel's universe is known as the 'Persian bet'. In the semi-dystopian not-too-distant future of the novel, certain airline companies have started offering low-fare flights but have scaled down on security measures, so that these flights now include a serious risk of crashing. The 'perishing bet' (or 'Persian bet' as Jeremiah calls it) involves buying life insurance and getting on one of these dangerous flights, so that if you arrive at your destination, you get a cheap flight, and if you perish, your family scores a hefty premium: 'Either way ye were a winner. If ye survived ye lost the bet but if ye perished yer family collected the cash' (93). As the masses who are willing to enter this bet increase in the novel, Jeremiah is hired as a security operative at an airport and observes the action from within.

The Persian bet is clearly a satirical portrayal of the way our society treats an underclass of precarious or terminally unemployed people, whose desperation and lack of dignity grows to the point where gambling away one's life seems to be the only honourable choice: 'People had originally bought them [raffle tickets] to enter the draw for a seat on one of the lower-end airplanes, hoping to win a honorable exit from this vale of woes, or a fair return on a lost-limb wager' (194–5). But again, the double meaning of gambling is immanent even in this most absurd of bets; on the one hand, Persian betters are forced to bet their lives away because of their poverty and deprivation; on the other hand, it seems to be a way for the precarious to retake a form of honour or dignity over their fates in the face of their deprivation and lack of agency. Schoene alludes to a certain utopian dimension in the communality implied in this multicultural mass of people that gathers in airports connected only by their utter deprivation and despair.[10] 'There is nay question it brought a solidarity' (118), Jeremiah claims at one point referring to the whole Persian bet affair and the public mood it created, but his comment seems more ironic than anything else. Having to gamble their lives away to retain a sense of dignity in a society based on a formalized system for the slighting of status, the precarious in the novel are so isolated and miserable that one can only laugh in the face of the absurdity of their misery.

Much like most of Kelman's earlier novels, including his classic *How Late it was How Late* (1994), *Careful* does not, on a thematic level at least, allude to many existing social communities or bonds of solidarity but only to small unrealized potentialities or openings. In his influential article 'Resisting Arrest', Cairns Craig characterizes James Kelman's fiction as a representation of a working-class culture 'which has become atomised, fragmented, and in which individuals are isolated from one another' (Craig 101). Whereas solidarity between these isolated individuals appears more or less impossible, Craig reserves a special place for a solidarity between text and character that he sees enacted through Kelman's use of voice. By resisting traditional bourgeois representations of the poor or the working classes – through a narrative voice that coalesces with the voice of the disenfranchised characters – Kelman's fiction: 'enacts at a linguistic level what it points to as absent in the world, a communality that transcends the absolute isolation of the individual human being' (Craig 103–4). Mirroring Craig's argument, one could claim that – because of *Careful*'s style – the reader stands squarely on the side of the precarious through her alliance with the protagonist Jeremiah. But in another and much more concrete sense, real political affiliation between people with a shared class disposition seems far from possible in *Careful*'s speculative universe. More than a blueprint for the establishment of solidarity among the precarious and the unemployed, the novel can instead be read as an indictment and a satire of a new globalized capitalism that exploits people on the grounds of their vulnerability and their mistrust of one another.

Class is, and has perhaps always been, a matter of distributing feelings and affect. In neoliberalism, painful feelings like anxiety are unequally distributed, as a result of various state and market forces that shield certain groups from danger while exposing others. In other words, as opposed to the claim from where I started this chapter, we are *not* all very anxious, or at least not equally so. The unequal distribution of anxiety is on display in a very visible way in the increase in gated communities and the lack of response of many affluent countries to climate changes from which they are relatively shielded. And as Judith Butler has pointed to, the distribution of precarity and security is increasingly becoming the battle ground for egalitarian political movements (Butler).

Kelman's writing is clearly not optimistic for the prospect of solidarity for the wretched in our new class system. *Careful* exposes a subtle but still rigid distribution of anxiety on class grounds, or what I earlier described as a formalized system for the slighting of dignity. As mentioned, in *Careful*, the hidden injuries that status anxiety cause often come to block the very prospect of solidarity. Rather, Kelman's speculative fiction should be read as unveiling the anxiety caused by the threat and experience of contemporary precarity and the brakes that these forms of emotional injuries put on community. Reading Kelman both makes you aware of the affective workings of class stratification and puts you in contact with some of the inevitable losers of our brave new class society.

Notes

1. According to the manifesto, former capitalist regimes relied on different reactive affects to quell dissent and create worker productivity – including misery in the early age of industrialization, and boredom in the Fordist and welfare state era – but in our age of precarious labour, these affects have lost relevance or been subsumed by new worker worries and affective dispositions. Similarly, Isabel Lorey argues that precarity has become a form of neoliberal biopolitics (Lorey).
2. Notice the problematic conflation of anxiety and precarity in quotes like the following: 'The present dominant affect of anxiety is also known as precarity' (The Institute for Precarious Consciousness).
3. In traditional Marxist thought, the 'reactive affects' of capitalism include misery and alienation, whereas the feelings imagined as progressive include anger and solidarity (or brotherhood). Not that this is necessarily wrong for our current moment, where more solidarity and anger would definitely be beneficial to combat wealth inequality or the destruction of the environment. But I still think we need a broader and more flexible register for understanding progressive emotional politics.
4. See for instance: Cottingham; Skeggs; Hochschild.
5. Autonomist Marxists have gone on to claim that immaterial labour and affective labour have become increasingly important industries in post-Fordist capitalism. According to Hardt and Negri, for instance, this creates advantages for new forms of dissent as workers are no longer intrinsically tied to manual labour and work–place solidarity, but it also creates disadvantages as workers are now more emotionally invested in their labour (Hardt and Negri).
6. See Neilson. Guy Standing also argues that the distribution of precarity in today's society is not at all equal but in fact fundamentally classed based on one's systemic relations of production, relations of distribution and relations to the state (Standing, *A Precariat Charter*).
7. Tom Boland has argued that unemployment leads to an acute loss of acknowledgement from the traditional channels through which people are rewarded recognition: 'if recognition is primarily given on the basis of what you do, then those who cannot give a clear answer to this question face difficulty' (Boland and Griffin 11).

8   Many sociologists and psychologists have thus identified the threat of unemployment as one of the main sources of status anxiety (May; Pahl; Kelly; Wilkinson).
9   'In Kelman's view contemporary humanity is at risk of giving in to globalisation as a purely economically determined process of agglomeration, both nationally and internationally, pushing cultures more closely together, yet rather than encouraging them to grow into convivial neighbourhoods, leaving them to cluster explosively in strictly segregated, fiercely competitive factions' (Schoene 93).
10 Schoene's reading particularly focuses on the strange character 'the being', who starts showing up in the airport where Jeremiah works and serves as a kind of messianic figure for the Persian betters when his/her grocery cart 'explode[s] into flames, including piles and piles of lottery tickets, auld betting receipts and scratchcards' (233). Schoene reads this manifestation as laying claim to a utopian potential of the Persian betters that share a form of solidarity through their fundamental form of despair (Schoene).

Works cited

Anderson, Ben. 'Neoliberal Affects'. *Progress in Human Geography*, vol. 4, no. 6, November 2015, pp. 734–53.
Berlant, Lauren. 'Nearly Utopian, Nearly Normal: Post-Fordist Affect in La Promesse and Rosetta'. *Public Culture*, vol. 19, no. 2, January 2007, pp. 273–301.
Boland, Tom, and Ray Griffin. *The Sociology of Unemployment*. Oxford University Press, 2015.
Butler, Judith. *Notes Toward a Performative Theory of Assembly*. Harvard University Press, 2015.
Casas-Cortés, Maribel. 'A Genealogy of Precarity: A Toolbox for Rearticulating Fragmented Social Realities In and Out of the Workplace'. *Rethinking Marxism*, vol. 26, no. 2, April 2014, pp. 206–26.
Cobb, Jonathan, and Richard Sennett. *The Hidden Injuries of Class*. Reprint edition. W. W. Norton & Company, 1993.
Connell, Liam. *Precarious Labour and the Contemporary Novel*. Palgrave Macmillan, 2017.
Cottingham, Marci D. 'Theorizing Emotional Capital'. *Theory and Society*, vol. 45, no. 5, October 2016, pp. 451–70.
Craig, Cairns. 'Resisting Arrest: James Kelman'. *The Scottish Novel since the Seventies: New Visions, Old Dreams*, edited by Gavin Wallace and R. W. Stevenson. Edinburgh University Press, 1993, pp. 99–114.
Ehrenreich, Barbara. *Fear of Falling: The Inner Life of the Middle Class*. Reprint edition. HarperCollins, 1990.
Graeber, David. 'On the Phenomenon of Bullshit Jobs'. *STRIKE!*, 17 August 2013, http://strikemag.org/bullshit-jobs/.
Hardt, Michael, and Antonio Negri. *Empire*. Harvard University Press, 2000.
Hochschild, Arlie Russell. *The Managed Heart: Commercialization of Human Feeling*. 3rd edition. University of California Press, 2012.
Kelly, Maura. 'Trickle-Down Distress: How America's Broken Meritocracy Drives Our National Anxiety Epidemic'. *The Atlantic*, July 2012.
Kelman, James. *The Busconductor Hines*. [1984]. Orion, 1995.
Kelman, James. *You Have to Be Careful in the Land of the Free*. Mariner Books, 2004.

Kelman, James. *A Chancer*. Birlinn, 2012.
Kelman, James. *How Late It Was How Late*. Random House, 2012.
Kelman, James. *Mo Said She Was Quirky*. Other Press, LLC, 2013.
Lorey, Isabell. *State of Insecurity: Government of the Precarious*. Verso Books, 2015.
May, Rollo. *The Meaning of Anxiety*. W. W. Norton & Company, 2015.
Neilson, David. 'Class, Precarity, and Anxiety under Neoliberal Global Capitalism: From Denial to Resistance'. *Theory & Psychology*, vol. 25, no. 2, April 2015, pp. 184–201.
Ngai, Sianne. *Ugly Feelings*. Harvard University Press, 2007.
Nussbaum, Martha C. *The New Religious Intolerance: Overcoming the Politics of Fear in an Anxious Age*. Reprint edition. Belknap Press, 2013.
Pahl, Ray. *After Success: Fin-de-Siecle Anxiety and Identity*. Polity, 1995.
Salecl, Renata. *On Anxiety*. Routledge, 2004.
Schoene, Berthold. *The Cosmopolitan Novel*. Edinburgh University Press, 2009.
Skeggs, Beverley. 'Exchange, Value and Affect: Bourdieu and "the Self."' *The Sociological Review*, vol. 52, October 2004, pp. 75–95.
Standing, Guy. *A Precariat Charter: From Denizens to Citizens*. Bloomsbury Academic, 2014.
Standing, Guy. *The Precariat: The New Dangerous Class*. Bloomsbury Academic, 2014.
The Institute for Precarious Consciousness. 'We Are All Very Anxious'. *Plan C*, 4 April 2014.
Wilkinson, Iain. *Anxiety in a 'Risk' Society*. Routledge, 2002.

Chapter 3

PERFORMING PRECARITY

THREATENING THE AUDIENCE IN GARY OWEN'S *IPHIGENIA IN SPLOTT*

Peter Simonsen

Theatre of the world and social class in the twenty-first century

In the introduction to *Social Class in the 21st Century*, a book framed as very much concerned with the societal risks of increasing class polarization stemming from increasing wealth among a small elite at the 'top' and new and grim, nineteenth-century levels of poverty at the 'bottom' of society, sociologists Mike Savage et al. recount an anecdote about theatre attendance in London in the context of the Great British Class Survey they conducted with the help of the BBC in 2011. The survey was based on feedback from 161,000 people answering a set of questions about class, and resulted in the proposal of a new class system made up of seven different social classes to better describe recent changes in the social fabric – among them the new super-rich elite class and the precariat class comprising the 'bottom' 15 per cent of the population in terms of income and fortune as well as most other resources such as cultural and social capital.

The BBC then, in April of 2013, created a class calculator whereby users of their website, by answering a few simple questions indicating economic, social and cultural capital, could find out what class they belonged to ('The Great British Class Calculator'). Within a week, no fewer than seven million people had taken the test. Not only did this solidly dispel with any remaining Thatcherite or Blairite notion that class had somehow ceased to matter because 'we were all middle class' or because the 'class war' was over, it also revealed a tremendous interest in and possibly also new insecurities about class structure and class identification in the new millennium. In the twenty-first century, the matter of class was back on the agenda and in the 'popular imagination' (Savage 6), but as a question as much as a given, as something under transformation rather than something settled. As such, class is obviously something contemporary art and literature also responds to and, critically, participates in making sense of.

The BBC's Class Calculator seems, additionally, to have produced a curious side effect Savage et al. mention in passing in the anecdote: 'Demand for theatre tickets in London increased by an average of 191 percent in the week after the GBCS launch' (6), they report, quoting a spokesperson for Seatwave saying that at first they were baffled 'until we realized that it corresponded directly with the BBC's Class Calculator' (6). In other words, many people seem to have realized that theatre attendance was an indicator of class belonging and that the more cultural capital you possessed – for example, from theatre-going – the less likely you were to find yourself aligned with one of the most negatively represented classes in Britain today, the precariat (often named by more explicitly derogatory terms such as 'underclass' or 'chavs'), a class very few people espouse or claim with any sense of pride. As its main contemporary UK theorist, labour market economist Guy Standing points out, 'People are not born in it [the precariat] and are unlikely to identify themselves as members with a glow of pride. Fear, yes; anger, probably; sardonic humour perhaps; but not pride' (*The Precariat* 22).

Paradoxically, if theatregoers around 2013 may have wished to increase their consumption of theatre to, at some level, escape precarity and the precariat and instead come to feel (if not in fact necessarily be) more securely middle class, the precariat was exactly what was on show at many notable theatre venues in London and across Britain. Theatregoers would indeed quite literally be facing deeply precariously employed members of the creative industry: professional or semi-professional actors many of whom identify with the precariat class due to short-term living and working conditions, instability and lack of orientation. These actors would in addition be performing roles as temp workers in cleaning or warehouse packing, or as unemployed high school dropout youths, as temporarily housed migrants, old-age pensioners, caregivers, students, etc. Indeed, individuals going to the theatre inspired by a sudden need to boost or consolidate their cultural capital might face angry and threatening actors performing *and* embodying precarity and the precariat, both in Mike Savage's sense and in Judith Butler's sense of living in response to 'the conditions of heightened vulnerability and aggression' (xi) of the present moment – conditions the bottom 15 per cent can hardly shield themselves against by purchasing theatre tickets.

For Butler, being precarious means 'That we can be injured, that others can be injured, that we are subject to death at the whim of another [. . .] One insight that injury affords is that there are others out there on whom my life depends, people I do not know and may never know' (xii). Precarity is something we all share as an ontological given, but also something we all (also members of the precariat) participate in distributing, in ways that increase certain groups' social and other suffering at the cost of another class fortifying its own feeling of relative safety. Many new plays indeed take as their subject matter lives and life experiences informed by precarity and experienced by members of the precariat. This tendency is no doubt inspired both by the precariat as a new social class as described by Savage and others and by the sense of precarity described by Butler and others, often directly in relation to theatre and performance studies and so present in the lives of contemporary performing artists in the age of neoliberalism, a phenomenon described by performance critics and theorists such as Jen Harvie, Katarina Pewny and Bojana Kunst. Indeed, 2013, the year of the BBC Class Calculator, saw the premiere of playwright Chris Dunkley's play, *The Precariat*, a play deeply informed by the emerging social class and even featuring a short preface written by Guy Standing. And recent years have seen the emergence of theatre criticism addressing some of these issues in work by Marissa Fragkou (*Ecologies of Precarity in Twenty-First Century Theatre* (2018)) as well as by contributors to the anthology *Of Precariousness* (2017), edited by Aragay and Middekke.

For Savage, though the precariat class is said to comprise 15 per cent of the population, it only made up 1 per cent of the survey respondents; in other words it eluded the BBC's statistical measurement. The precariat, though underrepresented in the survey, is not invisible as a class as far as attracting public attention is concerned. But it lacks a fair representation in the public discourse of tabloid press, political rhetoric, social media platforms and sensation-seeking reality television, where class members are portrayed in stigmatizing ways as 'idlers', 'scum' or 'chavs' (Tyler 9–10). As Savage puts it: 'It is rarely considered by the general public when observing working class people and neighbourhoods, that working class people, and especially the poor working class, the precariat, can know or understand themselves and their situation, and that they can articulate their understandings, perceptions and feelings extremely well' (335). Because so few from this class responded to the online query ('no one wants to come last', as Savage puts it (333)), Savage employed an ethnographer, Lisa McKenzie, to do a field study to describe the class in continuation of her study of council house life, *Getting By* (2015). Thus, according to Savage and based on McKenzie's ethnographic work, 'The precariat world is [. . .] one in which people are "knowing", but it is nonetheless also one which recognizes how people are placed on the receiving end of other people's definitions and initiatives' (342). The precariat is at the mercy of others, knows it and aims to guard itself from the consequences of this, and can therefore be difficult to get reliable insight into, even for trained ethnographers and sociologists. Literature offers another, supplementary way to approach knowing what's on the precariat's mind, enabling audiences or readers to take the necessary step of initiating the 'questioning of the stereotyping of those in the lowest rank of the social-class hierarchy' (Savage 404), which Savage sees as the main thing needed to decrease the social risks related to social fragmentation.

As a supplement to Savage's sociological and ethnographic studies of the precariat and thus with the shared ambition of nuancing the image of the precariat in order to prevent demonization, this chapter follows a suggestion made by Pierre Bourdieu in the introduction to his monumental study, *The Weight of the World: Social Suffering in Contemporary Society*. In this study, based on three years' of interviews with inhabitants of French council houses, Bourdieu himself gestures towards modernist literature as a model for a sociology that can understand the perspectives of individuals and groups who, like the precariat, are the victims of dangerous stereotyping and stigmatization caused by not being able to speak for themselves. He mentions modernist novelists (Joyce, Woolf and Faulkner) as artists who – compared to popular journalism – have experimented with giving 'a complex and multilayered representation capable of articulating the same realities [as those the popular press tries to account for] but in terms that are different and, sometimes, irreconcilable', arguing that (again as opposed to most popular journalism) 'we must relinquish the single, central, dominant, in a word quasi-divine, point of view that is all too easily adopted by observers – and by readers too, at least to the extent that they don't feel personally involved' (3). And as a last example in this framing of the study, Bourdieu mentions a well-known play by German writer Patrick Süskind (*The Double Bass*, a single-act monologue that premiered in 1981) which 'presents an especially striking image of how painfully the social world may be experienced by people who [. . .] occupy an inferior, obscure position in a prestigious and obscure universe' (4) relative to their surroundings, something he calls '*positional suffering*' (4). In my analysis of the theatre of the precariat in what follows, I emphasize how the audience becomes personally involved in the precariat's social suffering once this suffering is also shown as deeply personal via the specific perspective of a member of the precariat the audience comes to sympathize with. By virtue of its freedom to imagine the perspective and voice of the other, for example, marginalized individuals and groups on the fringes of society, even as it obviously must be careful when it aims to speak on behalf of the 'subaltern' (Spivak), literature can function as a strong source of insight into precarious living. Perhaps the specific form of literature that is drama can do so with extra force because of its close affiliation with political literature after Brecht, and because it has such a direct rapport with the precarity of those performing on stage and can directly invite the audience to (re)act to what is performed on stage.

Indeed, maybe theatre can do more than open the audience's eyes to the precariat to combat social suffering by busting stereotypical stigmatization. For Standing, the precariat is differently composed than for Savage because Standing explicitly includes two other groups than the relatively homogenous group that Savage seems to take to represent the precariat. For Standing, the precariat is internally at strife with itself since, in addition to members of the old, white working class, it includes migrant groups and creative freelancers, writers and artists (often not working class), and he nurtures a hope for progressive social change that rests on the latter subgroup's ability to imagine solidarity within the heterogenous and mutually suspicious precariat class-in-the-making and to articulate a programme for social reform that will lead to its recognition and inclusion in society. As he says on an almost prophetic note in *A Precariat Charter*: 'the biggest challenge for this part of the precariat [artists] is to induce the other varieties to share a common vision. There is no reason why that cannot happen, just as craftsmen and intellectuals acted as educators and leaders of "the working class" in the late nineteenth and early twentieth centuries' (30). This kind of hope is hard to find in the art and literature that engages with the precariat, but it may be there by sheer virtue of the strong interest in the precariat and precarity in much contemporary art and literature even as 'common vision' among artists and authors dealing with the precariat at the moment can be hard to discern.

The theatre of the precariat and contemporary political theatre

In recent years, several new significant works of British theatre by younger, often prize-winning playwrights, staged and produced on important national as well as regional stages, have participated in imagining the contours of an identity-information for the possibly newly emerging social class of the precariat. To situate the analysis of Gary Owen's play *Iphigenia in Splott*, which is my main concern in this chapter, in the context of contemporary theatre of the precariat I want to briefly mention three other playwrights working along similar lines. Two recent plays by Alexander Zeldin are squarely about the precariat and the feeling of precarity. In *Beyond Caring* (2015), we meet three very different but equally vulnerable zero-hour contract workers employed by a temp agency as cleaners in a meat factory, who, despite their differences, share appalling working conditions, never knowing if there will be work the next day, always under pressure to perform and under minute surveillance. As the blurb of the play text puts it, the play 'exposes stories of an invisible class', the precariat, whose labour conditions are very close to the condition of the meat in the machines they are cleaning. About the play Zeldin said in an interview: 'There are vast numbers of people called "the working poor". Their lives are dominated by one feeling: precarity. I wanted to look at what it means to live in that position: temporary solutions and temporary lives' (Trueman). In Zeldin's *Love* (2016), six precarious characters inhabit a precarious setting: temporary housing, which stresses them and puts them on the verge of mental breakdowns. They are an old-age, frail pensioner and her adult son who is her primary caregiver, a young, struggling family with children, and a Syrian and a Sudanese refugee – all hoping to move on to more permanent housing/lives. Thus, physical space, the material *site* of the play, embodies and instances the lack of permanence and predictability that defines the precariat's way of being in the world.

In Katherine Soper's award-winning debut, *Wish List* (2015), we meet seventeen-year-old Tamsin, who does zero-hour contract work packing boxes in a warehouse not knowing if there will be work the next day. She gets a text message from her agency if there are hours. Having lost her mother, she is trying to take care of her younger brother who suffers from a severe anxiety disorder and obsessive-compulsive behaviour and therefore fails to meet the requirements of the punitive workfare state and is kicked off social security. Tamsin is trapped and is under minute surveillance by the packing company's inhumane work regime, where everything is counted and measured and she constantly has to perform above her own possible best and face being told in neoliberal nudging management jargon that 'the only limitations are the limitations you set for yourself' (Soper 74).

Chris Dunkley's aptly titled *The Precariat* (2013) portrays fifteen-year-old Fin's life in a council house flat with his mother and his brother Leo. Fin is dropping out of school and working as a temp at the local KFC, where he has politically enlightening conversations with his co-worker Sally. Fin's younger brother Leo never gets a voice and is in the process of leaving the family and joining a dangerous street gang. In a climactic scene, Fin slashes a member of another gang in the hope of saving his brother, and he is arrested by the police and kept in youth detention. Yet the play ends with a vague hope of social change through new social media. Fin wants to start a blog and talks about a new 'we' that exists on the internet and that for him portends the possibility of political changes.

This body of theatrical work is evidence of what leading theatre critic Aleks Sierz points out when he argues that the 2000s saw increasing segregation between classes in the United Kingdom and the proliferation of stereotypes about class and poverty on stage, where 'the respectable working class was far less in evidence than the underclass, or chavs, the latest incarnation of the Victorian idea of the fearsome undeserving poor' (128). As social and political theatre, it is thoroughly embedded in the tradition dating back to John Osborne's *Look Back in Anger* (1956) and Edward Bond's *Saved* (1965) that reimagined anger and deprivation in new ways. These kitchen sink dramas aimed to disgust and alienate the audience in order, as Bond said in the early 1970s, to create a 'Rational Theatre' which 'interprets the world' and as such is able to show 'why things go wrong and how we could correct them' (qtd in Stevenson 304). The theatre of the precariat as practised by the playwrights mentioned earlier, however, and unlike those referenced by Sierz, is less concerned with alienating the audience than with transforming members of the precariat from disgusting, revolting 'types' into more credible human subjects that the audience can feel empathy towards and see themselves as sympathetically attached to.

The plays that constitute the theatre of the precariat most obviously have in common their shared thematic features and their concern with characters who belong to the precariat, whose lives are precarious, insecure, unstable, dangerous and in the hands of and at the mercy of others. But they are also marked by an interest in using different techniques for activating and engaging with the audience's sense of ethics and politics by staging an everyday lifeworld that is insecure or falling apart as an almost naturalistic part of what Jacques Rancière in his critique of Brecht calls 'the theatre of identification' (*The Lost Thread* 140). This is a theatre that supposes that a contemporary audience is less gullible and prone to illusion than a certain standard literary-historical understanding of Brecht's insistence on disenchantment and distance would have it. As Rancière points out in *The Emancipated Spectator*, we should be more critical of the notion of a passive audience wallowing unconsciously in identification with the represented illusion and uncritically internalizing its mode of false consciousness. Such a gullible audience is hardly imaginable, Rancière seems to suggest, to the extent that any audience obviously is, and is aware of itself as, an audience, even when not 'activated' by, for example, Brechtian strategies of *verfremdung*.

Further, it is questionable if art can programme an 'emancipation' (a correction) as one often feels in discussions of the impact of Brecht; for Rancière, it can at most make the audience consider the possibility of emancipation: 'It requires spectators who play the role of active interpreters, who develop their own translation in order to appropriate the "story" and make it their story. An emancipated community is a community of narrators and translators' (*The Emancipated Spectator* 22). The theatre of the precariat typically does break the fourth wall and address the audience *as audience* by interacting physically or verbally with it through strategies of *verfremdung*, thus making us aware of our role as observers: we feel awkwardly and uncomfortably complicit in the staged action. This is done, I suggest, not to imply that the precarious characters on stage are an illusion (it is not, as Brecht puts it, 'playing in such a way that the audience [is] hindered from simply identifying itself with the characters of the play,' 91), but exactly to make them feel real, to make us realize that they are not an illusion but part of the world we share – to enable the translation and appropriation of the story experienced in performance by the audience. In the theatre of the precariat, the audience is made to realize that it holds the lives of the precariat in its hands and the major point it makes is that these lives are human, vulnerable, exposed and grievable.

Critical work on theatre and precarity is, as mentioned earlier, emerging. This is not surprising. The world of theatre production and performance art more broadly is, as already suggested, one that tends to be deeply precarious and caught in the paradox that what it critiques is also what enables it. This existential condition has been analysed by Jen Harvie in *Fair Play* to also include the ways in which certain immersive theatre and performance art positions and uses the audience to make it share in the actors' experience of precariousness, which for Harvie becomes so many problematic means to 'rehearse audiences for, and naturalize them to, these harmful conditions of labour' (50) under new capitalism. This ubiquity and problematic of precarity in the world of theatre is surely a major reason why so much theatre in the early twenty-first century has taken up precarity and the precariat as its subject matter. Both Fragkou's *Ecologies of Precarity in Twenty-First Century Theatre* (2018) and *Of Precariousness* (2017) edited by Aragay and Middekke, focus, as I do in what follows, on the ways in which contemporary often post-dramatic theatre (under inspiration from Judith Butler in particular) engages and interacts with the audience by making it negotiate ethical and political questions and positions. Unlike Harvie, and inspired by Rancière, I want to at least hold forth the possibility that Gary Owen's play and others like it that immerse audiences in the felt experience of precarity through emotional appeals to identify with these 'others' – even as they are also threatening 'others' – do more than make the audience 'naturalize' the social suffering the play presents.

Gary Owen's Iphigenia in Splott, *anger and the threatening of the audience*

Gary Owen's *Iphigenia in Splott* (2015) premiered at the Sherman Cymru in Cardiff in May 2015 and won Best New Play at the UK Theatre Awards in 2015. It has toured the United Kingdom and was part of the American Brits Off Broadway in 2017, and reviewed in the *New York Times* (Brantley), after winning national critical acclaim upon its appearance at the National Theatre in January 2016. In a five-star review for *The Guardian* after the Cardiff premiere reviewer Andrew Haydon concluded, 'By any measure going, this is perfect theatre: intelligent, moving, and horribly, horribly relevant. Most of all, though, in those final moments, it feels like the start of a revolution' (Haydon). Most reviewers note the play's use of Greek myth via Euripedean tragedy (Iphigenia), its participation in the tradition of British political theatre as well as the very strong effect achieved at the close of the play. In what follows, I elaborate on the political dynamics of the play and place it in discussions of the precariat not noticed by the first reviewers, but relevant if its revolutionary, political appeal is to be taken more seriously.

The play is an hour-long monologue performed by Effie (played by Sophie Melville) on a bare stage with a few chairs and neon lighting as the only props. She is very blonde, heavily made-up, unemployed, uneducated, young, sexually attractive and promiscuous, dressed in tights, hoodie and trainers. The play portrays Effie as caught in an impossible life with no meaningful activities and no space or incentive to carve out a better future. She lives in a deprived area of Cardiff – Splott. The play's opening scene captures the locale of Splott and its recent transformation from a close-knit working-class neighbourhood to a dilapidated place of broken communities, closed shops and vacant meeting places, and it introduces Effie as aggressive and threatening vis-à-vis the audience.

Effie's Nan (significantly, we never hear a word or thought of Effie's parents; they seem to have completely abandoned her) remembers another time when 'this place used to have everything you need/Shops are gone, bingo hall burned down, pubs closed, doctors shut,/STAR centre getting pulled down and more flats thrown up' (2). Nan says: 'You could live here and live well./Now they're stacking us up, and we're supposed to just exist' (2). We get a clear sense in the play that Splott is the limit of Effie's geographical imagination; she never leaves it, can't imagine doing so. In the middle of the play she accidentally for the first time in her life visits the nearby beach, 'A beach a mile from where I grew up,/When the fuck did that happen?/It is the worst beach in the world, mind./Strips of metal, car wheels, half a toilet' (25). She has lived a twenty-odd-years' life centred around a place that is broken with no incentive to transgress its borders. She is being stacked and is stuck in a no-future place, a kind of no-man's land segregated from the rest of society. She is in a sense 'free to leave' this precariat 'ghetto' (Wacquant), but being born in a decomposing neighbourhood with absent parents and a generally dysfunctional public infrastructure puts Effie right at the centre of a negative social mobility curve: there is no way out for her.

While Nan seems nostalgic about the rupture with a past working-class community in the present of austerity, Effie is tough and disillusioned: 'I say: Nan wake up love./Everything changes, everything moves on' (2). Effie feels that Nan's moaning is directed reproachfully at her life, 'Cos I live my life a million miles an hour, do what I like, when I like and/Oh look, I've got – this – for you, if you can't deal with it' (2). A footnote added to 'this' informs the reader of the play script: 'Find some cute way to give the audience the finger' (2). The finger flashed at the audience is all Effie has to offer by way of resistance or 'revolt', in Imogen Tyler's sense of the way an 'abject subject' who 'repeatedly finds herself the object of other's violent objectifying disgust' (4) resists this subject position 'in forms of counter-political speech' (5). Of course, Effie giving us the finger makes no difference; at most it confirms us that she is a 'revolting subject'. Yet, as Imogen Tyler notes, 'it is often not events of protest or resistance themselves, many of which barely register within the public domain or are quickly forgotten or suppressed, but rather the *storying* of revolts – and the forms of aesthetics this affects – which *matters* most' (12–13). Effie giving us the finger makes no difference, but that she does it (in a cute way) in a 'perfect play' on a national scene, however, may matter and make a difference. It is this angry gesture directed at the audience that I take as point of departure for the following analysis of the play, which ends with Effie again confronting the audience, but this time with something much more gripping than a cute finger.

Before she gives it the finger, the audience is made uncomfortable by Effie's aggressive and scornful, taunting attitude as she opens the monologue by breaking the fourth wall and addressing the audience that surrounds her standing alone on the thrust stage: 'You lot./Sitting back, taking it easy, waiting for me/To – what? Impress you? Amaze you? Show you what I've got?/Well boys and girls, ladies and gents – I'm afraid not. You have got it back to front, arse about tit, and up your side / Is definitely down. See I know what you think/When you see me pissed first thing in the morning wandering around./You think -/ stupid slag. Nasty skank' (1). Instead of providing entertainment by 'playing herself' – that is, by living up to the audience's prejudiced anticipation of what 'someone' like Effie is all about, a 'revolting subject' who is drunk in the morning, uses foul language, is unemployed and therefore lazy, sexually promiscuous, tawdry and uninhibited – we, the audience, are present to give thanks to her, she says: 'Tonight/You all are here to give thanks/To me./Yeah I know it's a shock./But you lot, every single one/ You're in my debt./And tonight – boys and girls, ladies and gents – /I've come to collect' (1). What, we wonder, as the play begins, are we to give thanks for? And how can we repay the debt?

The play catches Effie on a bad day out of the ordinary, but as such also on a day of new potentiality for change: she wakes up *sober* on a Monday morning having somehow failed to get 'absolutely totally fucked' (4) the night before. The problem: she has a whole day to pass before she can escape her life through drink later in the evening, so she returns to the motif of aggressively threatening and insulting the audience: 'My body buzzing, all this energy and fuck all to do with it./This means one thing./Trouble. In the end for me/But before that, for . . . losers like you, basically' (5). Effie is not stupid; she knows she's on a path to disaster, and we know that as well from our knowledge of the classics: in Greek myth and in Euripides' tragedy, Iphigenia is sacrificed by her father Agamemnon to secure a safe passage of his fleet to Troy on a male pursuit of honour and riches. With the absence of Effie's real father in this play, we are left to wonder who will claim parental (ir)responsibility and sacrifice her?

The opening scene of the play has Effie describe herself walking down the street in the morning: 'I scan the streets for targets. Who's gonna volunteer? Who will be the victim of my fury?' (5). The immediate cause of her fury and initiator of the plot is her failure to drink herself to oblivion the night before; she therefore has a brain 'functioning on full power' (4), which she says is not normal, 'And it is definitely not safe' (4). She takes her fury out first on her boyfriend, the bodybuilder Kev, in what seem well-rehearsed and clichéd ways. She presents it to the audience as something we've heard and seen before, a well-choreographed act they tend to perform late at night and now perform in the morning, but is routine: he calls her 'slag' and she gets back at him for doing so (he thought he was allowed to use negative slang, but not this time) and they start shouting in the street, 'It's like a whole routine we got worked out,/We usually pull it – three in the morning?/ Screaming at each other, staggering up and down the street./You might have heard us. Or you might've been trying to sleep?' (6). Next she takes her furious anger out on a randomly chosen young mother with her baby in a carrier, 'Some fat mum with a massive buggy full of fat kids' (7), who asks Effie and Kev to lower their voices and stop swearing. Then all hell breaks loose and Effie scares the mum into silence by looking at the baby; the mother fears for her children who will have to walk these streets with Effie around in the future. Effie here performs the role which public media and discourse has prescribed for her; she is a core performer of the precariat's (self)destructive anger that makes the 'safe' middle class and 'respectable' working class fear her and her class, seeing her as unpredictable and guided by primitive and self-destructive instincts. She is, indeed, furious – out of or beside herself.

In a very short span of time we have moved from nostalgia for a close-knit solidary community to a future where kids can't play in the streets and feel safe. This aggression vis-à-vis the young mother and the newborn baby ('a wriggly red newborn' 8) is an important motif. We meet the young mother later in a GP's waiting room (where she herself is becoming violent, shouting at her child and striking his hand, 41) and at the very end as one member of the cast of broken, suffering, isolated individuals Effie has made us imagine during her monologue. They are all related to Effie in relations informed by betrayal, exploitation, aggression and lack of love, solidarity, tolerance and trust. And this moment with the baby crucially anticipates the culmination of the play where Effie herself becomes pregnant and experiences expectant motherhood as potentially transformative; it becomes an embodied corrective to her initial furious self. Effie *is* furious and uncontrollable to begin with in the play, but then she gradually becomes more and more angry in a disturbingly calm way as the play nears its tragic conclusion and she undergoes a transformation from furious and revolting to angry but sympathetic.

A bit later the word 'anger' rather than 'fury' is used to describe Effie's feelings, this time vis-à-vis her flat mate and 'friend', Leanne – who is really not her friend as she suggests the only reason for having a kid is to get benefits, and who gives pregnant Effie drugs without telling her. The only directly physical act of violence in the play is when Effie hits Leanne when she has realized she has drugged her: this is a key moment in the play's primary emotional strategy of making Effie seem sympathetic to a middle-class audience, one of whose basic moral values in the present moment is related to definitely not using drugs or alcohol while pregnant, a gesture that makes Effie imaginable as 'one of us' rather than a member of the dangerous and self-destructive precariat that (we believe) is oblivious to the health risks of using drugs and drinking alcohol while pregnant (as encouraged by Leanne).

Fury and anger are not the same. Anger theorists from Aristotle to Philip Fisher in *The Vehement Passions* typically distinguish between two kinds of anger, a dangerous one that is spontaneous and uncontrolled, where the subject is furious (out of herself) for no particular reason, and another, good kind of anger that is related to perceived injustice and may propel change (117ff.). The precariat is typically understood in terms of the first kind of anger, and hence as 'dangerous' as Guy Standing's subtitle suggests. This is indicated by Chris Dunkley using the London Riots as background for his 2013 play; Imogen Tyler would certainly see the riots as an expression of justified anger that was mediated or 'storied' as thoughtless and only destructive by the UK media from the kind of 'quasi-divine' point of view Bourdieu talks about. However, I want to explore the possibility Owen's play suggests that the precariat's anger might become socially transformative in less destructive ways. I want, in other words, to suggest that the slide from 'fury' to 'anger' in Owen's text marks a transition from the dangerous and spontaneous destructive behaviour in the opening scene towards an increasingly meaningful and justified anger that the audience can recognize, identify with but should be wary about, and has to understand as requiring its action in other ways than through ignorance or policing.

Instead of fleshing out a portrait of a totally unsympathetic character at the throat of single mums in the vein of Bond's kitchen sink drama, a stigmatized stereotypical member of the precariat blaming everyone but herself, in the course of the play, Effie wins our sympathy. Not least because she is 'knowing' in Mike Savage's sense, she knows that we think we know what she is all about (we see her through derogatory and stigmatizing slang expressions such as 'slag' and 'skank'), and she knows that we are hardly interested in really listening to what she has to say about what it actually might be like to be her. So, she acts out. 'You all know me' (1), she begins after the opening audience address and finger, a speech that is concluded by the threat of having come to collect. In the course of the play Effie betrays her bodybuilder boyfriend and falls for a wounded ex-soldier she meets in a pub. Having sex with him makes her feel not alone – a new feeling (24) – she becomes pregnant and transforms into a likeable character. She now feels 'glad' (33). However, the soldier is married, has a child and is not interested in her, yet she decides to have the baby and experiences the decision positively as a hopeful and transformative experience, which we might begin to imagine could help her out of her precarity. Nan helps Effie get a room of her own (50), Kevin tries to act like an expectant father (he says he believes parenthood can sort him out). For a moment, we can see a new, more stable, anchored life on the horizon, something good coming out of these miserably wasted lives. (On the precariat's desire for this kind of 'liveable life' as one that involves 'being able to lay down roots, to feel safe, to create a family and home, to belong to a community and to have some sense of a (better) future', see Tyler 12.)

But this is an instance of what Lauren Berlant would term 'cruel optimism', an instance where an attachment to something identified as promising a realization of the 'good life' (a baby, a home, a family, a future) actually, even if unintentionally, becomes an obstacle to realizing that life – even when as here we are dealing with one of the strongest objects of human desire. During premature labour at week 29, something goes wrong and Effie needs to be moved to another hospital. Because of snow, the ambulance has an accident and her baby dies during labour. The reason: due to cutbacks in the NHS, there was no capacity to treat her so she had to be moved. According to the rules, a midwife was supposed to have escorted her, but that midwife was compelled by the male part of a resourceful couple about to have twins to stay at the hospital and take care of them – otherwise they would call the boss. So, the midwife tells Effie that she won't be needing her after all and that all will be well. In a key moment, the initially very confrontational and talkative Effie is now at a loss for words by thus finding herself at the 'receiving end of other people's definitions and initiatives' (Savage 342): 'And I know I should argue./I know I should./But then the pain. I can't speak./And there is no one to speak for me, so . . .' (56); she has a miscarriage and the baby dies during transportation, and 'I go to hell', Effie says (60).

Inspired by Kevin, who she says rescues her, Effie sues the hospital which had made a mistake, and she actually stands to get compensation of several hundred thousand pounds that she envisions would change her life for the better: 'Get me a house./Get me a car./Get me by; for years and years' (61). Yet she declines because not only would it not bring back her baby, it would mean that others – she is now looking directly, threateningly at the audience, which must be feeling uncomfortable in its seats knowing that she has come to 'collect' – would get poorer treatment. Having been offered the compensation, she is told by the midwife that the only reason they had to transport her was that they didn't have a special care bed for her at the hospital, 'We don't have as many special care beds as we used to/ Cos of all the cuts' (62), and if Effie accepts the compensation, 'we'll have to cut some more./And more old people will die before they should. More young people will never get a chance to live./And more mums, just like you, will lose' (62). Effie does not decline the compensation simply to help others and for the common good. She is not naive. As Nan says and as Effie knows, 'the state you are in, will money help?' (63), and Effie knows it will not, 'But then what will help? Because I need something, I really fucking do/And she [Nan] says, you know./You know that too' (63). What it is she knows is not spelled out exactly but needs interpretation. By the logic of the transition towards sympathy for Effie, grounded in both her acts and sayings and her ever more just feeling of anger, I would suggest that a just and constructive anger is exactly what may be the compensation Effie gets from rejecting the system's attempt to buy her silence and compliance. Thinking about her loss, thinking about walking to the sea to drown herself ('that broken brick road to the sea/Not a mile away./I could walk it any day' (64)), she says: 'And what stops me [from going to the beach]/What gets me through is knowing/I took this pain,/And saved every one of you, from suffering the same' (64).

The Agamemnon figure in the play responsible for the human sacrifice is not just Austerity and neoliberal cuts in public welfare, but anyone with time and money enough to go to the theatre to watch the precariat act out instead of doing something about it. As she concludes, we should *thank* her when we see her in the street: 'Christ Effie, thanks. You took the cut for us' (64). Cut here is overdetermined and means both the cuts in welfare in the age of Austerity where incredible wealth accumulation is somehow logically linked to a rhetoric of needing to cut back government spending and lower taxation in the interest of growth, resulting in the creation of the precariat, and the personal cut of losing a child, a future, and having her life laid waste. Both are cuts that threaten the security of society, Effie seems to suggest. At the end of the play, Effie has found a sense of pride and identity that will get her through and that has won her a new independence from the system that has otherwise controlled her. By taking the cut and not accepting compensation for something that can never be compensated and that if accepted would only be another instance of 'cruel optimism,' as Effie's path to destruction would probably only be steeper with more money, she has earned the right to be angry.

Effie knows that we don't thank her, or her fellow sufferers. In the finale she mentions the other 'wasted' characters we have met in the play: the single fat mum, the wounded soldier, Nan, forced out of retirement to work at age seventy-plus in order to earn money to help Effie. These are characters who *should* be in solidarity with one another and form a class identity with common goals and demands against the oppressing elites; but instead, paradoxically, tragically, they are at one another's throats and exploiting one another: Effie screaming at the single mother, spending Nan's money on drink, being screwed by the disabled ex-soldier, abused and abusive of her friend Leanne. We do not thank them for always taking the hardest cuts in public welfare and in their personal, embodied lives. In fact, she suggests, we tend to blame them for being the *cause* of the destruction of the welfare system, rather than typically suffering the consequences of the cuts. Given this reality, she concludes:

> We can take it cos we're tough, the lot of us./But here's the fucking rub./It seems, it's always places like this/And people like us who have to take it,/When the time for cutting comes. And I wonder: just how long/Are we gonna have to take it for?/ And I wonder – /What is gonna happen/When we can't take it any more? (65)

With an allusion to Shakespeare's *Hamlet*'s 'to be or not to be' soliloquy ('there's the rub'), Gary Owen concludes this aesthetic intervention in current politics by making us think about the life choices of desperate people trapped in a situation where they can only ponder whether to kill themselves or those in power who they feel betrayed by (Claudius, Agamemnon, the rotten 'state you're in'). The play thus makes us see contemporary social suffering in a tragic light of both Euripides and Shakespeare. It shows how we still sacrifice vulnerable and defenceless humans to maintain a certain way of life when that way of living is making a whole social group feel trapped in a desperate position between choosing suicide (Berlant's 'slow death' through drug abuse, unhealthy life style etc.) or an equally destructive rioting and rebellion with no ideological or progressive agenda other than 'revolt' against a neoliberal consensus.

Conclusion

In his play *The Precariat*, Chris Dunkley is most explicit about addressing the precariat *as* precariat and experimenting with giving it a voice, collective identity and progressive agenda (Hogg and Simonsen). In his preface to the play, Guy

Standing notes that 'There is an energy building in and around the precariat, not just in Britain but across the world. It is organizing, and struggling to define a new forward march' (Dunkley 23–4). Standing believes that the precariat is a class-in-the-making and that it might be in the process of finding a new class identity to portend social change. As mentioned, Standing looks to the artists to take up the avant-garde. The plays discussed here, which appeared more or less simultaneously, can be understood as part of this new 'energy' and perhaps signal that parts of the precariat are finding a voice that, as Imogen Tyler puts it, can enable 'the *storying* of revolts' (13) through, for example, contemporary theatre and related media platforms that begin to make an impact beyond the theatre space via the processes of interpretation and appropriation Rancière describes in *The Emancipated Spectator*. Yet, in all these plays, the precariat speaks with many voices and has many mutually conflicting dreams and aspirations, which indicate that it might find it difficult to unite around one collective political set of goals – that it is still struggling to find ways to use its just anger to create social change.

In life, Effie is and remains all alone with her anger, and as such she is very vulnerable and easy to keep ignoring and to keep stereotyping; yet as 'storied' (Tyler) by the activating and absorptive but also threatening aesthetics of this play and as 'interpreted' and 'appropriated' by audiences (Rancière), she is deeply humane, deeply moving and easy to feel compassionate about, identify with, and not just take pity on. As one theatregoer and blogger, Debbie Johnson, said on her blog, *An Organised Mess*, after the play's premiere on 10 May 2015, the day after David Cameron and the Tories had won the general election:

> There is no doubt Gary Owen's adaptation of Iphigenia will be hard-hitting no matter what day of the week you get to see it. But watching it the evening after *that* morning it seemed so much more relevant, so much more like a call to action, an appreciation of community and the stark realities than ever. I wonder how I would feel watching if there had been a different government coming into power, would that sense of optimism make the reality of Owen's themes a little easier a pill to swallow? Maybe just maybe the one thing to come out of Friday's election result will be more people wanting to take decisive action, and maybe they will be fortunate enough to be near enough to the Sherman to see *Iphigenia in Splott* and maybe just maybe the community which we each have around us can rebuild and stand strong in response. (Johnson n.p.)

Thirty-four other bloggers/readers added their comments (one of whom was enthusiastic about the new government): most of them wished they had time to go to the theatre and thanked the blogger for making it present for them. Eight months later, the same blogger went to see the play at the National Theatre and was confirmed in the strength of the play and in its deep necessity in the present moment:

> This time, eight months on, I have less confidence that things are being fixed, things really aren't improving by those elected to look after our nation. This time

> I have more confidence in the strength of the human spirit, the ability to create change at grassroots [. . .] We failed to protect the cuts in the areas which can't take it, the cuts are going wider and deeper. Prodding and picking anywhere they can, and most commonly at the areas we value yet under appreciate, until it's too late. (Johnson n.p.)

This audience member and the many she represents who have seen Owen's play and experienced the impact of its performance of precarity in different ways may have come out of the hour-long experience slightly closer to engaging in political activity that in various ways might counter precarization and participate in the undoing of the conditions that underwrite the making of the precariat. Whether it is the revolution predicted by *The Guardian* reviewer, or an induction of us to share the 'common vision' desired by Guy Standing, is probably doubtful; but less may have to do, especially insofar as it as a minimum counters the bleak analysis that such performances of precarity merely 'naturalize' the audience's sense of the new economy.

Works cited

Berlant, Lauren. *Cruel Optimism*. Duke University Press, 2011.
Bourdieu, Pierre, et al. *The Weight of the World: Social Suffering in Contemporary Society*. Translated by Priscilla Parkhurt Ferguson et al. Polity Press, 1999.
Brantley, Ben. 'Review: A Mythic Force Rages in the Welsh "Iphigenia in Splott"'. *The New York Times*, 17 May 2017, https://www.nytimes.com/2017/05/17/theater/iphigenia-in-splott-review.html. Accessed 23 February 2020.
Brecht, Bertolt. *Brecht on Theatre: The Development of an Aesthetic*. Edited and translated by John Willett. Hill and Wang, 1964.
Butler, Judith. *Precarious Life: The Powers of Mourning and Violence*. Verso, 2004.
Dunkley, Chris. *The Precariat*. Oberon Books, 2013.
Fisher, Philip. *The Vehement Passions*. Princeton University Press, 2002.
Harvie, Jen. *Fair Play –Art, Performance and Neoliberalism*. Palgrave, 2013.
Haydon, Andrew. 'Iphigenia in Splott Five-Star Review – A Whirlwind of Aggression and Seduction'. *The Guardian*, 14 May 2014. https://www.theguardian.com/stage/2015/may/14/iphigenia-in-splott-review-sherman-cardiff-gary-owen. Accessed 27 January 2020.
Hogg, Emily and Peter Simonsen. 'The Potential of Precarity? Imagining Vulnerable Connection in Chris Dunkley's *The Precariat* and Amy Liptrot's *The Outrun*'. *Criticism*, vol. 62, no. 1, 2020, pp.1–28.
Johnson, Debbie. 'Iphigenia in Splott. May 10, 2015'. *An Organised Mess*. https://anorganisedmess.com/theatre/iphigenia-in-splott/. Accessed 18 February 2020.
Kunst, Bojana. *Artist at Work: Proximity of Art and Capitalism*. Zero Books, 2015.
Owen, Gary. *Iphigenia in Splott*. Oberon Books, 2015.
Pewny, Katharina. 'Performing the Precarious: Economic Crisis in European and Japanese Theatre'. *Forum Modernes Theater*, vol. 26, no. 1–2, 2011, pp. 43–52.
Rancière, Jacques. *The Emancipated Spectator*. Translated by Gregory Elliott. Verso, 2009.
Rancière, Jacques. *The Lost Thread: The Democracy of Modern Fiction*. Translated by Steven Corcoran. Bloomsbury, 2017.

Savage, Mike, et al. *Social Class in the 21st Century. A Pelican Introduction*. Penguin Books, 2015.
Sierz, Aleks. *Rewriting the Nation: British Theatre Today*. Methuen, 2011.
Soper, Katherine. *Wish List*. Nick Hern Books, 2016.
Standing, Guy. *The Precariat: The New Dangerous Class*. Bloomsbury, 2011.
Standing, Guy. *A Precariat Charter: From Denizens to Citizens*. Bloomsbury, 2014.
Stevenson, Randall. *The Oxford English Literary History: The Last of England? 1960–2000*, vol. 12, General editor, Jonathan Bate. Oxford University Press, 2004.
'The Great British Class Calculator'. *BBC News*, 3 April 2013, https://www.bbc.com/news/magazine-22000973.
Trueman, Matt. 'New Play Stages the "Temporary Lives" on Zero-Hours Contracts'. *The Guardian*, 27 June 2014, https://www.theguardian.com/stage/2014/jun/27/beyond-caring-alexander-zeldin-poverty-play
Tyler, Imogen. *Revolting Subjects: Social Abjection and Resistance in Neoliberal Britain*. Zed Books, 2013.
Wacquant, Loïc. *Urban Outcasts: A Comparative Sociology of Advanced Marginality*. Polity Press, 2008.
Zeldin, Alexander. *Beyond Care*. Bloomsbury, 2015.

Part Two

BODIES

Chapter 4

IMAGINED SOVEREIGNTY

MAPPING AND RESISTING PRECARITY IN INDIRA ALLEGRA'S *WOVEN ACCOUNT*

Marianne Kongerslev

In *Mark My Words: Native Women Mapping Our Nations* (2013), Mishuana Goeman (Tonawanda Band of Seneca) states: 'The imaginative possibilities and creations offered in the play of a poem, imagery of a novel, or complex relationships set up in a short story provide avenues beyond the recovery of a violent history of erasure and provide imaginative modes to unsettle settler space' (2). Taking these imaginative possibilities, of not only literature, but any artistic or creative practice, as a point of departure, in this chapter I focus on the complex artefact comprising a woven blanket as well as a filmic performance, *Woven Account* (2014), by performance artist, poet and weaver Indira Allegra (Cherokee and African descent). Set in the San Francisco Bay Area, the video depicts the artist in key locations weaving (or spinning threads for) the woven artefact. The performance and video coincide with the rise of the Black Lives Matter movement as well as social, political and academic movements to increase awareness of missing and murdered indigenous[1] women and girls (MMIWG[2]) in the United States, Canada and Mexico, and the two movements resonate with the performance in complex ways. The video is simultaneously a performance and a strange, queer sort of visual poem. It produces a performative, (auto)biographical mini-story that figuratively and literally weaves together precarity, place, trauma, disruption and bodies in a complex, multimodal artefact that holds in tension both pain and possibility.

Woven Account comprises an assemblage of images, sound, spoken words and the woven blanket itself. The establishing shot of the video is a black background with the artist's voice-over situating gay bashing as a widespread and underreported crime that the artist herself has survived. 'I needed to visit the places where people did not survive,' she states, linking her personal experience to a larger societal issue. Although there is no narrative as such, the video progresses from pain to healing through quick cuts between images of hands engaged in weaving, cityscapes and Allegra's body in key locations, culminating in the artist holding up the woven artefact, staring out from behind its gaps and holes to look at the viewer. The visuals are furthermore interspersed with sounds of the city as well as short narratives told by survivors in voice-over. *Woven Account* is featured as part of a series of woven projects under the umbrella term *Praxis Texere*, a project that focuses on the artist's corporeal intimacies and kinship with the loom, and on weaving as a form of writing and textile materials as a form of text. Although the woven cloth and the performance are separate cultural expressions, their shared origin ties them together. Mostly exhibited separately, the two artefacts stand alone as products, but the performance and the video representation of the performance both centre on the woven cloth (and its production) as it moves through the city and interacts with Allegra's body as a form of witnessing. By producing this artistic witnessing, Allegra accounts for herself and forces the spectator to apprehend – in Judith Butler's words – her life as livable, her body as mattering, and thus *grievable*. Moreover, the performance takes on a broader, symbolic characteristic, as it opens up a space for the articulation of precarity as a cultural silence, trauma as non-exceptional, and the possibilities for creative, imagined disruptions of precaritizing mechanisms.

In the context of precarious living and violent trauma represented artistically, several theoretical concepts are central. Judith/Jack Halberstam's *imagined violence* provides a point of departure for discussing what I call imagined sovereignty, a fantasy of embodied power and self-determination that allows poets and artists to produce a productive (albeit often imaginary) resistance or sense of futurity. In 'Imagined Violence/Queer Violence: Representation, Rage, and Resistance' (1993), Halberstam argues for a creative, queer, form of psychic violence that can 'harness the force of fantasy and transform it into a productive fear' (195). Central to Halberstam's argument is the notion of imagined communities, a phrase borrowed from political scientist Benedict Anderson, and through the use of 'imagining' as a descriptor of things that could be but might never be actualized, he analyses instances of queer violence as 'psychic counter threat' (Berlant and Freeman 162). Although this imagined violence does not become physical violence and does not necessarily transform the realm of the real directly, Halberstam argues, it has the potential to temporarily alter power structures. Analysing popular cultural productions such as *Basic Instinct* (1992), *Thelma and Louise* (1991) and Ice-T's 'Cop Killer' (1992), he illustrates how representations of violence towards white heteropatriarchy by 'subordinated' people are often met with harsh criticism and assumptions about the literalness of such violent fantasies, whereas mainstream violence by white men towards people of colour, women, queer people and other Others has been naturalized (189–90). As he states, 'white violence is not only permitted but legally condoned while the mere representation of black-on-white violence is the occasion for censorship and a paranoid retreat to a literal relation between representation and reality' (189). There is a power in the fantasy of the opposite kind of violence, therefore, in that 'violence against white men perpetrated by women or people of color disrupts the logic of represented violence so thoroughly that (at least for a while) the emergence of such unsanctioned violence has an unpredictable power' (191). In this context, like 'imagined violences [that] challenge white powerful heterosexual masculinity and create a cultural coalition of postmodern terror', to borrow Halberstam's words, imagined sovereignty 'create[s] a potentiality, a utopic state in which consequences are imminent rather than actual' (199). Imagined sovereignty is resistance to oppressive structures and processes, providing creative and productive ways to defy precarity.

It is important to note that the precarity which characterizes contemporary Native, black, brown and LGBTQI2S+[3] life in the United States is not the precarity of Standing's *Precariat*. If 'The precariat's foremost need is economic security' (Standing 157), there is a much more fundamental precarity at play for these communities: the right to life. Though disparate, one unifying feature of black, brown and Native lives is that they are often positioned as hyper-precarious and in very real danger of bodily harm and death, experiencing what Judith Butler calls 'highly exacerbated' vulnerability (*Precarious Life* 29). Thus, the precarity experienced by these groups in US society more closely resembles her definition in *Frames of War: When Is Life Grievable?* (2009): 'Precarity designates that politically induced condition in which certain populations suffer from failing social and economic networks of support and become differentially exposed to injury, violence, and death' (26). For instance, research funded by the United States Department of Justice shows that Native women are 2.5 times more likely than any other ethnic group to be sexually or violently assaulted in their lifetime. One in three Native women report having been raped or sexually assaulted (Bachman et al.),[4] and the third leading cause of death for Native women is murder, according to data published by Annita Hetoevėhotohke'e Lucchesi (Southern Cheyenne) and Abigail Echo-Hawk (Pawnee) (2018). The statistics for Native gay men, Two-Spirit[5] people and transgender persons suggest equally high overrepresentation of hate crimes and other assaults on these minority groups (Kilpatrick et al.; Bachman et al.). Even in the twenty-first century, violence and oppression, in other words, affect Native communities and people disproportionately. So when artists and poets express personal trauma visually, verbally or in poetic form, they not only reference personal experiences, but a communally occurring trauma and, possibly, a deep-seated genetic trauma.[6]

In this way, Butler's thinking about grievability in *Frames of War* and *Precarious Life* (2004) invites us to further consider how these processes of precaritization operate in other cases than those she uses as examples. However, Butler's phrasing in relation to grievability and precarity displays limitations from a Native-centred perspective. Being differentially 'exposed to' death and violence is not a passive process in the United States. Accompanying the disproportionate death and assault rates is also the necropolitical tendency towards invisibilizing these deaths and lives through negative or non-existent media representations, legal texts and historical amnesia. The media's vilification and dehumanization of African American victims of police murder is one example (Louine), and for indigenous people in a broader North American context, these representations are accompanied by a profound silence or disregard (Leavitt et al.; Schroedel et al.; Lucchesi and Echo-Hawk). For instance, Lucchesi and Echo-Hawk argue that MMIWG disappear three times: 'in life, in the media, and in the data' (2), and if Native victims are even portrayed at all, their murders are justified as self-protection (Robertson), extending the historical conception of Natives as dangerous savages into the present.

This foundational disregard for the Native Other echoes Butler's ruminations on Levinas' concept of 'the face' related to representation and the question of whose lives matter. In *Precarious Life*, she states,

> The media's evacuation of the human through the image has to be understood [. . .] in terms of the broader problem that normative schemes of legibility establish what will and will not be human, what will be a livable life, what will be a Grievable death. These normative schemes operate not only by producing ideals of the human that differentiate among those who are more and less human. (146)

Producing discourses about who counts as more or less human is a central mechanism of settler colonialism as Native peoples are discursively rendered as non-human and, ultimately, through cultural narratives and national expressions of power and history, as extinct.[7] Historically, as ideological as well as physical obstacles to expansion and nation building, the indigenous peoples of North America were constructed as 'native surplus' (Wolfe 404), and thus designated for elimination. Similarly, Achille Mbembe argues in 'Necropolitics' (2003) that such colonial logics produce 'peculiar spatial institutions' (26), such as reservations that were planned for the purpose of control and containment of the 'hated enemy' (*Precarious Life* 17). Native bodies have been subjected to analogous forms of erasure, dispossession and removal, including forceful sterilization, stolen children and other forms of 'invisible killing' (Mbembe 30). Thus, with its origins in colonialism, necropower cultivates various forms of population control or material destruction of bodies that are only possible if certain bodies become marked as ungrievable. Settler colonial logics of elimination provide this framing, or 'radical effacement' (*Precarious Life* 147), by 'relegating the colonized into a third zone between subjecthood and objecthood' (Mbembe 26). In *Frames of War*, Butler expands on her critical model about which/whose lives are posited as worthy of grief and mourning. Though her focus in this book is on the wars in Iraq and Afghanistan, and the ways in which they have been framed discursively in an American context, several of her points are relevant for the discussion of settler colonialism and Native, brown and black lives within the national borders of the United States itself. For instance, similar to the ways that Afghani lives are constructed as unworthy of grief/life (or not even considered at all), the dominant logics of settler colonialism construct Native lives as unlivable and invisible, and Native bodies as always-already-dead.

As a response, indigenous artists, writers and scholars often link the personal, gendered violence perpetrated against Native bodies to broader concerns about challenging settler necropolitics and promoting sovereignty for Native nations. In *The Beginning and End of Rape: Confronting Sexual Violence in Native America* (2015), Sarah Deer (Muscogee Creek) proposes what she calls 'sovereignty of the soul' and argues that 'Self-determination for individual survivors and self-determination for tribal nations are closely connected. It is impossible to have a truly self-determining nation when its members have been denied self-determination over their own bodies' (xvi). Similarly, in hir[8] 2004 article 'Stolen from Our Bodies: First Nations Two-Spirits/Queers and the Journey to a Sovereign Erotic', Qwo-Li Driskill (Cherokee descent) states that, 'as Native people, our erotic lives and identities have been colonized along with our homelands' (52). Trauma in Native America, therefore, is not a matter of personal, psychological trauma alone, but an embodied, bodily remembered cultural affect, which transgresses physical, biological and generational boundaries. Deer's personal experiences and sociological research into gendered violence leads her to the same conclusion: 'In Indian country, violence is not always experienced as an individual; some forms of violence manifest as systemic yet invisible structures that accomplish the trauma of violence on a large scale' (xvii).

Departing from traditional definitions of sovereignty as supreme authority over a territory, indigenous scholars have thus engaged in a reconceptualization of the term that transmutes national self-determination to personal and bodily self-determination. Producing bodies as coterminous with nations, these scholars insist on the inseparability of indigenous bodies and nations. For instance, by reclaiming power over Native sexualities and gender identities, Driskill argues that 'A Sovereign Erotic', as a poetic and artistic strategy, 'relates our bodies to our nations, traditions, and histories' ('Stolen' 52). On a larger scale, this conception of sovereignty as a bodily phenomenon entails freedom from any form of invasion, be it rape, assault, incarceration or other unwanted or unlawful occupation of another's body. Articulating land and embodied trauma, Driskill further explores the ways in which artistic practice (storytelling) may function as healing in Native communities and for traumatized Native bodies as well as disrupt settler logics. She/he asks and answers, 'How do we as Two-Spirits remain whole and confident in our bodies and in our traditions when loss attempts to smother us? I return to our stories' ('Stolen' 56). As a basket weaver and poet, Driskill defines stories in a broader sense than narrative literature so that poetic forms, visual expressions and other artistic practices also come to constitute stories. Thus, Allegra's performance, as a narrative, functions as a reclamation of confidence, wholeness and grievability. By physically moving through spaces and places of violence and death, Allegra artistically re-reclaims sovereignty, by re-situating LGBTQI2S+ lives as worthy of life, and LGBTQI2S+ bodies as worthy of grief. In this way, the performance seems to echo Butler, who, in *Frames of War*, asks the seemingly simple question, '*What is a life?*' (1), exposing the epistemological problem of the frames through which we understand grievability and livability. At the same time, the performance also becomes an artistic witnessing that promotes humanization, resonating with Butler's claim that 'those who gain representation, especially self-representation, have a better chance of being humanized, and those who have no chance to represent themselves run a greater risk of being treated as less than human, regarded as less than human, or indeed, not regarded at all' (*Precarious Life* 141).

Allegra's performance, as a form of self-representation, becomes an articulation of imagined sovereignty – an artistic assertion of sovereignty and a repossession of traumatized places as well as the recovery of precaritized and ungrievable lives. Where Halberstam's queer violence responds with often extreme retaliatory force (albeit still imaginary force), *imagined sovereignty* constitutes an alternative mode of rebellion, redefining what resistance might entail. *Woven Account* displays this form of imagined sovereignty in its total denial of violence, its redefinition of decolonization as non-violent and creative. The only explicit mention of violence comes as a brief account of an episode of non-binary/trans-bashing, in which the anonymous survivor explains that the violence was directed at their breasts. The voice recounts how the assailants, in attempting to rape the person, invaded their body by grabbing at breasts that are usually bound 'all the time' (*WA*). The practice of binding breasts in the transgender, non-binary or queer community provides a way to avoid an outwardly identifiable femme feature of bodies. In addition to the physical assault, the would-be rapists' targeting of that specific body part symbolically inflicts violence on a body that is seen as non-conforming, a way to discipline that body, to make it legible as femme and therefore violable. However, *Woven Account* does not 'bash back' through imagined counter-violence or angry feminist rhetoric.[9] The affective mood, in fact, throughout the performance is stubbornly calm, albeit melancholy. *Woven Account*'s mode of bashing back is in performance, with her act of weaving as a creative, pacifist response to hate and violence. This peacefully spiteful insistence on the right to (imagined) bodily and spatial sovereignty opens up for the possibility of survivance[10] and simultaneously provides a mode in which to critique violent colonialist heteropatriarchy. The video thus becomes a powerful intervention, a 'reverse discourse' (Foucault 101), that, in Halberstam's words, has the potential to threaten to 'destabilize the real' (199).

In this attempt to destabilize the real, Allegra also performs what Goeman calls (re)mapping. Through place-based weaving, Allegra maps the spaces and places where violence against subaltern bodies has been inflicted. Weaving is culturally significant as a specific femme art practice in a Cherokee context. As both Hill (1996) and Driskill (2016) explain, basket weaving traditionally belonged to the female sphere, but, most importantly, weaving is a way to maintain culture and the history of the people, while also creating new histories and 're-storying', a practice of storytelling in order to reimagine the past and transform the future (*Asegi Stories*). Furthermore, the 'profound association of women with weaving' (Hill 119) entailed not just creative work but significant changes to the landscape, as 'rivercane depends on disturbance for health and vitality' (Hill 120). The process of remapping in this sense calls to mind historical realities of women's central roles in ceremony and the importance of weaving for literally shaping landscapes (Hill). Colonial discourses of land and space, Goeman states, are 'not just about conquering Native lands through mapping new ownerships, but it is also about the conquest of bodies, particularly women's bodies through sexual violence, and about recreating gendered relationships' (Goeman 33). *Woven Account* narrates the stories of survival of LGBTQI2S+ people and people of colour through this kind of symbolic remapping of the scarred places, reinscribing them through creative power in order to witness the violence those places represent. As Allegra explains in voice-over in the beginning of *Woven Account*: 'I needed to visit other places [...] to weave in the voices of those like me who had survived bashings but whose stories never made the news' (*WA*). Both the weaving and the on-location performance function as ways of (re)mapping. That is, Allegra performs 'the labor Native authors and the communities they write within and about undertake, in the simultaneously metaphoric and material capacities of map making, to generate new possibilities' (Goeman 3). The invisibility of the trauma experienced by the ones who were bashed is represented through their disembodied voices, and, at the same time, their trauma is intricately tied visually to place. From downtown Oakland's business district to the Castro Street neighbourhood, all of the physical places visited as part of the performance matter and each symbolizes a different form of precarity. All of the sites are public places, but the occurrence of violence here poses the questions, whose presence do these public places afford and for whom are they safe? The first location in Oakland – the middle of the business district – places precarity within the spatial realm of neoliberal capitalism. Being violently attacked in such a location is an almost unrealistically apt way of illustrating the unsuitability of some bodies for those spaces. Furthermore, the violence perpetrated in non-places like BART stations and bus stops, hubs of human transience and transit, also stresses the gendered and racialized spatial constraints imposed on certain bodies.

The second location in Oakland is the Temescal neighbourhood, a part of the Bay Area that, like other places with names of Spanish origins, recognizably betrays the hidden genocidal history of the area. Californian cities contain layers and echoes of this history, from Spanish conquistadores to Mexican rule and finally US colonization in the mid-nineteenth century (Madley). The Temescal site makes these layers of colonization of the region visible, and the reminder of violence through repeated violent acts produces the space as an example of what Mbembe calls 'repressed topographies of cruelty' (40). The Bay Area is not the militarized death world that Mbembe portrays in 'Necropolitics', but the colonialist processes and mechanisms that produce such spaces of trauma are visible there. Temescal and its namesake creek are central sites of Ohlone culture and heritage, and although traces of Ohlone history are still present on the land, the creek and the area have been culverted and battered, and continue to be sites of struggle over belonging and rightful ownership (*Temescal Legacies*; Field). The painful, haunted history of the region echoes into the present, and it is this echo that Allegra's place-based performance taps into in *Woven Account*.

Thus, these locales remind us that the Bay Area as a whole is a colonially haunted space in which the processes and histories of the settler state are ever-present but invisibilized. In the East Bay, the Ohlone Trail, named after the still-present original owners of the land, is another palpable example of the problematic nature of this colonial erasure. While the Muwekma Ohlone Tribe was denied federal recognition in 2011 and therefore occupies a liminal space legally,[11] their presence is acknowledged culturally and symbolically, but also *historically*, as exotic inhabitants relegated to the past. In the early twentieth century, anthropologist Alfred Kroeber proclaimed that the Costanoan tribes, to which the Muwekma Ohlone belong, were extinct: 'The Costanoan group is extinct so far as all practical purposes are concerned. A few scattered individuals survive, whose ancestors were once attached to the missions San Jose, San Juan Bautista, and San Carlos, but they are of mixed-tribal ancestry and live lost among other Indians or obscure Mexicans' (Kroeber cited by Leventhal et al. 311). This discourse is integral to the settler colonial project, and, moreover, this rhetoric erases the indigenous presence by a racist sleight of hand that produces mixed-blood folks as 'obscure' and 'lost' Others. In response, Allegra uses her own body and the woven artefact to reinscribe a Native presence onto the landscape of the city. In one scene, she has placed the blanket over her prostrate body, so that, invisible to the general public and obscured by the myriad stories woven into the blanket, the contours of the body and face seem to fuse into the foreground as part of a landscape, becoming one with the terrain. The place becomes part of her and she becomes part of it.

Thus, throughout *Woven Account*, the interrelatedness of mourning, violence, silencing and place manifests through Allegra's body and its placement in and movement through the scarred and racially haunted landscape of the San Francisco Bay Area. Trauma and precarity are woven into bodies and embodied knowledge of spaces and places that are either regarded as safe or unsafe. As one voice-over explains, 'when you're in a certain environment, you know which street to walk down' (*WA*). The embodied knowledge that certain places do not accommodate you as a subject, the anonymous, disembodied voice explains, makes you keenly attuned to your own precariousness and your subjectivity as 'not quite recognizable as' a subject and your life as 'not quite [...] recognized as' a life (Butler, *Frames* 4).

It is not only her indigeneity that places her as anomalous in the dominant cultural imagination that constructs Natives as 'surplus' targeted for extermination (Wolfe), and narratively marked for extinction in US popular culture; Allegra's legibility as of African descent also entails a certain amount of spatial transgression. The video alludes to this on several occasions, as it uses the voices of survivors to narrate feelings of precariousness. As another voice states, 'I don't actually walk in the world assuming that there's a guarantee that the law's protecting me', alluding to juridical invisibility and precarious dehumanization. Protection under the law is thus exposed as a privilege only certain lives are awarded. A third voice describes walking in known unsafe spaces as a lack of sovereignty and freedom of movement: 'If you are a person who believes you have a lot to lose, you operate accordingly.'

Wilfully defying this received notion of insecurity, Allegra's is a body 'in dissent', a body that performs racialized identity in a 'specifically disruptive fashion', to borrow a term from Daphne Brooks' *Bodies in Dissent: Spectacular Performances of Race and Freedom, 1850-1910* (2006). Within the logic of white supremacist heteropatriarchy, Allegra is not supposed to take up space, and she is not supposed to make a spectacle of herself. In other words, the atypical use of public space as a place to create and to engage in this particular artistic practice (to weave) constructs her bodily performance as a form of insurgency. This 'strategy of critique' (Brooks 5) has a long history for displaced Africans and descendants of enslaved Africans in the United States and the Atlantic world. Although her performance is not spectacular in the same sense Brooks ascribes to nineteenth-century diasporic performers, it does provocatively engage in atypical behaviour for the locations she is in. Thus, her performance plays with the notion of 'displacement' in its multiple meanings and by weaving and spinning the strings for the weft in public places, she performs bodily acts that are not considered normative. In a central scene, this precarious positionality is visually represented by the intersection in which she sits, vulnerable to oncoming traffic and kneeling at the mercy of the surroundings, while still wilfully occupying that space. Furthermore, Allegra's body also refuses the logic of racial bifurcation, the notion that 'race' in the United States is a matter of black and white. By situating herself, as a femme, mixed-race woman, as an embodiment of the much more nuanced and complicated racial history of the United States, she opens up a space for bodies in dissonance and critique. It is not unimportant that Allegra uses her own intersectionally identified and racialized body as a stand-in, and it is not unimportant that she uses weaving as her artistic way to reclaim, rebuild, recapture and repossess place. In a sense, she is 'respatializing the Native body' to use Mishuana Goeman's words (Goeman 172), and insisting on a place in the world.

The physical artefact, the fragmented, woven blanket, functions as a visual and conceptual tie to body and place throughout the video. The narratives literally embedded within the fabric of the cloth, constructed as the weft of the weave, tie not only people but experiences together. The weft consists of strings of paper spun both prior to the construction of the blanket and on location of the performance, and some of them consist of stories from newspaper articles about people who were bashed and violated. However, most of the weft is blank paper signifying the stories of the many who were bashed, whose stories did not gain representation in the media (*WA*). In this way, the blankness of the weft resonates with Butler's assertion about the normative schemes of representation in *Precarious Life*, that 'sometimes these normative schemes work precisely through providing no image, no name, no narrative, so that there never was a life, and there never was a death' (146). The erasure of the stories signifies on a macro-level as well. Through the interplay of the woven cloth and the artist's body, the lack of visibility, like the physical locales of the performance, calls to mind the systematic erasure of the indigene throughout US history.

Furthermore, the hand-spun strips become a continuation of Allegra's body and as such an extension and merging of her experience with others' – the weft is the shared, common story of the survivors, whereas the warp strengthens the conceptual tie. The dual colours of these strong strings resonate with Allegra's body as the human hub, embodying multiple precarities. Some of the warp strings are beige and others are dark grey; they are organized in a seemingly random pattern, and in the final frames of the video, they partially cover the face of the performer. The face of the Other, staring defiantly into the camera, ends the video; however, the face is still obscured and only partially visible and recognizable as a face. The warp and weft enhance this tension between visibility and invisibility. While the warp looks almost carceral with its vertical strings mimicking prison bars, the weft exposes the double meaning of the woven fabric. The paper strips occasionally allow words and phrases from newspaper articles to be visible, but throughout the video none of the words are legible in full, with only syllables and single letters peeping through the holes and patterns. But the final frames of the video include a slow movement, progressing towards the semi-visible face, that finally reveals a few unconnected phrases and words. The most salient of these is the simple 'okay' that appears at the lower left side of the frame. Combining 'okay' with another visible phrase, 'are still', produces a sense of refusal of erasure and an insistence on survivance.

By appropriating the visual medium, Allegra speaks against a tradition in the United States of (mis)representing racialized Others visually. In *Going Native: Indians in the American Cultural Imagination* (2001), Shari M. Huhndorf notes how such representations of 'the Indian' establish various hierarchies (sexual, racial, gender), serving the colonialist purpose of violent erasure, both real and symbolic. This defiant gaze, therefore, is a sovereign act of self-determination, echoing Leslie Marmon Silko's notion of 'The Indian with a Camera'. Self-representation is not just an act of preservation and control over one's own image in the face of colonialist as well as symbolic violence, it is also threatening to the settler logic. As Silko states, 'the Indian with a camera is an omen of a time in the future that all Euro-Americans unconsciously dread: the time when the indigenous people of the Americas will retake their land' (178). By returning the viewer's gaze through the veil, Allegra defiantly forces us to acknowledge her 'face' as one among many. But the framing also suggests an unknowability, a perpetually shaded or veiled visage, signifying perhaps the refusal to be known or charted completely, yet still recognized and accounted for as a life.

Directly beneath the phrase 'okay', the blanket appears to make a promise of sorts. The simple infinitive 'to be' contains not just a static meaning of existence, but also projects into the future. Combined with the artist's defiant yet obscured gaze, this produces a sense of wilful survivance. If, as Mbembe states, 'the ultimate expression of sovereignty resides [...] in the power and the capacity to dictate who may live and who must die' (11), imagined sovereignty proposes a vision for the future in which black and brown people possess this capacity. Although it is not the futurity suggested by indigenous speculative fiction as such, *Woven Account* does suggest a kinship to the speculative philosophy that giving an account of oneself entails, according to Judith Butler. As she states, 'at the moment when we narrate we become speculative philosophers or fiction writers' (*Giving* 78).

Like the silenced and brutalized Philomela of the ancient legend exposing the identity of her rapist and telling her story of survivance by creating a woven account of it, Indira Allegra produces an account of violence and survival. Held up in front of 'the face of the other', the physical product resulting from the performance, the woven blanket, signifies the lens through which the survivor experiences the world while revealing oppression, violence and erasure. The frayed, tattered and fragmented blanket held together by newsprint, cotton and string is deceptive. It may look fragile and disjointed, but it is a communal artefact put together from the interlocking strings of the survivors' stories and strengths. It is being held up simultaneously as armour against the world and mirror to the world. The image forces the spectator to engage and to look beyond the surface to find the life behind the veil, to recognize and to regard. The woven blanket – the account of the violence and the reclamation of grievability of the lives represented – becomes, in a sense, an example of the ways in which 'One would need to hear the face as it speaks in something other than language to know the precariousness of life that is at stake' (*Precarious Life* 151), to borrow Butler's phrasing. The performative weaving becomes a way of speaking and representing in a way that is thus outside of language.

Through an analysis of Allegra's *Woven Account*, this chapter has suggested ways in which art and artistic practice can work towards 'destabilizing the real', as Halberstam phrases it. Extending Halberstam's concept of imagined phenomena that possess this destabilizing power, the chapter argued that imagined sovereignty suggests a vision for the future in which black, brown, Native and LGBTQI2S+ people possess power over their own images as well as bodies and communities. The imagined nature of this kind of sovereignty does not preclude actual sovereignty (now or in the future). Nor does it mean that it is imaginary or unrealistically utopic, though utopic it is. Nevertheless, artistic witnessing that possesses this destabilizing force is inherently revolutionary – imminent if not actual. As a decolonial strategy, therefore, imagined sovereignty destabilizes the logics of settler necropolitics, by insisting on humanization and grievability for 'the hated enemy'. Although this chapter focuses on a single cultural artefact, imagined sovereignty exists outside of this example as well. In indigenous speculative fiction, among Native and indigenous feminist thinkers, and in poetries, the often humorous and sometimes furious usage of imagined counter-violence, disruptions of eliminatory logics and visions of futurity thrive.

In the same way that Allegra's body comes to symbolize – in fact, embodies – the intersecting and interlocking precarities associated with being LGBTQI2S+, a woman, Native and African American, her woven testimony refuses a single form. By simultaneously producing a woven artefact, a performance and a film, Allegra articulates cultural practices to her embodied precarities and to modes of resistance. As Silko states, a Native person with the power to represent themselves is both threatening and a way to gain sovereignty. Although she does not expose assailants and perpetrators directly, Allegra uses the visual medium to reinscribe herself, and by extension of the woven cloth, her community, onto places where their 'ungrievable lives were lost' (Butler, *Precarious Life* 148), as a means to expose the workings of settler colonial logics and violence. Her insistence on placing her body in dissent, on narrating her own story of survivance in something other than language, becomes a 'challenge to the abusive patriarchal order' (Naples 1173), an order that is deeply anchored in US settler society. By giving a woven account of lives otherwise considered ungrievable, Allegra speculates on their futurity and imagines her own sovereignty.

Notes

1 There seems to be little or no consensus about terminology to describe and refer collectively to the indigenous peoples of what is now the Unites States of America, and whatever term one decides to use will invariably reveal some form

of constructedness of borders, nationhood or Indigeneity. The term 'Indian' or 'American Indian', although used by many, seems anachronistic, historically erroneous, essentialist and oppressive, in that it simultaneously constructs an identity category imposed from without that ignores differences and perpetuates a colonial erasure. I am aware that some Native people refer to themselves in this manner; however, that right to terminology does not necessarily transfer to non-Natives. The term 'indigenous', although in many cases preferable as it alludes to primacy and rightful ownership, is too broad a term which does not provide enough geographical specificity in this instance. Therefore, I will use the term 'Native' (or, rarely, Native American) when referring to pan-tribal, transnational aspects; however, in most cases I will strive to use sovereign Native national and tribal names, such as Cherokee and Muwekma Ohlone. Following the norms of standard English spelling for national adjectives, I will also use the capitalized 'Native' rather than the lower-case 'native' when referring to the sovereign 'nations within the nation' of the United States.

2   Although indigenous women disappear and are murdered by the thousands in the United States and Canada, their stories are silenced and often go unacknowledged by law enforcement and are frequently missing in federal agencies' databases. For a more thorough discussion of this crisis, see Annita Hetoevėhotohke'e Lucchesi and Abigail Echo-Hawk (2018).

3   Lesbian, Gay, Bisexual, Transgender, Queer/Questioning, Intersex, Two-Spirit and others. I use this acronym to denote the diversity of gender and sexual identities. It is not, however, meant to be exhaustive, and other subjectivities are not meant to be excluded. I will use this acronym to signify subjectivities and identities, whereas I will use 'queer' to denote the oppositional energy that is not necessarily associated with a sexual orientation or gender identity.

4   In comparison, about 18 per cent of women in the United States in general report being sexually assaulted or raped in their lifetime (Kilpatrick et al.).

5   The neologism Two-Spirit refers to Native persons whose gender or sexuality falls outside the settler colonial heteronormative matrix and denotes a departure from colonialist terminology about sex, gender and sexuality. Qwo-Li Driskill (2005) calls Two-Spirit 'a sovereign term in the invaders' language' (62). The term originated in the late 1980s Native lesbian and gay movements—and specifically at the 1990 Native American Gay and Lesbian Conference in Winnipeg—when Indigenous LGBTQI2S scholars coined it as an umbrella term to replace the derogatory and homophobic 'berdache' (Tatonetti, 'The Emergence' 150–1). Unlike 'berdache', Two-Spirit more closely mirrors the important social, economic and spiritual roles third- and fourth-gender persons played in ancestral tribal communities. It is not an unproblematic term, but I use it here to refer to those Native people who self-identify as such. See Tatonetti ('The Emergence' and The Queerness of Native American) or Jacobs et al. (Two-Spirit People) for a fuller discussion of the term and its history.

6   Recent studies of/in trauma and genetics have demonstrated that trauma can traverse generations, biologically and literally speaking, since traumatic events can alter genomes, which parents can pass on to their children. This 'transgenerational transmission of trauma' (Kellerman) has been studied in mice and other laboratory test animals, but studying Holocaust survivors and their offspring, in recent years, researchers such as Rachel Yehuda and Tania Roth have concluded that epigenetic transmission of trauma can also occur in humans (Roth; Kellerman; Braga et al.). The news of this research was presented on the online news site Indian Country Today Media Network in an article by Mary Annette Pember that linked these findings to

an indigenous context. Pember concludes that although the research is new, it is not a new phenomenon to indigenous peoples. She writes, 'Folks in Indian country wonder what took science so long to catch up with traditional Native knowledge' (n.pag.). For instance, scholars such as psychiatrist Maria Yellow Horse Brave Heart, who called this phenomenon 'historical trauma', have worked with indigenous communities since at least the 1980s producing research on the effect of historical trauma, especially as it relates to substance abuse (Brave Heart; Brave Heart et al.).

7   See for instance Shari M. Huhndorf's *Going Native: Indians in the American Cultural Imagination* (2001), Philip Deloria's *Playing Indian* (1998) and Elizabeth Cook-Lynn's *Anti-Indianism in Modern America: A Voice from Tatekeya's Earth* (2001).

8   Driskill has used several alternatives to the he-she binary pronouns on different occasions, sometimes using they/their, ze/hir, and she/he/hir. I use the pronouns found at the faculty homepage at Oregon State University website: http://liberalarts.o regonstate.edu/users/qwo-li-driskill.

9   Recent feminist scholarship and activism have focused on the role of anger and rage as feminist strategies of resistance. See for instance Rebecca Traister's *Good and Mad: The Revolutionary Power of Women's Anger* (2018), Soraya Chemaly's *Rage Becomes Her: The Power of Women's Anger* (2018) and Brittney Cooper's *Eloquent Rage: A Black Feminist Discovers Her Superpower* (2018).

10 Often described as a portmanteau of 'survival' and 'resistance', the term 'survivance', which now has a central position in Native/Indigenous studies, refers to 'an active sense of presence, the continuance of native stories, not a mere reaction [. . .]', as Gerald Vizenor states in *Manifest Manners* (vii). Survivance entails a rejection of mere survival and an insistence on active resistance. In narrative terms, Vizenor suggests that 'Native survivance stories are renunciations of dominance, tragedy and victimry' (*Fugitive Poses* 15). Survivance is inherently decolonial in its rejection of colonialist logics, and like 'Two-Spirit' it is an indigenized term 'in the invader's language'.

11 While federal recognition could also be construed as another form of colonial violence (see for instance Coulthard, *Red Skin, White Masks*), its absence both legally and symbolically erases the presence of the tribe and prevents access to federal services, protection under the Native American Graves Protection and Repatriation Act and possibilities for land-rights cases. For a fuller discussion of federal recognition, see Lightfoot et al. ('The Study of Indigenous Political Economies') or Myers ('Federal Recognition of Indian Tribes').

Works cited

Allegra, Indira. *Woven Account (Full)*. indiraallegra.com, 2014. https://www.indiraallegra.com/woven-account.

Bachman, Ronet, et al. 'Violence Against American Indian and Alaska Native Women and the Criminal Justice Response: What Is Known'. U.S. Department of Justice, 2008. https://www.ncjrs.gov/pdffiles1/nij/grants/223691.pdf.

Berlant, Lauren and Elizabeth Freeman. 'Queer Nationality'. *Fear of a Queer Planet: Queer Politics and Social Theory*, edited by Michael Warner. University of Minnesota Press, 2007, pp. 193–229.

Braga, Luciana Lorens, Marcelo Feijó Mello, and José Paulo Fiks. 'Transgenerational Transmission of Trauma and Resilience: A Qualitative Study with Brazilian Offspring of Holocaust Survivors'. *BMC Psychiatry*, vol. 12, 134, 2012, https://doi.org/10.1186/1471-244X-12-134.

Brave Heart, Maria Yellow Horse. 'The Historical Trauma Response Among Natives and Its Relationship with Substance Abuse: A Lakota Illustration'. *Journal of Psychoactive Drugs*, vol. 35, no. 1 (2003), pp. 7–13. doi:10.1080/02791072.2003.10399988

Brave Heart, Maria, et al. 'Historical Trauma Among Indigenous Peoples of the Americas: Concepts, Research, and Clinical Considerations'. *Journal of Psychoactive Drugs*, vol. 43, no. 4, 2011, pp. 282–90, doi:10.1080/02791072.2011.628913

Brooks, Daphne. *Bodies in Dissent: Spectacular Performances of Race and Freedom, 1850–1910*. Duke University Press, 2006.

Butler, Judith. *Precarious Life: The Powers of Mourning and Violence*. Verso, 2004.

Butler, Judith. *Giving an Account of Oneself*. Fordham University Press, 2005.

Butler, Judith. *Frames of War: When Is Life Grievable?* Verso, 2009.

Cook-Lynn, Elizabeth. *Anti-Indianism in Modern America: A Voice from Tatekaya's Earth*. University of Illinois Press, 2001.

Coulthard, Glen Sean. *Red Skin, White Masks: Rejecting the Colonial Politics of Recognition*. University of Minnesota Press, 2014.

Deer, Sarah. *The Beginning and End of Rape: Confronting Sexual Violence in Native America*. University of Minnesota Press, 2015.

Deloria, Philip J. *Playing Indian*. Yale University Press, 1998.

Driskill, Qwo-Li. 'Stolen from Our Bodies: First Nations Two-Spirits/Queers and the Journey to a Sovereign Erotic'. *SAIL*, vol. 16, no. 2, 2004, pp. 50–64, doi:10.1353/ail.2004.0020

Driskill, Qwo-Li. *Asegi Stories: Cherokee Queer and Two-Spirit Memory*. University of Arizona Press, 2016.

Field, Les W., et al. 'Mapping Erasure: The Power of Nominative Cartography in the Past and Present of the Muwekma Ohlones of the San Francisco Bay Area'. *Recognition, Sovereignty Struggles, and Indigenous Rights in the United States: A Sourcebook*, edited by Amy E. Den Ouden and Jean M. O'Brien. University of North Carolina Press, 2013, pp. 287–310. *JSTOR*, www.jstor.org/stable/10.5149/9781469602172_obrien.14.

Foucault, Michel. *The History of Sexuality: Vol. I: An Introduction*. Translated by Robert Hurley. Pantheon Books, 1978.

Goeman, Mishuana. *Mark My Words: Native Women Mapping Our Nations*. University of Minnesota Press, 2013.

Halberstam, Judith. 'Imagined Violence/Queer Violence: Representation, Rage, and Resistance'. *Social Text*, no. 37, 1993, 187–201, doi:10.2307/466268.

Jacobs, Sue-Ellen, et al. *Two-Spirit People: Native American Gender Identity, Sexuality, and Spirituality*. University of Illinois Press, 1997.

Hill, Sarah H. 'Weaving History: Cherokee Baskets from the Springplace Mission'. *The William and Mary Quarterly*, vol. 53, no. 1, 1996, pp. 115–36. JSTOR, www.jstor.org/stable/2946826.

Huhndorf, Shari M. *Going Native: Indians in the American Cultural Imagination*. Cornell University Press, 2001.

Kellermann, Natan P. F. 'Epigenetic Transmission of Holocaust Trauma: Can Nightmares Be Inherited?' *Israel Journal of Psychiatry and Related Sciences*, vol. 50, no. 1, 2013, pp. 33–9.

Kilpatrick, Dean G., et al. 'Drug-Facilitated, Incapacitated, and Forcible Rape: A National Study'. National Crime Victims Research & Treatment Center, 2007. https://www.ncjrs.gov/pdffiles1/nij/grants/219181.pdf.

Leavitt, Peter A., et al. '"Frozen in Time": The Impact of Native American Media Representations on Identity and Self-Understanding'. *Journal of Social Issues*, vol. 71, no. 1, 2015, pp. 39–53, doi: 10.1111/josi.12095.

Leventhal, Alan, et al. 'The Ohlone: Back from Extinction'. *The Ohlone Past and Present: Native Americans of the San Francisco Bay Region*. Compiled and edited by Lowell John Bean. Ballena Press, 1994, pp. 297–336.

Lightfoot, Kent G., et al. 'The Study of Indigenous Political Economies and Colonialism in Native California: Implications for Contemporary Tribal Groups and Federal Recognition'. *American Antiquity*, vol. 78, no. 1, 2013, pp. 89–103. JSTOR, www.jstor.org/stable/23486386.

Louine, Jeannice L. *Media Portrayals of Police-Involved Deaths in U.S. Newspapers, 2013–2016*. Mississippi State University, 2018. *ProQuest Dissertations Publishing*, https://search.proquest.com/docview/2100114517

Lucchesi, Annita Hetoevėhotohke'e, and Abigail Echo-Hawk. *Missing and Murdered Indigenous Women & Girls: A Snapshot of Data from 71 Urban Cities in the United States*. Urban Indian Health Institute, 2018. http://www.uihi.org/wp-content/uploads/2018/11/Missing-and-Murdered-Indigenous-Women-and-Girls-Report.pdf

Madley, Benjamin. *An American Genocide: The United States and the California Indian Catastrophe, 1846–1873*. Yale University Press, 2016.

Mbembe, Achille. 'Necropolitics'. Translated by Libby Meintjes. *Public Culture*, vol. 15, no. 1, 2003, pp. 11–40. *Project MUSE* muse.jhu.edu/article/39984.

Myers, Mark D. 'Federal Recognition of Indian Tribes in the United States'. *Stanford Law & Policy Review*, vol. 12, no. 2, 2001, pp. 271–300. *HeinOnline*, https://heinonline.org/HOL/P?h=hein.journals/stanlp12&i=282

Naples, Nancy A. 'Deconstructing and Locating Survivor Discourse: Dynamics of Narrative, Empowerment, and Resistance for Survivors of Childhood Sexual Abuse'. *Signs*, vol. 28, no. 4, 2003, pp. 1151–85.

Norman, Jeff. *Temescal Legacies: Narratives of Change from a North Oakland Neighborhood*. Shared Ground, 2006.

Pember, Mary Annette. 'Trauma May Be Woven into DNA of Native Americans'. *Indian Country Today Media Network*, 28 May 2015, https://newsmaven.io/indiancountrytoday/archive/trauma-may-be-woven-into-dna-of-native-americans-CbiAxpzar0WkMALhjrcGVQ/

Robertson, Dwanna L. 'Invisibility in the Color-Blind Era: Examining Legitimized Racism against Indigenous Peoples'. *American Indian Quarterly*, vol. 39, no. 2, 2015, pp. 113–53. JSTOR, www.jstor.org/stable/10.5250/amerindiquar.39.2.0113.

Roth, Tania L. 'How Traumatic Experiences Leave Their Signature on the Genome: An Overview of Epigenetic Pathways in PTSD'. *Frontiers in Psychiatry*, vol. 5, article 93, 2014, https://doi.org/10.3389/fpsyt.2014.00093

Schroedel, Jean Reith, and Roger J. Chin. 'Whose Lives Matter: The Media's Failure to Cover Police Use of Lethal Force Against Native Americans'. *Race and Justice*, October 2017, doi:10.1177/2153368717734614.

Silko, Leslie Marmon. *Yellow Woman and a Beauty of the Spirit: Essays on Native American Life Today*. Simon and Schuster, 1996.

Standing, Guy. *The Precariat: The New Dangerous Class*. Bloomsbury Academic, 2011.

Tatonetti, Lisa. 'The Emergence and Importance of Queer American Indian Literatures; or, "Help and Stories" in Thirty Years of SAIL'. *Studies in American Indian Literatures*, Series 2, vol. 19, no. 4, 2007, pp. 143–70. https://www.jstor.org/stable/20737397

Tatonetti, Lisa. *The Queerness of Native American Literature*. University of Minnesota Press, 2014.
Vizenor, Gerald. *Manifest Manners: Narrative of Postindian Survivance*. University of Nebraska Press, 1994.
Vizenor, Gerald. *Fugitive Poses: Native American Indian Scenes of Absence and Presence*. University of Nebraska Press, 2000.
Wolfe, Patrick. 'Settler Colonialism and the Elimination of the Native'. *Journal of Genocide Research*, vol. 8, no. 4, 2006, pp. 387–409. doi:10.1080/14623520601056240.

Chapter 5

PRECARIOUS BODIES ON THE MOVE, PRECARIOUS BODIES UNDER ATTACK[1]

Katharina Pewny and Tessa Vannieuwenhuyze

The current surge of right-wing politics and ongoing discussions about stricter migration policies add a controversial layer to our understanding of solidarity. In this chapter, we will introduce terminologies and activist discourses around precariousness in the first decennium of this millennium, in order to zoom in on two recent performances of 'precarious bodies on the move'. These performances are centred around groups of people who are faced with (forced) migration and therefore live under unstable conditions. Although migration is a reality from which precarious conditions can emerge, migration precarity remains an overlooked aspect in performing arts discourse. Analysing a particular aesthetics of connectedness present in the discussed performances, we finally work towards a spiritual reconsideration of solidarity in relation to these 'precarious bodies under attack', which might encourage an encounter with the Other from within.

Performances of the precarious as de/precarization[2]

The changing working conditions in the New Economy, the worldwide economic crash in the autumn of 2008 and increasing poverty created a variety of uncertain and unstable circumstances, which could be labelled as 'precarious', and precariousness is frequently staged in contemporary theatre, performance and dance. The word 'precarious' can be traced back to the French adjective *précaire*, which in turn originates from the Latin word *precarius*, meaning 'sensitive, difficult'; the Latin verb *precare* means to 'beg' (Pewny, 'Theatrum Europeaeum Precarium' 30–47). In 2004, Judith Butler launched an influential discourse on vulnerability as a human ontology of precariousness, drawing on Emmanuel Lévinas' writing about the precariousness, that is, vulnerability, of the other. In Lévinas' ethics, the encounter of the self with the other is central because *it constitutes the subject status of the self through responsibility for the other*. Lévinas' thinking, which was shaped by his witnessing of the Holocaust, is very relevant today, as we are being confronted, most often through extensive media representation, with people dying while attempting to reach Europe. Restricted access to the European Union (EU) produces a specific precariousness, as many risk their lives trying to reach European shores. Following Lévinas, we can ask: What is the historical responsibility of people holding European passports and other members of majorities in this situation? Both aspects are indivisibly interconnected because, for the philosopher, the self becomes human by acknowledging the other (Lévinas 78). In Lévinas's thinking, acknowledging the other means that the self steps out of relatedness to itself and into difference to itself. The humanity of the self exists in the acknowledgement of the mortality of the other and in making the other's concerns one's own. The exposure of the other is an invocation, command or assignment for the self to show responsibility (Lévinas 163). Judith Butler's thoughts have been referenced in theatre and dance studies and in performances that deal with war and other traumatic events (Pewny, *Das Drama des Prekären* 'Performing the Precarious'). The term 'precarious', as it has been developed by Butler, denotes an ontological vulnerability of the human being/of all humans. Of course, this concept could be extended to include non-human beings and ecological questions in the light of contemporary concern about the climate.

In activist and sociological discourses after the Millennium, the precarious includes several aspects. It embraces human vulnerability arising from unsecured working and living conditions within current economic developments, as well as bodily vulnerability and, in the end, mortality. Despite all their political, social and economic differences, the 'multiple loci of Europe' (Chakrabarty 17) provide comparatively wealthy and secure contexts of living – at least for those who hold a European passport. However, the economic shift from Fordism to post-Fordism from the 1970s onwards set a destabilization of living and working conditions in motion. French writers Anne and Marine Rambach's book *Les Intellos précaires* already initiated debates on precariousness in 2001. They spread rapidly from France to other Mid- and Western European countries such as Germany, Spain and Italy. In 2003, the German-Swiss theorist and artist collective Kleines postfordistisches Drama released the video *Kamera läuft* [Camera rolling] (2003), in which the collective stages casting situations with performers who read texts on precarious work. The texts consist of samples from previously conducted interviews with the producers and their friends. Looking for an alternative to the union-led strike that took place in Madrid in 2003, the Spanish feminist network Precarias a la Deriva launched the video 'A la deriva (por los circuitos de la precariedad femenina)' on the precarious lives of both migrant and Spanish women. Both videos create visual identities that make the working and living methods of their producers visible, and they perform a 'narration of the self', which Richard Sennett claims is a strategy for coping with the insecurities of New Capitalism. Both these videos were circulated widely between 2000 and 2010 within the discussion forums surrounding precarious work. Many temporary work situations demand skills traditionally important for work in the arts, such as creativity, excellent self-performativity and flexibility. Consequently, people living under precarious conditions have started to discuss their living and working situations in publications, in visual media, on the internet and at public gatherings (see Pewny, 'Performing the Precarious'). Migrated persons, people of colour and female-marked persons publicly circulate their visual self-narrations in the first decade of this Millennium, but their individual (artistic) identity stays invisible in the nameless groups of *precarias*. From the people and productions observed between 2000 and 2010 in Europe, no female artist and/or artist of colour became famous and/or financially stable with their work on precarity. They were not able to turn their vulnerability into stable productivity. Curiously enough, however, as we will show in the upcoming section, performances of precarity were successful (during that period) when they were staged as a crisis of white masculinity.

De-precarization through performances of the precarious in European theatre

Among the choreographies of precariousness after the turn of the millennium was the solo-trilogy *Perform Performing* (2004–5) by Jochen Roller. After many successful performances of this piece, Roller managed to turn his unstable working conditions into full-time employment, as he was dance dramaturge at the renowned Hamburg performance venue Kampnagel from 2007 to 2010 and was afterwards appointed artistic director of its well-known live art festival. Consequently, Roller finally sold his own performance at the Kampnagel summer festival in 2009 entitled *Wir können uns nicht aus der Krise shoppen* (We cannot shop our way out of the crisis, 2009). One of the most well-known theatre makers who successfully transformed his own precarious living and working conditions into a flourishing career is René Pollesch (Volksbühne Berlin), who explicitly referenced the reality of his own living and working situation in the theatre in his early works. However, these theatrical performances do *not* refer to more complex levels of insecurity and to fundamental precariousness in the living and working situations of those illegalized and migrant persons portrayed in the video *Las Precarias* and in the online representation of the fictive saint *San Precario*. The success of the aforementioned theatre makers and their successful de-precarization can thus be read as exceptions of a few privileged white/male subjects who inhabit the territory of the globalized knowledge society, rather than as profound expressions of solidarity among those sharing the vulnerable state of precarity. We only witness processes of de-precarization in the careers of male, *white*/European theatre makers and dancers.

From 2010 and onwards, precariousness and performances of precarity have become the object of a broad range of academic surveys. Many of them are written by (former) feminist researchers, and they show how some Gender Studies researchers are increasingly preoccupied with a more general critique of capitalism and a plea for humanism: these include Shannon Jackson's *Social Works* (2011), Bojana Kunst and Gabriele Klein's *Performance as Labour* (2012), the TDR (*The Drama Review*) issue on precarity (2013), Lauren Berlant's monograph on *Cruel Optimism* (2011) and, last but not least, Bojana Kunst's book *Artist at Work: Proximity of Art and Capitalism* (2015). The 'precarious' – be it understood as precarity or precariousness – is a link between the performing arts, activism and academia. For white intellectuals – both female and male, if we think of Guy Standing – reflections on precarity serve as a successful step within their academic careers. Lauren Berlant turned reflections on grassroots-movements in which migrated people united with freelancers and the unemployed into an influential theory in her book *Cruel Optimism*. The Italian Mayday-demonstrations inspired her, when she was travelling through Europe in 2001, with her ideas on precarity and precariousness, which she now terms 'slow death'. Berlant describes precarity as an ongoing instability that works across social stratifications and across bodies, affects, economies and aesthetics (194–6). Her idea of precarity takes psychic processes into account, and she underlines the fact that the precarious subject is haunted by the fantasy of what seems lost (and what maybe always was a phantasy), that is, stability. Precarity is, according to Berlant, a collective state of being, a general condition of/in Western societies. For Berlant, the aesthetics of precarity are characterized by 'glitches' and 'disturbances' (198). Her description resembles what Nicolas Bourriaud defined in 2004 as precarious aesthetics: relational, flickering, blurring, as well as transformational and posttraumatic (Pewny, *Das Drama des Prekären*). All these analyses highlight disturbance, fragmentation and irritation: unbinding effects. The connecting, networking and enclosing aspects of precarious aesthetics are yet to be researched. However, within our contemporary ecosystem of connective media, media scholar José van Dijck has rightly pointed out the conflation of meaning between human connectedness and the automated connectivity that social media platforms encourage (12).

In what follows, we therefore decided to turn to the binding, connecting and stabilizing aesthetics of precarious art today as a possible re-negotiation of a correlated fragmented sense of solidarity: an aesthetics of connectedness, enhancing complex human connection. We propose a holistic understanding of an interconnectedness between humans and other beings and their surroundings, that is, plants, the earth and the cosmos: 'Spirituality concerns what is holistic – that is, a fully integrated approach to life' (Sheldrake 5). This holistic understanding, which implies a concern about the wellbeing of the other, is at work at times when the polity fails to protect the basic rights of humans (see Agamben; Rancière). By referring to a holistic, or even spiritual, understanding of art, we point out the political and emancipatory aspects of a holistic understanding of being, which could reinstate solidarity. To further demonstrate this argument, we now continue with a discussion of Tanja Ostojić's performance project *Misplaced Women?* and Yael Ronen's 'This Situation' as precarious works of art characterized by this particular aesthetics of connectedness, set in a shared context of right-wing politics.

Connectedness in/of Tanja Ostojić's art project Misplaced Women?

Working since 1994 from a feminist perspective on issues of migration and displacement recently earned Tanja Ostojić a place in British newspaper *The Guardian*'s list of most influential artists of the twenty-first century

(Searle 'The Best Art of the 21st Century'). The Berlin-based, Yugoslavian-born artist and cultural activist, who studied Visual Arts in Belgrade and Nantes, crossed the Schengen border in 2000 between Austria and Slovenia during the performance 'Illegal Border Crossing'. In the same year, she placed an advertisement online containing a picture of her naked, shaved body and a text declaring she is looking for a husband with an EU passport. The advertisement, the search, the wedding with a German artist and, finally, the divorce party in 2005 were part of the project 'Looking for a Husband with EU Passport'. In her project *Naked Life 1* (2004–08), Tanja Ostojić reports on the deportation of Roma from Germany. With the camera running, she reads out the 'Written Comments of the European Roma Rights Centre Concerning Germany For Consideration by the United Nations Human Rights Committee at its 80th Session, 2004'. In these documents, deported Roma share their experiences of the structural violence and chicanery which go on around the deportation-process. In 2011, Ostojić produced a new version of this project named *Naked Life 2* and performed it in the Second Roma Pavilion 'Call the Witness' exhibition at the UNESCO office at the Venice Biennale. Here she reads out disturbing individual stories of diverse kinds of discriminations against Roma from across Europe, including racist serial killings of Roma in Hungary. The entire 'Naked Life' project from 2004 to 2016 comprised around seven performances in total, each based on new research. In this project, she performs the role of ambassador for people who are not able to speak for themselves in the EU, since they have experienced over 500 years of systematic and racist discrimination across Europe. She answers to the vulnerability of the other by exposing herself to the spectators. Throughout the performances and video performances she takes off her clothes until she is naked in the end. 'Ostojić considers how it is possible that in contemporary Europe certain ethnic groups are constantly exposed and stripped of their political, social, and human rights' (Ostojić, 'Naked Life 2' n.p.). With the clothes she loses protection by and by until the gaze of the spectators can scan the contours of her body. Ostojić's nudity further quotes the visual exploitation of the suffering of the other in contemporary mass media.

In 'Naked Life 1-7', Ostojić engages as a messenger of those who have been deported from the EU already. The working title 'Call the Witness' is both a declaration of the artist's position as a witness and a call to the spectators to testify. Since 2000, Tanja Ostojić has consequently worked (like many others today) from the perspective of a migrated, freelance (female) artist. Multilinguality, mobility and critique of the isolationist policies of the EU are integral to her work. She publicly visualizes her own path towards a European passport and she portrays herself as a switchboard between whites/artists with an EU passport and migrated persons who live without a valid residence permit in the specific precarity of *sans-papiers*. A position like that of Ostojić therefore unites 'precarity' in the sense of economic instability, with the 'slow death' which Lauren Berlant calls 'precarity', as well as with the ontological vulnerability of all humans, discussed by Judith Butler in 2004. *Misplaced Women?* is a clearly outlined script for a performance that is distributed by the artist online and acted out herself and supervised in various workshops in public spaces globally since 2009. It is one of the 'series of [. . .] strategic products that span a period of several years' developed by her (Ostojić quoted in Gržinić 161).

Score 1 of *Misplaced Women?* reads as follows:

1. Select a migration specific place that resonates to you (public transportation, central bus station, airport, border, aria affected with gentrification . . .)
2. Get there and unpack a bag of your own (such as your own purse or back pack or a bag with empty plastic bags, or packaging from consumers articles . . .).
3. Take every single item out and turn it inside out. Take all out of your pockets. Turn your pockets inside out. Take your shoes off. Ones you unpacked all, search to see if you discover something.
4. For advanced and additionally motivated: You can do the same action at a variety of places and see how different it is being perceived at different times and locations. In such a case, draw a map of where you have performed. (Ostojić, 'Score #1: unpacking a bag of your own') [sic]

These instructions constitute the main score. Since 2009, *Misplaced Women?* has been performed in over twenty-five cities in Europe, Switzerland, the United States and Canada (and there is one written contribution from Gaborone, Africa) by Tanja Ostojić and contributors who developed their own versions of *Misplaced*

Figure 5.1 *Misplaced Women?* Project (2009–20). Dedicated to the missing and murdered indigenous women in Canada. Performed by Tanja Ostojić, October 2016, in front of the Art Gallery of Ontario, Toronto, Canada, 7a*11d. Photo: Henry Chan. Copyright / Courtesy: Tanja Ostojić.

Women? in workshops offered by Ostojić or who simply borrowed the concept. Texts and visual documentation are accessible on an online platform – which can also be seen as a blog on precarious work – on which Ostojić calls for realizations of the scores: 'You are invited to perform *Misplaced Women?* and to share your experience on the web and during public discussions. Tanja Ostojić would like to hear from anyone performing this delegated piece: please send your contributions in the form of images, notes, texts, drawings or videos for this blog' ('About'). Because one can perform exclusively one's own experiences or invent an artistic personality with a fictional biography, and all variations in between, *Misplaced Women?* has an infinite number of possible realizations. Ostojić herself refers to the aesthetics of authenticity, which is, especially in performances of migration, a crowd magnet, namely when migrated people share their authentic migration experiences. Some artists deliberately refuse to do so, for example Mohammad Al Attar in *Iphigeneia* (Volksbühne Berlin 2017), where women refugees onstage discuss why they are silent about their flight from Syria to Germany in the theatre, in order to avoid a voyeuristic aesthetics.

The simple score of *Misplaced Women?* provides a spatial arrangement next to or around the suitcase and prescribes the timing of unpacking and packing the suitcase. These are the fixed dramaturgical elements of the performance. It resembles a ritual act performed by a 'ritual agent' by manipulating ritual objects in a delineated space. The ritual unpacking and packing of the objects connects the performer with other misplaced women, and it also connects the performer and other misplaced women with transcendental elements such as hope (on arrival), memory of the dead (escape from war). Transversal connections are established, both to the earth (most performers sit on the ground) and to a virtual space (through the internet platform). However, unlike the shaman or the priest, the ritual agent here, the performer, is not authorized to perform her actions, but appears as a disturbance in the zones of transit where she performs *Misplaced Women?*; in other words, she appears as being misplaced. Therefore, this art project stimulates a reflection on public space as (private) property, on displacement and on the specific vulnerability of female (and other non-male) bodies, under the condition of migration. To quote Judith Butler:

> So we do have to stay critical about modes of political resistance that do not simply resignify an existing public sphere, but instead dissolve the lines that demarcate the private, private enterprise, from the public, public security. We have to think anew about these threshold zones, including the internet, that sometimes traverse those distinctions and other times retrench both military and securitarian power, corporate control, and censorship. (Butler in Butler and Athanasiou 153)

Ostojić, who never asks for permission for her performances in public spaces, advises, for example, to always bring another person to the performance, someone who 'talks the security out (of the performance)'. According to Sara Ahmed, spaces are designed for specific bodies, and anybody who does not belong to this norm has restricted ability to move in (public) space (546). The search or quest is the central dramaturgical engine of *Misplaced Women?*, and as this search seems to have no end, I suggest, therefore, that the performance should be understood as an actualization of identity as 'orientation towards something', as Sara Ahmed explains this phrase (553), rather than using any fixed notion of identity. The objects we surround ourselves with bring out the identity that distinguishes us. Therefore, *Misplaced Women?* is a call to give shape to one's identity, even though 'women' are often 'misplaced' in zones of transit. As Ahmed writes, 'Phenomenology asks us to be aware of the "what" that is around. After all, if consciousness is intentional, then we are not only directed toward objects, but those objects also take us in a certain direction. The world that is around has already taken certain shapes, as the very form of what is more and less familiar' (545). The objects that we direct our attention towards reveal the direction we have taken in life. If we face this way or that, then other things, and indeed spaces, are relegated to the background; they are only ever co-perceived (546). The suitcase and the other objects shape the bodies that handle them, and they determine in which direction the bodies move. Sara Ahmed emphasizes, drawing on Heidegger and Husserl, that 'Phenomenology hence shows how objects and others have already left their impressions on the skin surface':

> The tactile object is what is near me or what is within my reach. In being touched, the object does not stand apart; it is felt by the skin and even on the skin. In other words, we perceive the object as an object, as something that has integrity and is in space, only by haunting that very space, by coinhabiting space, such that the boundary between the coinhabitants of space does not hold. The skin connects as well as contains. (551)

The presence of *Misplaced Women?* in the zone of transit is precarious because representatives of state authorities or private companies can intervene at any time. Nevertheless, the connecting qualities are very prominent in this art project. The combination of different experiences of migration (the performers), the outspoken connection with the place it is performed, the circulation of the scores and the documentation on the internet and the conscious practice of self-connection with the selected items, which comes about in the act of packing and unpacking, counterbalance previous critical approaches emphasizing disruption and crisis by adding instead the precious connective element of constant re-actualization.

Yael Ronen's The Situation *as interreligious communion of hummus (Maxim Gorki Theatre Berlin, 2015)*

In Yael Ronen's *The Situation* (Maxim Gorki Theatre, Berlin), the act of eating hummus functions dramaturgically as a conciliating activity between members of different hostile religious communities and language groups (namely, Arab and Hebrew). We proceed from the hypothesis that, as in many other contemporary

Figure 5.2 *Misplaced Women?* Project (2009–20). 'Which Colonial Comfort Would You Like to Consume Today?' Developed and first performed in the frame of *Misplaced Women?* performance workshop in the public space by Tanja Ostojić, Berlin. Performed by Rhea Ramjohn at Tempelhoferfeld, Berlin, January 2018. Photo: Alice Minervini. Copyright / Courtesy: Ostojić, Minervini, Ramjohn.

performance and theatre pieces in Europe, a longing for connectedness can be observed here, proposing an alternative to the dominant aesthetics of precarity mentioned earlier. The act of eating together can be read as a materialization of connectedness, which brings us to the issue of the transpersonal and the spiritual (Dox 46). The migrated artists are cultural translators between the various precarious groups such as German-born intellectuals, cultural workers and artists, artists who migrated to Germany and live there under comparatively stable working and living conditions, and migrated persons who do not have a residence permit and so on. 'Precarity' as 'a general condition in Western societies' (Berlant 192) is the condition that connects people whose conditions of working and living strongly differ from each other.

Yael Ronen is resident playwright at the Maxim Gorki Theatre, the smallest city theatre in Berlin, where Shermin Langhoff has been intendant since season 2013–14. The start of Langhoff's (and Jens Hillje's) intendancy was a sign that the issue of coexistence of different 'cultures' and religions is not simply confined to a niche of post-migrant theatre, but has become a matter that concerns the city theatres and the German theatre repertoire. Langhoff gathers people from 'countries in crisis' in the studio of the Maxim Gorki Theatre, in line with her statements, such as: 'In Berlin leben Menschen aus 168 Nationen. Wir müssen nicht mehr weggehen, um die Welt kennenzulernen. Die Welt ist längst bei uns' ('People from 168 different nations live in Berlin. We do not have to go abroad to come to know the world. The world has already been for a while among us', Widmann 2015). Her ensemble of actors from a migrant background and her way of programming attract a mixed audience, which consists of many second- or third-generation migrants. Within this frame, director Yael Ronen is known for her work with ensembles of actors from different cultural and religious backgrounds. Ronen's name is also connected with the Berlin city theatre scene coming to terms with diversity, and she is precisely in this scene a resident and the most prominent playwright at this moment. Ronen became known in 2008 with the production *Die Dritte Generation* ('The Third Generation'), in which Israeli, Palestinian and German actors, who were born after the Holocaust and the Nakba, perform at times intense discussions on their different perspectives and identity concepts, but also on canonical discourses on victims and offenders (Tropper 7). This struggle for reciprocal understanding bears witness to grave conflicts that unfold along politicized lines of religions and languages and to the difficulty of coming to reciprocal understanding and connectedness.

Common Ground is a later work on the war in Bosnia, which Ronen wrote at Langhoff's request.[3] The quest for connectedness or the 'common' of the people involved is, according to the programme booklet of the Maxim Gorki Theatre, the cornerstone of *Common Ground*: 'What do they share? What is their common ground?' (*Gorki #9*, 30). At first glance, *Common Ground* appears to be an autobiographical work, since the actors seemingly perform their own life stories. However, this impression of authentic presence is subverted, for example when actors Jasmina Music and Mateja Meded exchange their identities onstage: The 'Serbian' and the 'Bosnian' characters, descendants of a Serbian perpetrator of war crimes and a Bosnian victim (of Serbian cruelty) perform each other. Ronen's recent work at the Maxim Gorki Theatre is an example of the so-called 'Post-migrant' (Foroutan) theatre in Germany, which touches upon the trope of authenticity that is commonly expected from migrant performers.

'Postmigration or 'post-migrant society' in Germany can be characterized as a state in which society is deeply and profoundly shaped by migration in all its aspects. Although social science scholars like Foroutan use the term to refer to a historical (contemporary) period, its initial use by artists and scholars was more like an analogy of the other post-conditions of the twentieth century. The concept of *post-migration* or *post-migrant* is highly influenced by the field of postcolonialism and its approach to the politics of knowledge, identity and cultural belonging, for example. Post-migrant theatre established an aesthetic and intellectual space for subaltern artists to speak for themselves, in their own voices, and thus to produce theatrical discourses (Langhoff, Kulaoğlu and Kastner 400). Nowadays post-migrant theatre is considered its own genre within the German theatre and has been an influence on other (West)European countries with similar immigration flux. In 2013, Shermin Langhoff became the artistic director of Maxim Gorki Theatre, located in the historical eastern part of Berlin. At Maxim Gorki Theatre and especially at the studio Studio я, intersectionality became very present within the narratives' aesthetics as well as the artists on and off stage. Since then, the theatre has twice been awarded the title 'Theater des Jahres' (Theater of the Year) by the German theatre journal 'Theater der Zeit', in 2014 and 2016.

Consuming hummus as cultural translation

In its intersectional approach, the Gorki Theatre Berlin is highly inclusive towards formerly marginalized audience members, such as second- and third-generation migrants and other postcolonial people and queers. Multilinguality, language switching and non-native utterances of German are now trademarks of the Gorki performances, making it a 'syncretic' stage where elements across several religious and political beliefs converge. A good example of how seemingly opposing and conflicting characteristics of different beliefs co-exist in a fusion of aesthetic and intellectual intersectionality, is the award-winning performance piece *The Situation*, which premiered on 4 April 2015. Like other productions by Ronen, the dramaturgy relies on biographical research, multilingualism and short improvised scenes, which were translated into different languages and reworked multiple times during the rehearsals (Tropper 9). In the following, we will refer to the staging of 1 January 2016 and the manuscript of 15 September 2015, which was written in German, English, Hebrew and Arabic. In this respect, it is telling that the manuscript mentions that it is authored by 'Yael Ronen und Ensemble (Dimitrij Schaad, Ayham Majid Agha, Orit Nahmias, Yousef Sweid, Maryam Abu Khaled and Karim Daoud)'. In seven scenes, seven 'lessons' of a course in German are staged, in which the performers from Israel, Palestine, Syria and Kazakhstan each tell a (seemingly) biographical story and present themselves as a heterogeneous group of people that seriously disagree on religious themes. The only performer that seems to be a German, Stefan the teacher, reveals in the fifth scene that he is the son of Russian immigrants (Ronen et al. 65).

The production reaches its climax when Stefan is exposed as an assimilated migrant who can pass as a 'real German', after which the performers eat hummus together, which seems to function beyond former religious borders. The theme of religion is addressed in an ironic way in the first scene, when Noa (played by Orit Nahmias) tells a story in the German class that is critical of her homeland Israel. The following part is taken from her class lecture entitled 'Wer bist du? Who are you?':

NOA: we have a sea of potable water – where Jesus –
AMIR: Jesus.
NOA: Jesus went under . . . on the water – and everyone pisses in it. And the/people are not secure in their houses, because there are cockroaches everywhere. That result in/a rat alert. (Ronen et al. 9)

After this, religion is discussed from different perspectives. In this discussion, conflicts and the relation between religion and politics dominate. Jerusalem is, for example, represented as a war-torn city bathing in blood, but the play also deals with the problem of being Jewish in Berlin (Ronen et al. 13) and the issue of how 'being Jewish' can actually be defined. The second 'lesson' – and second scene in the text – is entitled 'Wo kommst du her?', or 'Where are you from'. One of the students, Hamoudi, says he is a Syrian refugee, while the teacher is uncertain whether or not he was active in IS. Hamoudi tells about his plan to order hummus and sell it during the pause of the German course to his fellow students (Ronen et al. 33). Religion and politics converge when he thinks out loud about shaking the hand of Noa, the Israeli woman: 'I don´t know if it's legal for me to shake her hand, I don't know if she's legal to eat humus!' (Ronen et al. 35). *The Situation* deals with political issues through religious conflicts and is therefore described as a 'political comedy'. The comical elements are mostly wordplay and alleged grammatical errors. Laughing is thereby a reaction to the opening-up of unequivocal contexts that both separate and bring together groups of people on the stage but also in the audience (Tropper 10).

However, behind the comical, self-ironical aspects of the performance, there lies a bitter conflict between members of various religious groups. This is represented through a tragic love story between the Jewish Noa and the Palestinian Amir, whose marriage comes close to divorce but is still laden with hope at the end of the performance: Noa: 'There is still hope for us' (Ronen et al. 82). Their son, who has been brought up in two languages, carries a conflicting identity. Depending on the religious context, the boy is treated as Israeli (speaking Hebrew) or Palestinian (speaking Arabic). His father Amir, for example, speaks about the difficulties he encounters in the Berlin neighbourhood Neukölln – where Amir is seen as a Palestinian – when his son speaks Hebrew in public: 'The waiter looked at me like I was Jew, who learned Arabic in the Moussad. FUCK YOU! How dare you! What? Do I have to come and apologize for my son's Hebrew? Do I really have to say "I am not Israeli!" I'm your Palestinian brother and my son too. I'm just married to a Jew' (Ronen et al. 22). The religious conflict is represented through the languages (Arabic and Hebrew) and addressed by the heterosexual marriage and the relation between people, which can occur between individuals, but at the same time transcends the personal level and is therefore not tangible. The motif of hope is connected with the hope for a peaceful coexistence between people of all religions and sexes. In the last scene, for example, Noa compares the hope of the salvation of their love with the hope that all people can live a peaceful life.

The Situation is one of many examples of contemporary theatre and performance art concerned with creating communities beyond social differences and political conflicts and achieving connectedness among people. In the programme of the Maxim Gorki Theatre of winter 2015–16, one can read a 'Letter to Society', which ends with the following words:

> Dear society, we will not cease to criticize you, to explain and to postulate your changeability. Maybe because we want to conjure up the hope that there is a connection that can eventually be described and disrupted somehow. Do you think that we mean you, when we talk about you? Please answer, it would be of great help to us. (*Gorki #9*, 3)

The issue of connectedness, which is apparent in the call for replies in the programme of the Maxim Gorki Theatre, and the longing for all living creatures being connected in love, is transpersonal. Here, it goes beyond the political and concerns the realm of the spiritual. In the last scene, entitled 'Konjunktiv' – the grammatical conjunctive form that is used in German to signify possible actions – the performers form a group that eats hummus together, bought 'live' onstage from Hamoudi. The eating of hummus is a dramaturgical tool that functions across religious differences. The act of eating together materializes the longing for connectedness that is difficult to put into practice and that pervades the whole performance and the dramaturgical practices of seeking and realizing durable connections between people at the Maxim Gorki Theatre. Here, in this scene, the differences between meat-eaters and vegetarians, vegans and flexitarians, religions and origins are played off against each other. The dramatic character 'Hamoudi' distributes the hummus, and a pita bread, in a priest-like manner among the performers, who consume it onstage. The political differences that were constructed and acted out before, most prominently between 'the Jew' and 'the Arab', are mutually translated and incorporated through the joint consumption of this meal. The dramaturgy of shared hummus therefore works as a cultural translation on the bodily level. However, by not including the audience members in this intercultural, multilingual and interreligious communion, the director and her ensemble re-establish the classical division between performers and audience that the performance tried to overcome in previous parts through staging multilinguality. All performers move around an enormous yellow staircase in the otherwise empty black box stage. The yellow is exactly the same colour as the well-known cover of the *Duden*, the most prominent lexicon of German language and grammar, which, since 1880, serves as the go-to authority for language questions about German. The teacher's costume partly resembles this shade of yellow, whereas the other characters are dressed in the colours of the flags of their native countries.

The text and the performance are written and spoken in German and easily switch to English, while there are also some utterings in Hebrew, Arab and Russian:

> Als mein Sohn war kleiner, ich versuchen zu sprechen Arabisch mit mein Sohn. Aber es war schwer – we lived in Tel Aviv and all around where Jews who spoke Hebrew. There are hardly any Arabs in Tel Aviv. But when my son was a baby I tried. His first word was Arabic: Baba. (Ronen et al. 21)

The language switching resembles everyday practices in today's superdiverse urban contexts, such as Brussels, where more than half of the population is of migrant origin. Furthermore, the applied languages resemble the diverse and conflicting religious backgrounds, namely Arab and Hebrew. Significantly, German and English do not stand for a specific religion, but they rather serve as unmarked norms, in which traces of Christianity pass unseen and thus not reflected upon – comparable to 'whiteness' as unmarked norm on stages (see Joy Kristin Kalu). On a more general level, the multilinguality employed reflects the mobility of the sign on theatrical stages, for theatricality is characterized by an increased mobility and shifting of meaning (Fischer-Lichte). Tracy Davis and Thomas Postlewait highlight the fact that '[i]f theatre and life are inseparable, our behaviour is a series of roles. And if we are merely playing roles, there is no "original" to the mimesis, we are caught in an inescapable condition of imitating a false ideal' (10–11). What does this mean for multilingual performances and for utterances of 'incorrect' German?

These utterances of 'incorrect' German highlight the fact that, according to Davis and Postlewait's definition, there is no 'original', that is, a homogeneous German language. The German of a native speaker as 'original' language is uncovered as a product of learning, rather than innate knowledge. It is only logically consistent to the plot that the teacher of German, Stefan, is by no means a native speaker, but reveals himself as the son of Russian immigrants. In the last few years, the Gorki theatre makers have managed to attract an audience of people of various origins and languages. German, English, Hebrew, Arab and Russian are spoken on the stage, which becomes a 'macaronic stage' (Carlson and Balme, quoted Meerzon 44,), or 'theatrical syncretism'. Still, the theatre makers imply that everyone can see, read and understand either German or English, because subtitles in these two languages are projected on the back wall of the stage, whereas no Arab, Hebrew or Russian subtitles are used when someone is speaking in German or English. Audience members can choose to cognitively follow the narration or let their minds wander through the sounds, while understanding some parts of the text, and other parts not. Consequently, there is no longer one 'implied reader' (Iser) who can fill the gaps between meanings. Rather, this syncretic theatre forms a collective body that encounters itself 'as self' and 'as other' (Meerzon 44). This is reflected on the bodily level of affective utterances, when waves of laughter sweep across the seat rows and mark the sometimes simultaneously and sometimes suspended affective reactions to jokes, language 'mistakes' and other comic elements. The collective subjectivity comes to being through this performance that is an act of cultural translation: not a cultural translation between two, let us say, theatre systems or languages, but a cultural translation within the group of theatre makers, and between theatre makers and audience members.

At this point, we would like to refer to Gabriele Klein's definition of cultural translation, which indicates that translation can never be a reproduction of an 'original'. Rather, it is always a process of mediation and negotiation. Cultural translation is haunted by the paradox that translation conceals difference, whereas identity can only arise from difference (Klein 17). This means: the gesture of translating a script necessarily produces identity different from the 'original'. 'Culture' only becomes a unity in a retrospective manner, during the translation process, as the translation creates the imagined unity and nation. In *The Situation*, the Gorki theatre makers perform a multilingual, interreligious culture in which German and English pass, alongside with (traces of) Christianity, as unmarked norms. At the same time, they distribute the 'pockets of not knowing' within the collective body of a syncretic stage, that might privilege migrated audience members because of their multilingual capacities (in contrast to North-Western Europeans who are capable of speaking their native language, plus English). We read these ruptures, which are caused by not-understanding, as 'disturbances' and 'glitches', which are, according to Berlant, distinctive features of precarious aesthetics.

The ritual of eating simultaneously acts as an explicitly connecting element. The acceptance of the other's vulnerability, which Levinas and Butler call precariousness, is realized through the collective body of the audience, which is affectively involved, even if the epistemic understanding due to the multilingualism sometimes fails. The collective eating of the hummus onstage teases the audience with an interreligious ritual that involves them, as hummus is a popular and successful product of today's hip, Mediterranean or vegan urban food politics in Western metropolises. Again, some migrated artists, just as Tanja Ostojić, choose to act as switchboards between more or less precarious people. This means that the 'vulnerable other' is no (longer) to be found outside of one's own person, but also in one's self. Therefore, precarious artworks such as *Misplaced Women?* and *The Situation* switch between seemingly authentic material and multiple levels of fiction. These realizations indicate that both performances bring a (future) reality full of possibilities to the extended stage, where spiritual connections with our daily surroundings transcend a superficial demand for connectivity and its fragmented sense of solidarity.

Nevertheless, we cannot ignore the many (violent) acts that disrupt these intentions of solidarity. Bringing 'precarious bodies on the move' to the stage, unfortunately, also means acknowledging how, oftentimes, they remain 'precarious bodies under attack'.

Precarious bodies under attack: (How) to perform under conditions of right-wing politics

During a recent performance of *Misplaced Women and the Tourist Suitcase* that took place at the historic location 'Goldenes Dachl' in Innsbruck, Tyrol, Austria, on 12 May 2018, Tanja Ostojić packed herself inside a suitcase, that she partly carried on her upper body. When she crossed the street, carrying the suitcase on her back with only her lower body and legs sticking out, a woman violently pushed her away. As Tanja Ostojić told Katharina Pewny on 18 December 2018:

> There were actually two interventions during the performance: one was in the first part while I was sitting inside the suitcase creaming myself with sun cream and eating fruit yogurt. A catholic activist was trying to discipline me by slapping me gently on the face with church leaflets. Later while I was walking around with my upper body inside the huge suitcase, the second woman who was dressed in a dirndl and had wooden barrel filled with schnapps on her [approached me]. She belonged to a traditional orchestra that was there in support of [a] celebration of a local right wing party event to whom my performance was obviously disturbing.

The attack by the second woman put Ostojić's body in danger as she had to struggle not to fall on the street. This is a striking example of how migrated and other artists in precarious states are being physically attacked and/or harassed by members of right-wing parties and groups in more than one European country. We quote from the *Financial Times*, 29 July 2018:

> Few cultural figures have been as personally affected by the rise of the German right as Shermin Langhoff, artistic director of Berlin's Maxim Gorki Theater. In the latest indignity, an AfD MP has demanded to see her contract. 'It is harassment, pure and simple,' she says. 'Anyone who speaks out publicly against the ideologues of the New Right is being attacked.' [...] [The] Gorki represents a vision of Berlin as a cosmopolitan melting pot that warmly embraces foreigners and refugees. For the right it is a symbol of how German national identity has been replaced by the 'hippie state', a melange of diversity, open borders and rainbow flags. (Chazan 10)

Also in Vienna, the members of the migrant theatre group 'The Silent Majority' have been attacked by members of the 'identitarian', that is, a right-wing group, as well, during a performance at Vienna University. Apparently, it is possible today to walk into a performance, push performers, throw fake blood and threaten people in various ways such as shouting without being convicted by the state afterwards. We are sure that many more such examples could be told. This is Europe today, and these are 'Precarious Bodies under Attack'.

The porous borders of these performances of precarity need to be safeguarded. Throughout this chapter, we argued that defending this is intrinsically linked with an embodied notion of solidarity and intensified spiritual sensibilities – in the sense of being through interconnectedness – of our surroundings. The discussed performances are examples of attempts to resurrect moments of encounter in which the audience can acknowledge and share a trace of the vulnerability of the other, instead of trying to mask it under the veil of a distant reality. The aesthetics of connectedness residing in multilingualism and shared food consumption on a syncretic stage, as well as self-connection through performing precariousness in zones of transit facilitate an encounter from within, and even the more rudimental human emotion of empathy, a characteristic that should remain at the core of performance.

Notes

1. Our considerations are informed by the outcomes of Katharina Pewny's research project 'Theatre of the Precarious', funded by the Austrian Academy of Sciences from 2003 to 2009. They are also informed by our cooperation with Yana Meerzon around dramaturgy and multilinguality, and by the research project 'Choreographies of Precariousness' conducted by Annelies van Assche and funded by the Research Foundation – Flanders. See also: Meerzon and Pewny *Dramaturgy of Migration*.
2. An earlier version of this section was published in *Forum Modernes Theater* (Pewny, 'Performing the Precarious', 2011).

3   *Common Ground* was invited to the Theatertreffen Berlin and received the public award at the Mühlheimer Theatertage in 2015.

Works cited

Agamben, Giorgio. *Homo Sacer. Sovereign Power and Bare Life*. Translated by Daniel Heller-Roazen. Stanford University Press, 1998.
Ahmed, Sara. 'Orientation. Towards a Queer Phenomenology'. *GLQ: A Journal of Lesbian and Gay Studies*, vol. 12, no. 4, 2006, pp. 543–74.
Berlant, Lauren. *Cruel Optimism*. Duke University Press, 2011.
Bourriaud, Nicolas. 'Precarious Constructions. Answer to Jacques Rancière on Art And Politics'. *Open 17: A Precarious Existence*. Nai Publishers, 2009.
Butler, Judith. *Precarious Life. The Powers of Mourning and Violence*. Verso, 2004.
Butler, Judith and Athena Athanasiou. *Dispossession: The Performative in the Political*. Polity Press, 2013.
Chakrabarty, Dispeh. *Provincializing Europe. Postcolonial Thought and Historical Difference*. Princeton University Press, 2000.
Chazan, Guy. 'Germany's Increasingly Bold Nationalists Spark a New Culture War'. *Financial Times*, 29 July 2018, www.ft.com/content/348a1bce-9000-11e8-b639-7680ced. Accessed 8 August 2018.
Davis, Tracy C., and Thomas Postlewait. *Theatricality*. Cambridge University Press, 2003.
Dijck, Jose van. *The Culture of Connectivity: A Critical History of Social Media*. Oxford University Press, 2013.
Dox, Donnalee. 'Spiritual Logic from Ritual Bodies'. *Religion, Theatre, and Performance*, edited by Lance Gharavi. Routledge, 2011, pp. 42–63.
Fischer-Lichte, Erika. 'From Theatre to Theatricality – How to Construct Reality'. *Theatre Research International*, vol. 20, no. 2, 1995, pp. 97–105.
Foroutan, Naika. 'Postmigrantische Gesellschaften'. *Eindwanderungsgesellschaft Deutschland*, edited by Hans Ulrich Brinkmann and Martina Sauer, Springer, 2016, pp. 227–54.
Gorki #9. Dezember/15-Februar/16. Programme Booklet of the Maxim Gorki Theater. Berlin, 2015.
Gržinić, Marina. *Integration Impossible?: The Politics of Migration in the Artwork of Tanja Ostojić*. Argobooks, 2009.
Iser, Wolfgang. *Der implizite Leser: Kommunikationsformen des Romans von Bunyan bis Beckett*. W. Fink, 1979.
Kalu, Joy Kristin. 'Estrangement Effect. Constructions of Color in Contemporary German Theatre'. S:PAM lecture, 6 May 2014, Ghent University.
Kamera läuft. Kleines Postfordistisches Drama, 2003.
Klein, Gabriele and Hanna Katharina Göbel. *Performance und Praxis. Praxeologische Erkundungen in Tanz, Theater, Sport und Alltag*. Transcript Verlag, 2017.
Langhoff, Shermin, Tunçay Kulaoğlu and Barbara Kastner. 'Dialoge I: Migration dichten und deuten. Ein Gespräch zwischen Shermin Langhoff, Tunçay Kulaoğlu and Barbara Kastner'. *Das Drama nach dem Drama. Verwandlungen dramatischer Formen in Deutschland seit 1945*, edited by Artur Pelka and Stefan Tiggers. Transcript Verlag, 2011, pp. 399–408.
Lévinas, Emmanuel. *Ethik und Unendliches. Gespräches mit Philippe Nemo*. Böhlau, 1982.

Meerzon, Yana. *Performing Exile, Performing Self. Drama, Theatre, Film.* Palgrave Macmillan, 2012.

Meerzon, Yana, and Katharina Pewny, eds *Dramaturgy of Migration. Staging Multilingual Encounter in Contemporary European Theatre.* Routledge, 2019.

Ostojić, Tanja. 'About'. *Misplaced Women?*, https://misplacedwomen.wordpress.com/about/

Ostojić, Tanja. 'Naked Life 2'. *Call the Witness*, https://callthewitness.net/Testimonies/NakedLife2

Ostojić, Tanja. 'Score #1: Unpacking a Bag of Your Own'. *Misplaced Women?* https://misplacedwomen.wordpress.com/2018/03/15/score-1-unpacking-a-bag-of-your-own/

Pewny, Katharina. 'Theatrum Europeaeum Precarium'. *Theater Und Ökonomie. Ästhetik, Produktion, Institution*, edited by Franziska Schössler and Christine Bähr. Transcript Verlag, 2009, pp. 39–55.

Pewny, Katharina. *Das Drama des Prekären. Über die Wiederkehr der Ethik in Theater und Performance.* Transcript Verlag, 2011a.

Pewny, Katharina. 'Performing the Precarious: Economic Crisis in European and Japanese Theatre'. *Forum Modernes Theater*, vol. 26, no. 1–2, 2011b, pp. 43–52.

Precarias a la Deriva. 'A la deriva (por los circuitos de la precariedad femenina)', 2003, https://vimeo.com/3766139. Accessed 26 February 2020.

Precarias a la Deriva. 'A Very Careful Strike – Four Hypotheses'. Translated by Franco Ingrassia and Nate Holdren. *Caring Labour*, February 2005, https://caringlabor.wordpress.com/2010/08/14/precarias-a-la-deriva-a-very-careful-strike-four-hypotheses/. Accessed 26 February 2020.

Rambach, Anne and Marine. *Les Intellos prècaires.* Fayard, 2001.

Rancière, Jacques. *The Politics of Aesthetics: The Distribution of the Sensible.* Translated by Gabriel Rockhill. Bloomsbury, 2004.

Ronen, Yael and Ensemble. *The Situation.* Maxim Gorki Theater Berlin, 2015.

Searle, Adrian. 'The Best Art of the 21st Century'. *The Guardian*, 17 September 2019, https://www.theguardian.com/artanddesign/2019/sep/17/the-best-visual-art-of-the-21st-century

Sennett, Richard. *The Culture of The New Capitalism.* Yale University Press, 2006.

Standing, Guy. *The Precariat: The New Dangerous Class.* Bloomsbury, 2011.

Standing, Guy. *A Precariat Charter: From Denizens to Citizens.* Bloomsbury, 2014.

Tropper, Elisabeth. '"I Always Look for Groups That Challenge Each Other." Improvisation und kollektives Schreiben als Prinzipien interkulturellen Theaters'. Manuscript of a lecture at University of Luxembourg, 27 July 2014.

Van Assche, Annelies, and Katharina Pewny. 'The Brussels Dance Swarm on the Move: Precarious Bodies (Not) at Home'. *Forum Modernes Theater*, vol. 28, no. 2, 2013, pp. 117–32.

Widmann, Arno. 'Shermin Langhoff im Interview mit Arno Widmann'. *Frankfurter Rundschau*, 8 January 2015, http://www.fr-online.de/theater/shermin-langhoff-im-interview-das-theater-muss-sagen--was-sache-ist,1473346,29512184.html.

Chapter 6

DEATH KNELLS AND DEAD ENDS

LATENT FUTURITY IN MASANDE NTSHANGA'S *THE REACTIVE* AND MOHALE MASHIGO'S 'GHOST STRAIN N'

Sophy Kohler

South Africa has long considered itself a special case – during apartheid, as a pariah on the world stage; after apartheid, as an unparalleled democracy under the banner of a 'rainbow nation'. The country's literature is no exception; caught in a binary that distinguishes only then from now, it is frequently viewed as either unusually harrowing or uniquely hopeful and almost always inward-looking. However, the twenty-first century has seen the emergence of what loosely constitutes a new category of literature, referred to as 'post-transitional', which rebuffs the myth of South Africa's exceptionalism by interacting with global social realities.[1] One of the ways in which it does this is by representing issues of social stagnation, or precarity, that are not unique to South Africa but rather evidence of a more universal condition. Consequently, this writing after transition allows us to consider South African literature as global literature, something that is of importance considering the country's former political and cultural isolation.[2]

The contemporary debates around the concept of precarity originated largely in US academic circles in the twenty-first century, and although the discussions have been enthusiastically picked up in Europe, they remain considerably absent from cultural criticism in, and concerning, the so-called Global South.[3] Precarity's reference points are therefore distinctly 'Northern-centric' (Munck 752), largely linked to events in recent economic history, of which the most significant is perhaps the 1973 oil crisis and the resulting breakdown of Fordism. This chapter moves towards remedying this gap by taking up some of Lauren Berlant's theorizations of precarity and attempting to relocate them into a context that sees itself as uniquely affected by precarity and yet remains somewhat outside of contributions to these debates – that is, South Africa after its transition to democracy. It does so by turning to writing of this period-in-process, exploring how this new literature aims to perform what Meg Samuelson refers to as the scripting of connections by creating ties with what comes before it and with what is happening elsewhere in the twenty-first century.

One of these points of contact is precarity; post-transitional literature attempts to participate in the global by reorientating itself, whether consciously or not, to the widespread condition of uncertain and unpredictable livelihoods, characterized by a lack of job security and an otherwise tentative social existence. I will call this new engagement, after Samuelson, the scripting of precarity. This turn seems apposite, as South African society is certainly one in which precariousness, as a more general or shared 'ontological condition of vulnerability, displacement and insecurity' (Kasmir 1), is pervasive. As one of the most unequal countries in the world,[4] South Africa also presents as a highly saturated example of Judith Butler's distinction between precariousness and precarity, where the latter is understood as a differentially distributed, 'politically induced condition' (25). Nonetheless – and in contrast to the contexts of the Global North in which precarity theory has usually been articulated – South Africa experiences precarity as its norm and less a recent phenomenon with specific economic ties. As Ronaldo Munck argues, 'for the millions of workers and urban poor in the global South [. . .] precariousness has always been a seemingly natural condition' (747), and the 'stable working class with full social and political rights' (Munck 752) often posited as precarity's opposite has always been somewhat mythical in South Africa. However, I argue that South Africa is not a place for which, as Munck tentatively claims, the terms are irrelevant (757). By choosing to co-opt the term 'precarity', and adapt it to a discussion of the South – replacing, say, 'politically' with 'historically' in Butler's phrasing – we can in fact avoid it becoming, 'a colonising concept [. . .] in classic Eurocentric mode' (Munck 751). This would involve acknowledging precarity as intellectual category while paying attention to its reality as a lived experience.

Two recent works of South African fiction that foreground precarity as embodied, by leveraging the more graspable phenomena of illness and infection, are Masande Ntshanga's debut novel, *The Reactive* (2016), and Mohale Mashigo's short story 'Ghost Strain N' (2018). Using these two texts as my starting points, I will engage variously with Berlant's concept of 'slow death', which she qualifies as the 'structurally motivated attrition of persons notably because of their membership in certain populations' ('Slow Death' 761), and the texts' own relationships with ideas around latency and a kind of deferred or even ongoing death originating from modes of infection – in *The Reactive*, the human immunodeficiency virus; in 'Ghost Strain N', an imagined and rather ephemeral contamination akin to a form of substance-induced psychosis. Both of these can be conceived of as 'etymologically [diseases] of time' ('Slow Death' 763) and deterioration, whose definitions, as Susan Sontag argues of AIDS, '[depend] on constructing a temporal sequence of stages' (108). With this, my claim is that these two texts convert disease into a metonym for precarious living and deteriorating social conditions in contemporary South Africa, and, in doing so, engage with, and contribute to, a growing body of academic literature on vulnerability.[5]

Although illness, owing largely to the work of Sontag, is primarily read alongside metaphor, metonym would seem to me a better point of discussion with respect to both *The Reactive* and 'Ghost Strain N', and perhaps post-transitional literature more broadly. However, several critics have pointed to the difficulty of distinguishing metaphor from metonym (see, for example, Radden in White 310), and the two are at best overlapping in their definitions. In order to differentiate them, I will therefore rely on Susan Niemeier's claim that essentially all metaphor begins as metonymy, that is, metaphors 'are dependent on conceptually prior metonymic conceptualisation' (in White 311). We might therefore think of the two terms as being on a continuum, where 'metaphor' has a greater level of abstraction than 'metonymy'. As a consequence of their differing degrees of abstraction, metaphor has the potential to make concepts further dematerialized and metonymy has the ability to bring us back to things themselves. If we were to conceive of virus as a *metaphor* for precarity, we might run the risk of making precarity even less understandable or tangible as a phenomenon, which may then lead to it becoming further intellectualized. It is for this reason that metonymy appears better suited to a discussion of precarity, which is a decidedly concrete phenomenon despite its varying definitions. To see a virus instead as a *metonym* for precarity means understanding it as a component part of a broader complex, rather than something that merely replaces or stands in for it.

To make the argument that virus in the two texts functions in this manner, I borrow from Andrew van der Vlies's idea of the atmosphere of 'blocked futurity' (17) that attends South African literature after transition, recasting it as 'latent futurity' after the viruses' own respectively real and imagined incubation periods and appropriate to how they are conceptualized both within and outside of the texts. I then build on readings of *The Reactive* by Van der Vlies and Lara Buxbaum, and in attempting to make a case for the turn to precarity across South African literature of this period, provide a way in which we might read Mashigo's work under this same rubric.

A history of disappointment

Before considering the kind of work done by the two stories within the context of precarity, it is necessary to delineate the period or moment in which they were written, particularly as the category of what is being called 'post-transitional literature' is new and still rather amorphous.[6] When speaking about post-transitional literature, the transition being referred to is, of course, South Africa's transition to democracy following the country's historic 1994 election, which saw the African National Congress come to power under Nelson Mandela. However, transition is a process rather than an event with clearly defined temporal parameters; the category of the post-transitional is therefore itself transitional and should not be regarded in a strictly linguistic sense, that is, as 'occurring after a period of change' (Frenkel and MacKenzie 2), because change is ongoing and an inevitable part of history. Similarly, it marks less a breaking with the past, than it does a stage of progression; it has a reconfigured relationship with the past – and the blocks of South African history that constitute it – rather than no relationship with the past.

Although this period might be more broadly categorized as post-apartheid, it more accurately constitutes a kind of 'second wave' (McGregor and Nuttall in Buxbaum 523) of post-apartheid writing; the works of literature that fall under this category-in-the-making of the post-transitional are largely those written after the tentative conclusion of the court-like Truth and Reconciliation Commission (TRC) in 2002 and the impetus it was supposed to provide, through a process of restorative justice, for South Africa to move out of a sense of impasse.[7] It is thus not simply post-apartheid literature, as it appears outside of the interregnum period between the end of apartheid and the dawn of a comparative degree of democracy.

Instead of dealing directly with this particular historical interim, post-transitional literature explores the way in which this stagnation inheres in the country's present, attributable to the gap that has developed between imagined and possible realities, in which citizens' hopefulness is constantly undermined by rampant corruption and the government's chronic inability to answer basic service-delivery demands. Building on Berlant's 'slow death' as a symptom of precarity, Van der Vlies calls this atmosphere of disappointed hope and deteriorating optimism, after Jane Elliot, 'blocked futurity' (17), arguing that it is a key characteristic of post-transitional literature. By reproducing the stasis that results from violated expectations and a disjuncture between the magical future of the past and the mundane future of the present, South African literature after transition is something of a poster child for what Emily J. Hogg refers to elsewhere in this collection as 'the problem of the unimaginable future [being] related to difficulties making sense of the past' (160).

The Reactive

One of the events of South Africa's recent past that arguably most requires making sense of is the spread of HIV, which arrived in South Africa at the same time the country was negotiating a new future for itself as a democratic country. The idea that post-apartheid reparations would take decades, that change on such a large scale happens slowly, was anathema to the rapture attending Mandela's release from prison in 1990 and the jubilation accompanying the country's first democratic election in April 1994. And it was into this space between possibility and reality that HIV/AIDS entered, 'threatening extinction at the *very* moment that freedom affirmed life and possibility' (Ndebele 172; emphasis in original).

Under the shadow of the epidemic, coupled with endemic poverty, South Africa's transition to democracy came to be defined by the social problems of this period and most notably the way in which they were dealt with by government. The most significant moment in this regard was former president Thabo Mbeki's infamous mishandling of the HIV epidemic, and the estimated 330,000 lives lost in the delay of rolling out antiretrovirals (ARVs) and nevirapine, a drug proven effective in the prevention of mother-to-child transmission of the virus. The devastating scourge moved the realm of possibility further away from reality, producing a scenario in which South Africans witnessed their optimism atrophy and were made to 'adjust to the loss of fantasies of the good life promised by liberal democracy' (Van der Vlies 17).

The Reactive signals its intention to cross-reference South Africa's historical present – particularly the HIV/AIDS crisis – with global concerns as early as its paratextual matter. Standing as epigraphs to the American edition of the book are quotes from Mbeki and Franz Kafka.[8] The first of these is a response given by Mbeki to a question asked in Parliament on 20 September 2000, in which he expresses doubt over the scientific consensus that HIV causes AIDS.[9] While Mbeki's response takes place after the South African government has already stopped providing nevirapine to HIV-positive pregnant woman, *The Reactive* is set before the mass roll-out of antiretrovirals to HIV-positive South Africans. Although the quote works primarily to set the context for the story that follows, it also unknowingly returns us to what Njabulo Ndebele has said about the challenges of an unfolding reality and, in doing so, foregrounds the atmosphere of stasis and the sense of an unclear future that play out on a smaller scale in Ntshanga's debut novel. Situating the book broadly within the timeline of HIV treatment in South Africa is key, as the novel's main events revolve around the black market in ARVs.

The Reactive follows narrator Lindanathi Mda (nicknamed 'Nathi') and his two friends, Ruan and Cecelia ('Cissie'), in Cape Town in 2003. Of the three, Nathi tells us, he is 'the one who's supposed to be dying' (Ntshanga 16). By dying, Nathi means that he is HIV-positive, a diagnosis then regarded as inevitably ending in an untimely death. Nathi's belief in his own continuing or deferred death is as much a response to the death of his half-brother, Luthando ('LT'), for which he feels responsible, as it is to his HIV status. In 1993, at the age of seventeen, LT had gone 'to the hills', at Nathi's encouragement. To *go to the hills* is to embark on the amaXhosa initiation ceremony *Ulwaluko*, during which young men are circumcised and ushered into 'manhood', almost always in a rural, non-clinical setting. Nathi, who was then sixteen, had promised to follow after LT, but then changed his mind for reasons we are not made aware of. We learn then that LT became the victim of a botched circumcision and that subsequently, nearing the end of his days on the mountain, he had 'taken his death' (Ntshanga 2).

After LT's death, Nathi had tried to make a new life for himself in Cape Town – and his telling of 'what [his] hands had made' and 'how it broke' (Ntshanga 2) is what occupies the rest of the novel. After dropping out of a university journalism degree, Nathi enrolled at the city's technikon,[10] where he was employed as a lab assistant. His job here was to test blood samples for HIV antibodies, in the hope of finding 'a genetic mutation that gave a small percentage of the population immunity' (Ntshanga 132), dividing the samples into one of two categories depending on whether they were 'reactive' (testing positive for HIV) or not. It is here that Nathi contracts HIV, deliberately infecting himself with the virus in the lab. Nathi suggests a wealth of reasons for having done so, not least of which is the desire to make himself experience something of the vulnerability he imagined LT to have experienced in the days leading up to his death. Nathi points to this directly, recalling: '[A] week before the sixth anniversary of LT's death, I infected myself with HIV in the laboratories. [. . .] I never had the reactions I needed for myself, and I couldn't react when LT called to me for help, so I gave my own body something it couldn't flee from' (Ntshanga 161).

The implication is, as Van der Vlies suggests, that Nathi's 'decision to infect himself with HIV, to become "a reactive", was an attempt to find a way out of inaction, a way of restaging a reaction in his own body that he should have had in the world' (158). It was also, presumably, a way of punishing himself for his perceived complicity in LT's death. However, the infection in the laboratory works to counteract the kinds of associations usually accompanying HIV/AIDS. As Buxbaum reminds us, a 'story of laboratory self-infection is unheard of in South African fiction, where the virus has been depicted as spread through sexual transmission' (527). This method of contraction violates any sense of Nathi being the victim, and both matches and goes against the assumption of guilt. This is not sexual deviancy and it is not, ironically, drug use, as we shall see. Ntshanga presents instead illness as self-punishment, at the same time uncoupling HIV from sexual risk and risk from sex, 'usually inextricably paired together in the context of the spread of HIV/AIDS' (Buxbaum 526).

Nathi's infection with HIV is what allows him to operate in South Africa's large informal economy in a time of severe job shortages, and provides him with a way of navigating what Berlant terms 'the forced improvisation of a contemporary life that is increasingly not only without guarantees but without predictables' ('Austerity' 2). After using his severance pay and compensation money to buy a medical-aid plan, under which he is provided with ARVs, he works with Cissie and Ruan to sells his ARVs into a market created by the fact that the drugs have not yet been made widely available in South Africa, and are not yet provided for free by the government. They thus find themselves making their own labour, supplementing the income they get from working precarious, low-paying jobs. Nathi, Cissie and Ruan put their sales plans into action at sessions of some of Cape Town's many free HIV- and drug-counselling groups. It is at one of these sessions, 'in the basement car park of the free clinic in Wynberg' (Ntshanga 26), that the three first met. Cissie, who works as a teacher, was attending the meeting because the school she worked at had just accepted its first openly HIV-positive pupil, while Ruan, who was working for his uncle's IT firm at the time, was there 'to shop for a social issue they could use for their corporate responsibility strategy' (Ntshanga 27). Being HIV-positive, Nathi is the only one of the three mandated to attend – it is one of the requirements in order for his medical-aid scheme to continue to cover the costs of his ARVs.

We are first introduced to Cissie and Ruan when the three friends have just woken up hungover in Cissie's apartment in Newlands and are dosing themselves heavily with ibuprofen, less as a cure than as a small routine in a life largely devoid of structure. It is not insignificant that the scene opens in Newlands, a wealthy, leafy suburb of Cape Town. But with its stained walls and cracked floors, Cissie's place violates the aesthetic Newlands promotes for itself as manicured and sophisticated and, above all, clean – and it is the dirt and defects that are precisely 'what makes it affordable for her to rent a flat in this area' (Ntshanga 10). The trio's sniffing of industrial-strength glue, smoking of *tik* (a cheap and particularly dangerous form of crystal methamphetamine) and chewing of *khat*, the first two of which are seen as pastimes of the poor or the homeless, are in contrast to the location in which these scenes play out, and in contrast, too, to the fact that Nathi and his friends are intellectuals – reading Camus, listening to Brian Eno, obsessively contemplating their existence – who graduated from some of the country's first Model C schools (Ntshanga 20).[11]

Yet despite a solid education, they find themselves caught in a situation where their future is uncertain and today becomes almost indistinguishable from tomorrow; and the amount of time spent getting high in Cissie's apartment means that it comes to feel like 'an old tomb around [them]' (Ntshanga 13). This sense of disintegration is evident in the drifting and languid scene that begins the novel proper and outlines a day in the life of the three friends. As Nathi tells us, 'We drift through whatever passes for early afternoon here at Cissie's place' (Ntshanga 10), later describing the unfolding of the day as 'like riding on the back of a large, dying mammal. It matches the tepid warmth, and I close my eyes against it' (Ntshanga 12). In this same scene, Cissie is in the kitchen cooking up a batch of glue, which they will use to paste up posters advertising the availability of ARVs for sale – although we can assume that some of it will go towards their own recreational use. Nathi's detailed description of the cooking of glue reinforces the sense of stuckness or stagnation. But what is significant is that it is not just their today that moves at the pace of a dying mammal, it is their everyday; and it is perhaps no coincidence then that these scenes are set in the city known colloquially as 'Slaapstad', literally 'sleep town'.[12] *The Reactive* points to this with the suggestion that the city's sense of languidness 'is what they mean when they call Cape Town the city of slumber' (Ntshanga 48).

It is within this early spaced-out sequence that we learn more about the adhesive connection between the three friends, a relationship that foregrounds more literally the priority given by post-transitional literature to the importance of establishing connections (see Chapman in Samuelson 114). Nathi's seemingly endless state of suspension is partly the result of his perceived role in the death of his half-brother and his HIV-positive status. In fact, as he tells us, 'In order to do as much standing around as I do, you need to be one of the forty million human beings currently infected with the immunodeficiency virus' (Ntshanga 17). In a sense, having HIV is what allows Nathi to live this precariously middle-class life, one that aligns with what Berlant refers to as the 'continuing now'[13] (*Cruel Optimism* 7) of precarity, that is, the sensation of an 'enduring present that is at once overpresent and enigmatic [and] requires finding one's footing in new manners of being in it' (*Cruel Optimism* 196). However, Nathi's endless standing around might also be viewed as the consequence of his refusal in 1993 to undergo initiation rites. As Van der Vlies argues, Nathi is 'trapped in a version of minor waithood' (161), because according to amaXhosa custom, he has not transitioned into a man; he is therefore alienated from both a masculine identity and a black identity (having attended a historically white school).[14] This waithood is present even at the level of Nathi's name; the name Lindanathi, we are told, means 'wait with us', but as the narrator reveals, 'What I'm meant to be waiting for, or who I'm meant to be waiting with, I was never told' (Ntshanga 16).

In fact, reading *The Reactive* might itself be conceived of as a process of waiting. The novel's apotheosis comes when a mysterious masked man offers to buy out Nathi's supply of ARVs, and having agreed to the transaction, the three friends set out to uncover the man's identity. When the climax arrives, it occurs in the same dreamlike sequences and with the same bleeding between days that characterize the protagonists' dazed everyday, where the distinction between being high and not high is poorly defined, and we are ultimately left with little to help us differentiate between climax and anti-climax. Berlant argues of this mode of existence that it is 'where life building and the attrition of human life are indistinguishable, and where it is hard to distinguish modes of incoherence, distractedness, and habituation from deliberate and deliberative activity' ('Slow Death' 754). Nathan Goldman picks up this same uncertainty around agency in *The Reactive*, referring to how the manner in which the plot unravels moves further towards 'exposing the characters as ultimately without agency in the anti-drama of their lives' (*Full Stop*). Thus, this equivocal climax, which we hope will destroy the impasse, merely reiterates the novel's holding pattern of uncertainty and insecurity.

However, the palpable sense of 'waithood' present throughout *The Reactive* also acts to acknowledge and offer subtle but decisive challenges to the stigma and normalized opinions surrounding HIV. In place of ideas of sexual deviancy, for one, Ntshanga favours imagery that speaks to the general condition of uncertainty and levels of precarity that characterize the reality of South Africa's present, thus upturning the traditional narrative of HIV that belies the government's many safe-sex campaigns.[15] In doing so, Ntshanga allows HIV to become instead a metonym for the country's many social ills, under which HIV/AIDS has become 'the generic rebuke to life and to hope' (Sontag 109). With its window period between infection and illness, HIV as metonym for precarity gets us closer to an understanding of what I've called 'latent futurity' as an aspect of Berlant's 'continuing now' (*Cruel Optimism* 7). Through his conceptualization of infection with HIV as a kind of ongoing death, in which 'people are understood as ill before they are ill' (Sontag 119) or indeed dead before they are dead, and the novel's drug-infused denouement, Ntshanga effectively represents the lives of young South Africans navigating their country's fast-tracked but insufficient change, whose future has become frozen in the present. In representing this atmosphere of stasis, *The Reactive* participates in the scripting of precarity as disappointed hope that I argue is a key characteristic of South African literature after transition.

'Ghost Strain N'

Some of the historical and social ghosts that hang over *The Reactive* are made more literal in the reconfigured reality of Mashigo's 'Ghost Strain N'. The story, set primarily in an unnamed South African township and its surrounding suburbs, concerns a fast-spreading virus that is turning young people into 'Ghosts' – or 'living-dead thing[s]' (Mashigo 37) – around the world. The infected are referred to as Ghosts because, we are told, they 'were virtually dead before they had it – broken people who turned to a life of oblivion and homelessness even when they had places to lay their heads at night' (Mashigo 39–40). One of the more destructive aspects of the virus is that it leads Ghosts to attack other people, but the particular way in which this kind of violence manifests depends on the strain. Although it is apparent from the story that Ghosts are appearing all over the world, the narrator tells us only of the strains that are affecting some South African provinces; we discover, for example, that 'Ghost Strain T in the Western Cape made the Ghost chew the hands and arms off people', T standing for *tik*, and 'Ghost Strain W hit farm workers on Wine farms where Ghosts ripped the throats out of people and ate them' (Mashigo 39–40).

Mashigo's description of Ghost Strain W, in particular, gives us a clear indication that the strains of the Ghost virus are acting as metonyms for societal problems. Koketso decides that 'Strain W made Ghosts rip out the oesophagus from people because they had wine poured down their throats instead of being compensated and invested in by those who profited from their labour' (Mashigo 40). With this strain, Mashigo makes reference to the 'dop system', an exploitative truck system in which labourers on South African wine farms, particularly in the Cape, would receive a daily *dop* (tot or measure) of cheap wine to supplement their low wages. The practice began as early as the seventeenth century, with the arrival of settlers from Europe; and although it is now officially outlawed, it has not been completely eradicated. It has resulted in devastating social damage to the Cape's rural communities, in particular, leaving a legacy of alcohol abuse and related birth defects. Similarly, with the T strain, Mashigo sheds light on the effects of methamphetamine use, in particular of the highly addictive and easily available form *tik* and its correlation with sharp increases in crime and sexual violence, among other highly destructive behaviours (see, for example, Watt, et al.), particularly in South Africa's gang-ridden Cape Flats communities.

However, the strain that dominates the narrative is, as the title suggests, the N strain. The story follows Koketso and his attempt to track down and care for his best friend, Steven, who has become infected with Ghost Strain N – named for the equally problematic street drug *nyaope*, because 'in his neighbourhood it was Nyaope that had sustained the Ghosts; it kept them alive and in search of the next fall down a bottomless pit, until the high ended and yanked them back into a world they hated' (Mashigo 40). Having the kind of connection with Steven that transcends normal relationships, Koketso is already intimately familiar with his friend's destructive habits – which range from trainsurfing to using his uncle's disability grant to buy alcohol – as well as his precarious living situation. In a country with one of the highest unemployment rates in the world, 'Steven [had] found himself dealing with a complication that had become common in his neighbourhood: dreams deferred and idle days' (Mashigo 30). This manifests physically in Steven's appearance; Koketso had begun noticing changes in Steven, particularly in his eyes, which were now 'in a perpetual state of waking up, turned down and glassy' (Mashigo 33). Despite these clues, it is only when Koketso learns that Steven hasn't been home in two weeks that he fears Steven may have become infected.

After witnessing one of the many acts of vigilante justice that are being perpetrated against Ghosts, primarily in the townships, Koketso senses that Steven could be the next victim of a mob killing, and his search for him takes on a great deal of urgency. Koketso, who works at a funeral home, exploits the trust his employer has in him (he regards Koketso as too dull to do anything dangerous) to 'borrow' the company's hearse. After just a few hours of driving around in the hearse searching for Steven, knowing he would have been drawn to 'the most colourful street' (Mashigo 37) in a life now devoid of colour and adjectives (Mashigo 27), Koketso finds him hiding in a bush outside someone's house. When Steven tries to claw at and bite Koketso, Koketso wraps a chain around him and drags him to the hearse, 'heaving [his] living body into a coffin' (Mashigo 38). After months of travelling in stolen cars, with Steven in a coffin in the back, and after raiding a food-canning factory for supplies to survive, Koketso eventually settles down with Steven in an abandoned farmhouse.

Even without food, Steven's half-dead existence continues to stretch out, and Koketso, as his protector, becomes faced with the possibility that he might have to carry his friend around with him in a coffin for the rest of his life. He senses that '[s]omewhere inside the Ghost mind [. . .] Steven was trapped' (Mashigo 46), and with the yearning to break Steven out, spends his evenings talking to him in 'a soliloquy peppered with hope' (Mashigo 44). As the situation becomes exacerbated, and the country turns into 'a Ghost Town where most of what made people feel secure, fell away. There were no more jobs to wake up for' (Mashigo 40), the army is dispatched to exterminate the burgeoning Ghost population, and Koketso is forced to keep on the run in order to continue protecting his friend.

Although conceptualized as ghosts, Mashigo's description of the infected more often aligns with the kinds of images we popularly associate with zombies; we are told, for example, that '[s]aliva dripped from their mouths as their muscles relaxed, eyes half shut, some bent over in the kind of ecstasy and agony that oblivion brings' (Mashigo 30). However, these associations are frequently mixed; as Koketso observes of a Ghost at a traffic light, he was 'graciously suspended in a moment of sliding down a pole [. . .] he looked like a life-sized photograph frozen in that position. There was nothing in his eyes, nothing but oblivion. Drool fell from his mouth, just missing the tattered shoes he had probably stolen from another Ghost' (Mashigo 31). This idea of 'suspended in time' (Mashigo 31) provides a strong connection to Van der Vlies's description of South African youths as 'trapped in an imperfect present' (viii), and functions as a literal manifestation of Berlant's 'continuing now' (*Cruel Optimism* 7).

The Ghost virus carries the same sense of death as an ongoing process, or death as a condition of living, as HIV does. It too functions in the story as a metonym for the kind of precarity generated by social issues – in this case, all of the circumstances that underlie the turn to drugs and alcohol. Koketso is, in fact, sceptical of whether it is a virus, despite scientists calling it such; as the narrator tells us: 'he [Koketso] had seen with his own eyes its genesis. In just a few months, things had fallen apart all over the world' (Mashigo 39). Koketso is wise to the virus's metonymic power; it is apparent from the narration that he recognizes the genesis of the N strain in the gap the drug has filled in a society facing endless disappointments: 'Nyaope was just another name for an opportunist. Where society left a gap, this opportunist took over' (Mashigo 39).

We learn, additionally, that the devastating epidemic that became the Ghost virus was the result of a build-up of smaller problems; that, like all major events, this one was 'really just a string of small, overlooked events holding hands' (Mashigo 26). It is perhaps for this reason that the epidemic appears to have gone unnoticed for some time, despite the serious signs of infection present, and that '[b]y the time national newspapers, radio stations and TV stations were covering the "outbreak" it was too late for many' (Mashigo 35). Although it is suggested that Koketso may have been one of the first to notice the symptoms of the outbreak, as 'a young person whose observations were not valued, [he] knew nobody would believe him' (Mashigo 26). Not only is there a reluctance to speak up out of the fear of not being heard, but infected with the Ghost virus, young people literally lose 'their ability to stand up straight or speak' (Mashigo 30).

With this literal depiction of degeneration, Mashigo directs us to Berlant's idea that the 'living precarity of this historical present' is no longer masked by '[t]he promise of the good life' (*Cruel Optimism* 196). With its focus on epidemic as 'part of an argument about classification, causality, responsibility, degeneracy' ('Slow Death' 763), 'Ghost Strain N' depicts an evolving disquietude in an imagined township while implicitly commenting on the dangers of real social ills affecting marginalized South Africans, and the accompanying sense of an imperfect present that is without the compensation of a hopeful future.

Conclusion

Now without its main enemy and primary source of inspiration in the form of apartheid (Frenkel and MacKenzie 1), and no longer needing to respond to the narratives of trauma and hope coming out of the TRC, South African literature after transition has been afforded the space to engage with some of the subjects being dealt with around the world. The global concern with precarity sees contemporary South African literature paying attention to such affects as 'uncertainty, scepticism, doubt' (McGregor and Nuttall in Buxbaum 523), modes of feeling dominant in a country where the promises of freedom, democracy and equality have gone unfulfilled. Although precarity is a condition widely represented in this new literature, it has scarcely been dealt with directly in critical work done on literature after transition – two notable exceptions to this being analyses by Van der Vlies and Buxbaum, whose observations I have sought to develop in this chapter.

Having the privilege of no longer needing to be protest literature, and therefore able to shift the focus away from the 'moral earnestness [and] the dominance of race' (Frenkel and MacKenzie 2) of an earlier literature, *The Reactive* and 'Ghost Strain N' work with a political impetus and often clear underlying social commentary that is not lessened by the embracing of imagination. In their explorations of precarity, the two texts can be seen to have dual functions. The first of these is their avoidance of metaphorizing illness in favour of using illness metonymically in a way that speaks to the condition of 'waithood' experienced by many South Africans; instead of guilt, indulgence and sexual deviancy, they foreground a language of precarity whose victims are primarily without blame. The second of these is the scripting of connections identified by Samuelson, which, in part, involves a literary shift 'from nation to transnational relations' (Frenkel and MacKenzie 3) and an engagement with the concept of precarity, in particular. Under this, subject matter turns, for example, to 'the seeming dead-ends to which many young South Africans have been consigned by the legacies of structural inequalities fostered by apartheid and by the accommodations with local and global capital of the post-liberation government' (Van der Vlies 153). I have called this phenomenon 'latent futurity' and the burgeoning engagement with it 'scripting precarity'.

Both *The Reactive* and 'Ghost Strain N' conceptualize the country's disaffected youth as versions of the 'living dead' in an effort to represent the feeling, now ubiquitous in South Africa, of being 'trapped in an imperfect present that is not as the future was imagined, a present beyond which it might be a struggle to see' (Van der Vlies viii). Although widespread and experienced by the majority of the population, this is a condition that is still unevenly distributed and lived with to different degrees. It is certainly the case in 'Ghost Strain N', where Steven has become a zombie-like Ghost, infected with a virus that stands in place of the abuse of the illicit street drug *nyaope*. It is also the case in *The Reactive*, where the protagonist's HIV-positive status places him in a category of people who are considered 'ill before they are ill' (Sontag 119). As Goldman argues of Nathi, he 'haunts his own life, which he drifts through, drugged and dazed. He understands himself as undead and refers to his HIV-positive status as a state of being between life and death' (*Full Stop*). What all of this points to is the larger sense of latent futurity, rife with dead ends, and the persistent tolling of both literal and symbolic deaths.

The Reactive and 'Ghost Strain N' are important works in a recent set of socially conscious fictions that seek to deconstruct the idea of a South Africa for all and that complicate the rainbow nation mythology. They are representative of the way in which South Africa, essentially given a new lease on life after apartheid, attempts to participate in the global and bust the myth of its singularity. Instead of providing evidence of a South African uniqueness, they reveal stasis to be a widespread condition and are therefore in dialogue with other works of global literature, in a way that confirms 'a shared horizon of expectation, or disaffection' (Van der Vlies 153).

Both texts address precarity-as-disappointment under the metonym of illness – a specific, embodied and more graspable phenomenon largely unlinked from economic specificities. But although they utilize illness to great effect, they are less concerned with illness, viruses or disease than they are with people engaged in 'the on-going work of living' (Berlant in Puar 163) and experiencing claustrophobic lives, forced to reconfigure 'the relation of living to a fantasy life' ('Austerity' 4). Through an atmosphere of drifting, disintegration and slow demise, they emphasize the persistent disappointment and uncertainty faced by South African youth – in particular, in the decades after 1994 – while situating themselves 'in conversation with representations of precarity and disappointment that extend beyond South Africa's particular conditions' (Van der Vlies 162). At the heart of South Africa's grappling with the present, and at the heart of post-transitional literature, is therefore a general enthusiasm for and commitment to the future felt alongside 'the challenges of an unfolding reality' (Ndebele 171).

Although critics such as Munck would argue that theorizations of precarity may be ill-suited to discussions of the South, to refuse the terms here would seem to merely reiterate the divide between North and South and bolster the case of South Africa's exceptionalism. Instead, 'precarity' as an intellectual term allows us to reconsider South African literature as global literature, and precarity as an embodied concept brings to the wider international discussion the indispensability of a lived experience. In studying post-transitional literature through the lens of precarity, we therefore go some way towards highlighting what analyses of contemporary vulnerability may otherwise miss – that 'as part of a broader process of dispossession' (Munck 757) and the consequence of inimical historical forces in the South, precarity has a complexity that extends it well beyond the economic specificities of the North.

Notes

1. Although the term has so far only been used to describe South African literature that is in some ways distinct from an earlier post-apartheid literature, it is one that could come to accommodate literature written 'after' postcolonialism and, more generally, literature after conflict. After all, South Africa's release from the grips of apartheid coincided with several other moments of dramatic change, of which the fall of the Berlin Wall and the end of the Cold War are two of the most significant.
2. I avoid using the contested term 'world literature' here, as, to my mind, it merely reiterates the divide between Western literature and literature of the South.
3. This is not something that is necessarily deliberately overlooked, but rather the result of a hesitancy to use the term outside of US or European contexts. Although precarity in literary studies skews North, other academic disciplines in South Africa have engaged with the term, to varying degrees, and it is most often explored within the domains of sociology and public health. I use the terms 'Global South' and 'Global North' with the awareness that both constitute a problematic homogenization of diverse historical and political contexts.
4. According to findings by Statistics South Africa in 2019, some 55 per cent of South Africans live below the upper-bound poverty line (defined, in April 2019, as subsisting on R1227/month or roughly €75) and 20 per cent live below the food poverty line (R561/month or €34). It would therefore be offensive, in the case of South Africa to rally behind Richard Seymour's cry, 'We are all the precariat' (in Munck 753).
5. To the extent that both texts deal with the impairing effects of a disrupted or changed temporality, they can also be read within the framework of disability studies.

However, it is important to note that the particular relationship between chronic illness (here, HIV and addiction) and disability is far from straightforward. For more on disability and 'chrononormativity', see Marie-Elisabeth Holm's discussion of Paul Kalanithi's memoir *When Breath Becomes Air* (102–33). For more on the connection between HIV and disability, see Evans, Adjei-Amoako and Atim.

6 A series of attempts towards defining the 'post-transitional' were made in a special issue of *English Studies in Africa* published in 2010 – see vol. 53, no. 1.
7 It is difficult to provide an end date for the TRC, as several of its cases are unresolved, but it is usually considered as concluding in 2002 or 2003.
8 The American edition of *The Reactive*, published by Jacaranda Books, is the one used throughout this chapter.
9 The quote given by Nsthanga is, 'We need to look at the question that is posed, understandably I suppose: Does HIV cause AIDS?' Although this statement has been widely reproduced, I have been unable to locate a primary source for it, and am therefore unable to corroborate it. Nevertheless, footage of the same session of Parliament, provided by GroundUp News, features Mbeki saying something similar: 'When you ask the question, "Does HIV cause AIDS", the question is "Does a virus cause a syndrome?". How does a virus cause a syndrome? It can't.' The second quote is taken from Franz Kafka's 1903 letter to his friend Oskar Pollak; it reads: 'We are as forlorn as children lost in the woods.'
10 In South Africa, a technikon is a tertiary education institution that focuses on vocational training. The technikon in the novel is named as Peninsula Tech, one of the institutions included under the banner of Cape Peninsula University of Technology since 2005.
11 The term Model C was used during the final years of apartheid to refer to South Africa's historically white, government-aided or semi-private schools; the name is now defunct.
12 'Slaapstad' is a play on the Afrikaans word for Cape Town – 'Kaapstad'.
13 Berlant also uses the terms 'ongoing present' and 'ongoing now' (see, for example, *Cruel Optimism* 54 & 196).
14 Adding to this is the fact that Lindanathi is a name usually given to a woman. Ntshanga clarifies this on p. 16 of *The Reactive*.
15 By emphasizing the disruptiveness of a particular set of social conditions rather than chronic illness specifically, *The Reactive* and 'Ghost Strain N' speak to the need for a more inclusive definition of disability, complicating its description as either 'personal limitation' or 'social imposition' (see Oliver).

Works cited

Berlant, Lauren. 'Slow Death (Sovereignty, Obesity, Lateral Agency)'. *Critical Inquiry*, vol. 33, no. 4, 2007, pp. 754–80.
Berlant, Lauren. 'Austerity, Precarity, Awkwardness'. *Supervalent Thought*, 2011, https://supervalentthought.files.wordpress.com/2011/12/berlant-aaa-2011final.pdf.
Berlant, Lauren. *Cruel Optimism*. Duke University Press, 2011.
Butler, Judith. *Frames of War: When Is Life Grievable?*. Verso, 2009.
Buxbaum, Lara. 'Risking Intimacy in Contemporary South African Fiction'. *Textual Practice*, vol. 31, no. 3, 2017, pp. 523–36.

Evans, Ruth, Yaw Adjei-Amoako, and Agnes Atim. 'Disability and HIV: Critical Intersections'. *Disability in the Global South*, edited by Shaun Grech, and Karen Soldatic. Springer, 2016, pp. 351–64.

Frenkel, Ronit, and Craig MacKenzie, 'Conceptualizing "Post-transitional" South African Literature in English'. *English Studies in Africa*, vol. 53, no. 1, 2010, pp. 1–10.

Goldman, Nathan. 'The Reactive – Masande Ntshanga'. *Full Stop*, 16 August 2016, www.full-stop.net/2016/08/16/reviews/nathan-goldman/the-reactive-masande-ntshanga.

GroundUp News. 'Thabo Mbeki Questions Whether HIV Can Cause AIDS', YouTube, 7 March 2016, https://youtu.be/RCb9tdPIxoU.

Hogg, Emily J. 'The Future Is a Ghost: Precarity, Anticipation and Retrospection in Anneliese Mackintosh's "Limited Dreamers" and Lee Rourke's *Vulgar Things*'. *Precarity in Contemporary Literature and Culture*, edited by Emily J. Hogg and Peter Simonsen, Bloomsbury, 2021, pp. 160–75.

Holm, Marie-Elisabeth. *Recognition Redefined: Using Literary Texts to Get Social Acknowledgment*. PhD diss., University of Southern Denmark, 2020.

Kasmir, Sharryn. 'Precarity'. *The Cambridge Encyclopedia of Anthropology*, edited by F. Stein, S. Lazar, M. Candea, H. Diemberger, J. Robbins, A. Sanchez, and R. Stasch, 2018, pp. 1–14. https://www.anthroencyclopedia.co; https://www.anthroencyclopedia.com/printpdf/282.

Mashigo, Mohale. 'Ghost Strain N'. *Intruders*. Picador Africa, 2018, pp. 26–46.

Munck, Ronaldo. 'The Precariat: A View from the South'. *Third World Quarterly*, vol. 34, no. 5, 2013, pp. 747–62.

Ndebele, Njabulo S. 'AIDS and the Making of Modern South Africa'. *Fines Lines from the Box: Further Thoughts About Our Country*. Umuzi, 2008, pp. 170–89.

Ntshanga, Masande. *The Reactive*. Jacaranda Books, 2017.

Oliver, Mike, 'Social Policy and Disability: Some Theoretical Issues'. *Disability, Handicap & Society*, vol. 1, no. 1, 1986, pp. 5–17.

Puar, Jasbir. 'A Virtual Roundtable with Lauren Berlant, Judith Butler, Bojana Cvejić, Isabell Lorey, Jasbir Puar, and Ana Vujanović'. *The Drama Review*, vol. 56, no. 4, 2012, pp. 163–77.

Samuelson, Meg. 'Scripting Connections: Reflections on the "Post-transitional"'. *English Studies in Africa*, vol. 53, no. 1, 2010, pp. 113–17.

Sontag, Susan. *Illness as Metaphor and AIDS and Its Metaphors*. Penguin, 2002.

Statistics South Africa. *National Poverty Lines*, 31 July 2019, http://www.statssa.gov.za/publications/P03101/P031012019.pdf.

Van der Vlies, Andrew. *Present Imperfect: Contemporary South African Writing*. Oxford University Press, 2017.

Watt, Melissa H. et al. 'The Impact of Methamphetamine ("*tik*") on a Peri-Urban Community in Cape Town, South Africa'. *International Journal of Drug Policy*, vol. 25, no. 2, 2014, pp. 219–25.

White, Michael. 'Metaphor and Metonym at the Crossroads. A Cognitive Perspective / Antonio Barcelona (ed.)'. *Estudios Ingleses de la Universidad Complutense*, vol. 10, 2002, pp. 309–15.

Part Three

TIME

Chapter 7

PERIODIZATION AND PRECARIOUS LABOUR

THE WORK OF GENRE IN *LA LA LAND* AND *SORRY TO BOTHER YOU*

Alissa G. Karl

In the context of the films in which they appear, Figures 7.1 and 7.2 depict struggle in today's labour markets. Figure 7.1 is from the 2018 film *Sorry to Bother You* (dir. Boots Riley), which has been described as science fiction, magical realism and 'wildly dystopian satire' (Scott), and is set among the rampant economic inequalities of contemporary (or perhaps near-future) Oakland, California. The image is of the film's protagonist, Cassius 'Cash' Green, in a cubicle at his poorly paid telemarketing job. Figure 7.2, from the opening song to the 2016 musical *La La Land* (dir. Damien Chazelle), captures a large cast singing and dancing atop cars stuck in a Los Angeles (LA) highway traffic jam; their song, 'Another Day of Sun', is an ode to the singers' collective striving in the Hollywood entertainment industry. Both images refer to conditions of contemporary labour markets – job scarcity, low pay and the perpetual reach for better working conditions rather than their eventual attainment – yet each presents a distinct scopic effect. 'Another Day of Sun's' expansive view echoes the imperative of the song's chorus: 'climb these hills I'm reaching for the heights/and chasing all the lights that shine'. Like the optimism of the singers, the shot is quite literally massive, and can be indexed to the professional ambitions that animate much of the rest of the film. *Sorry to Bother You*, on the other hand, depicts Cash's work in repetitive, stifling architecture that viewers can nonetheless imagine extending far into the distance, and that aptly frames the film's affective blend of cynicism, anger and comic absurdity. The visual parameters of these two screenshots not only track onto the larger visual and narrative tropes of each film; they reference the imaginaries of labour and of the labour markets that I argue are mobilized by each film's generic features – including, but not limited to, their visual rhetorics and affective postures.

In this chapter, I examine how *La La Land* and *Sorry to Bother You* entail divergent accounts of precarious labour in the contemporary economy as a function of their generic forms. The versions of labouring precarity that the films generate involve both its periodization (i.e. historical and structural accounts of the sources from which our present moment derives) and an identification of what counts as labour and work in the first place. I'll detail how *La La Land*'s musical form

Figure 7.1 Cash in his cubicle in *Sorry to Bother You*, directed by Boots Riley © Annapurna Pictures 2018. All rights reserved.

Figure 7.2 Overpass choreography in 'Another Day of Sun', in *La La Land*, directed by Damien Chazelle © Lionsgate 2016. All rights reserved.

diagnoses current precarious labour as a function of so-called de-industrialization and a loss of the kinds of 'job security' that are often associated with Fordist labour regimes of the mid-twentieth century, while *Sorry to Bother You*'s combination of science fiction, absurdist comedy and magical realism rejects the anachronistic thinking offered by the musical form. Instead, Riley's film uses its generic resources to literalize labouring conditions; as a result, *Sorry to Bother You* demonstrates how periodizing and defining our precarious labour today must revolve around a longer-range awareness of our near-total dependency on the markets.

I hope, then, to lay the ground for rejecting a 'hard' periodizing thesis of de-industrialization that emerges in the generic features of a text like *La La Land*. I argue instead that precarious labour today is subtended by the same conditions that it has been in earlier phases of capitalism – by what Marx identifies as the worker's 'double freedom'. I proceed by first mapping the de-industrialization thesis that is embedded within the anachronistic form of the contemporary musical, including some of its more troubling racialized valences. I then interrogate some of the presumptions of that de-industrialization thesis and read the alternative imaginary of *Sorry to Bother You*'s fantastic, fantasy and absurdist forms as offering a literalized account of the structural conditions of precarious labour today.

Another day of looking for a job

La La Land's full-blown musical revival was in wide cinematic release; the film won five Oscars and was nominated for seven more.[1] I will focus here on the film's opening number, 'Another Day of Sun', though my reading applies to the film as a whole. This first scene of the film begins in the manner of mid-twentieth-century musicals, with an opening CINEMASCOPE banner in black and white that fades to reveal a scene saturated with colour, yet thoroughly mundane: a present-day traffic jam on the exit ramp connecting the 100 and 105 freeways in LA. The music starts, and an ensemble cast of mostly young, multiracial singers and dancers dressed in colour-blocked street clothing emerge from their stationery cars to sing and dance among and atop them. Their song is dedicated to the art of perseverance in the entertainment industry: about moving to LA in search of a life in the movies and the imperative to 'get up off the ground' when the job market doesn't go your way. The number culminates with a coordinated dance on the roofs of the cars as the camera pans back to reveal dancers and highway stretching as far as the eye can see, with the skyscrapers of downtown LA in the sunny, hazy distance.

This song – which is fundamentally about work – is organized by contending labour imaginaries and periodizing impulses as the number's generic and thematic elements simultaneously lament for the bygone days of industrial Fordism and celebrate our more contemporary regimes of immaterial and affective labour.[2] I'm arguing that it is the song and the film in general's generic status *as musical* that promotes a largely anachronistic and nostalgic, yet also ambivalent, response to today's precarious labouring conditions – an economic imaginary that is appropriate to our current political moment, but that I also want to challenge and ultimately read against its dominant generic grain, in part through a reading of *Sorry to Bother You*. My reading thus proceeds in the vein of prominent thinking on the Hollywood musical from Jane Feuer, Rick Altman and Richard Dyer, who have variously pointed out that the genre is invested in resolving the ideological contradictions with which it deals. 'Sun' engages in a full-throated nostalgia for

Fordist industrial capitalism on numerous levels; most immediately, the heyday of the Hollywood musical – roughly the 1930s through the 1960s – coincides with the Fordist economic moment in high-GDP countries, and we can link *La La Land*'s revival of the musical genre to the Fordist economic organization to which the musical form is native.

Indeed, *La La Land* has faced criticism for its appropriation of the musical genre, and what one reviewer called its 'formula[ic]' application of older forms that merely 'venerates and celebrates bygone methods and mannerisms' (Brody). Beyond the complaint that the film is derivative, Geoff Nelson argues that its 'politics of nostalgia and whiteness are inextricable'. Nelson claims that *La La Land*'s anachronistic escapism to the heyday of the musical also entails a return to a time of flagrant white supremacy in the United States, before desegregation and the Civil Rights Act; he calls *La La Land* 'a regressive effort at time travel with no sense of shame for America's many historical sins' (Nelson). I concur with Nelson's analysis, and would add that we can't separate the film's racial and economic nostalgia. For where *La La Land*'s generic form hearkens back to Fordist industrial capitalism, Nikhil Pal Singh and Thuy Linh Tu demonstrate in their study of the decline of textile manufacturing in the US South that those decades of well-paying and secure manufacturing work were enjoyed disproportionately by *white* workers and their families (104). Singh and Tu's analysis clarifies how claims about the so-called de-industrialization or the loss of 'manufacturing' jobs in the United States – and the changes in labour conditions that such a shift has inaugurated – are also expressions of racial exceptionalism regarding a perceived recession in standards for white workers. I'll revisit how white exceptionalism is related to the de-industrialization thesis later in this chapter, but for now I wish to emphasize that purported racial nostalgia in texts like *La La Land* is at the same time a form of economic periodization – that is, a diagnosis of our present economic condition as a function of 'decline' from a Fordist peak.

There is a strong argument to be made, then, that 'Sun's' anachronistic generic form *in itself* generates a nostalgia for the time of that genre's inception. At the same time, references to high Fordism inhere in the number's sheer scale and scope, which are themselves generic features of the musical. It is no small feat to shut down the intersection of two major LA highways for two days to film a scene like this, and one of the effects of this number is the awe of simply seeing it done. Michael Goddard and Benjamin Halligan read classical Hollywood cinema as conjoined with the economic imaginary of the mid-twentieth century, classifying such works – and especially musicals – as Fordist based upon the 'lavish products' that emerge at the end of a hierarchical production line. Goddard and Halligan also point out that the musical 'displaces' the hierarchies of the production process – the strict discipline and stratification of the shop floor – onto the linear-seeming formation of the chorus line or ensemble musical number (174). In this line of thinking, 'Sun's' Fordist imaginary inheres in how it characterizes the work products of the movie industry; the song sees the movies as massive technological marvels, or 'technicolor world[s] made out of music and machine'. 'Sun' pines for a version of manufacturing in which big things get made, and presents the production process as spontaneous and horizontal: the cast members hand the verses of the song off to one another and for the first part of the number the camera tracks each singer at street level before the shot widens to show the ensemble singing and dancing in unison. Occupying the narrow, linear space of the freeway, 'Sun' is a visual assembly line, the 'big product' of which is the image of horizontal, mass-manufacturing itself.[3] 'Sun', thus, allegorizes 'big manufacturing' in and through its deployment of the musical's generic tropes.

The film's self-referentiality (as a musical about the industry that makes musicals) is also a double reference to the Fordist past: via one of its dominant genres, and in reference to older, 'industrial' labour regimes and the supposedly 'good jobs' – namely, union jobs – associated with them. Yet 'Sun's' reference to industrial jobs and union jobs specifically remains ambivalent given the anachronism that the musical entails. The height of the musical's popularity coincides with peak unionization in the United States – about 27 per cent in 1953 (Flippen). While that rate now hovers around 10 per cent, long-established unions hold sway in the professional film, television and stage industries in all parts of the production process, from writing, acting and directing to all aspects of technical work. Mostly operating on a guild model, union membership in the stage and screen industry is earned through experience and is a mark of the kinds of success to which 'Sun's' singers aspire. So, the specific types of work sought by the singers resemble the 'big manufacturing' and industrial jobs that occupy the imagination of the Fordist era as they are likewise structured around the collective bargaining models associated with mid-century industrial labour; indeed, the singers' implied objective is entry into such labour collectives. But 'Sun's' location on the freeways of LA presents another conflicted reference to the Fordist-era industrial work that it might seem to covet, since Los Angeles County *currently* has the most manufacturing jobs of any metropolitan area in the United States.[4] My point is that even as this number is actually set within the highest concentration of contemporary 'industrial' labour in the United States, its formal and generic anachronism references a *prior* moment of industrial labour instead (i.e. Fordist work regimes referenced by the musical). Such nostalgia for 'big manufacturing' suggests a fixation on the recent economic past and its attendant labour and social formations – which amounts to an outsized emphasis on de-industrialization (and while one could certainly argue that the dream of success in the screen industries indicates a preference for union work in the present, I contend that the generic form of the musical renders that contemporary aspiration anachronistic).

'Sun' also looks past actual contemporary industrial work through its focus on other facets of labour: those of immaterial, affective, creative and flexible work. For where the song and film are formally Fordist, they provide a clear picture of the prominent restructuring of labour in recent decades. The setting on the freeway at what appears to be mid-day emphasizes the flexibility of the contemporary worker and the mutability of her work arrangements: everyone is quite literally in transit. A few people in the song are actively on the job (like the workers in the back of a moving truck who play instruments while the rest of the cast dances), but we imagine that everyone else is either on their way to work, looking for work, travelling between multiple jobs or engaging in gig work (how many of those cars are Ubers?). The freeway is thus the definitive site of flexible work in a car-based infrastructure like Southern California. Furthermore, the actors sing about the struggles of finding and maintaining work ('I bang on every door [. . .] Even when the answer's "no"'), and they do so through references to personal subjectivity and personality ('I did what I had to do/'Cause I just knew'). 'Sun' scrambles and conflates work and personality, job and self, paid and unpaid (the first singer wants to 'live inside each scene' that she watches at the movies).

Such is 'Sun's' recognition of the immaterial and affective forms of labour that dominate the service and creative industries – forms of work that often skirt the waged workday and shift structure of industrial capitalism and allow (or require) the worker's simultaneous flexibility and her personal, often emotional immersion in job tasks. While immaterial and affective labour are not synonymous terms and emerge from different conceptual genealogies, I talk about them together here because they are both involved in the restructuring of labour worldwide in recent decades as part of expanded service, tech, creative and communications lines of production.[5] 'Sun' is optimistic about these kinds of work and the ways in which they extract value from what Sarah Brouillette calls the 'ongoing affective social production of self-sacrificing and self-motivated workers, people who freely offer their labour because it is experienced as non-laborious pleasure or moral compulsion' (39). The moving crew in the back of the truck is an exaggerated case in point: on their way to another back-breaking work site, they're engaged in joyous self-expression, playing music on the job! Likewise, the song's emphasis on personal ambition posits each individual as an entrepreneur, each self as capital.

The overlapping references to Fordist industrial and contemporary immaterial and affective modes of labour in 'Sun' in fact reference the restructuring of labour in response to critiques of industrial work as alienating and repetitive. As scholars including Kathi Weeks and Jasper Bernes have recently documented, management discourses from the 1970s onwards appropriated the critique of work as alienating into human resources protocols that emphasize worker wellbeing and what many workplaces call 'work-life balance'. By encouraging workers to 'bring themselves' to their jobs, and in some cases to participate in management decision-making, managerial practice has orchestrated the fusion of work and subjectivity that marks immaterial and affective labour. In other words, the features of flexibility, responsibility and personal investment and empowerment are not just attached to the *kinds* of work underway, but to an enforced orientation towards our labour – and ourselves – more generally. The effect of such management discourse, as Weeks puts it, is that 'programs presented under the rubric of work enrichment are also methods of work intensification. In a kind of bad dialectic, quality becomes quantity as the call for better work is translated into a requirement for more work' (107).

The co-location of Fordist and immaterial modes in 'Sun', then, points not to a *choice* of one mode over the other (a simple casting off of the Fordist past in favour of an immaterial future, or a rejection of the latter in favour of the golden age of the former). Rather, the two modes merge in our contemporary economic imaginary in multiple ways. The song longs for 'past' forms of work and the tangibility of their products at the same time that its form seems completely comfortable with a subsumption of subjectivity by the job task. In this second feature, where the boundaries of work and non-work, subjectivity and job performance are increasingly blurred, it becomes difficult to clearly identify what exactly labour *is*, or for labour to speak for and as itself. For instance, Jasper Bernes suggests that the recent restructuring of labour 'provides fewer opportunities for [workers to] struggle *as workers*', instead offering 'the space of circulation rather than production' as the site of contestation over exploitative practices and conditions (196, original emphasis) – think a consumer boycott rather than a strike. So whether a reckoning with labour has, as Bernes claims, been pushed into the realm of circulation for people in higher-GDP countries who primarily consume the products that workers in lower-GDP locations produce,[6] or onto that of the aesthetic as workers confront the confusion generated by having to fulfil so many capacities (intellectual, affective, personal and interpersonal) at once,[7] the underlying point that emerges from the overlapping labour imaginaries of 'Sun' is that we currently face an increasing challenge in defining our own labour as such, and consequently in identifying exploitative conditions. We might speculate that such a challenge in defining work itself forms part of the appeal – along with the often-insufferable conditions of current labour – of the anachronistic imaginaries of which *La La Land* is an example. Given its generic status as musical, then, the film is disinclined to document work as such in the present; instead, the musical form casts its labour imaginary into the past, or merges work with subjectivity itself. Generic anachronism is therefore the dominant mode in which *La La Land* operates and through which the viewer is encouraged to organize all of the film's references to precarious labour. However, later in this discussion I do consider how, in light of the structural awareness of precarious labour made available in *Sorry to Bother You*, we can in fact read 'Sun' against its prominent generic grain. As I suggest at the end of this chapter, 'Sun' does overlap various forms of labour in a provocative manner that is nonetheless obscured by the film's generic tendencies.

Why 'the only thing worse than being exploited is not being exploited'

'Another Day of Sun' exposes the present confluence of economic imaginaries under which precarious labour is posited as a counterpoint to Fordist security, and yet the modes of that very same precarious labour are accepted as integral to subjectivity. In the de-industrialization thesis as it emerges in *La La Land*, we witness the conceptual limits of our periodizing concepts and of our definitions of work writ large. I wish now to address the pitfalls of such thinking and to turn to what I believe is a more productive approach to reading precarious labour today. I have already alluded to the white exceptionalism that inheres in a narrow diagnosis of current precaritization as a function of de-industrialization in high-GDP, long-industrialized locations. Yet positioning formerly industrial whites as a new precariat class quite simply ignores today's international division of labour.

There is evidence that manufacturing work has declined *globally* during the last thirty years – and not just in formerly dominant industrial countries.[8] There is much commentary on the causes and ramifications of this de-industrialization trend in global labour, and I am unable to do that conversation justice here. I will, however, emphasize two themes: the first is that given flat and declining manufacturing labour, capital increasingly requires fewer aggregate workers in manufacturing – thus busting a simple narrative that 'good' manufacturing jobs in places like the United States are simply being shifted to foreign locations (whether industry is more 'productive' due to technology, automation or other developments in production management is a matter of debate).[9] As Benjamin Kunkel puts it, 'the *systemwide* tendency, for almost four decades now, has been to add jobs more slowly than population [. . .] [such that] a proportionally shrinking body of laborers is ever more heavily exploited' (Kunkel, emphasis added).

Second, while de-industrialization is not geographically (or racially) unique, it isn't historically unique, either. De-industrialization – part of a larger process of the development and (de)skilling of certain labour techniques, and their eventual obsolescence – merely indicates, as Leigh Claire La Berge puts it, 'the devaluation of a certain place and its built environment', and has been a part of capitalist history since the inception of industrial labour (La Berge). The British textile industry of the nineteenth century is case in point, when 'labor-process innovations such as the spinning jenny, spinning mule and power loom meant that eventually this industry [. . .] began to throw off labor and capital' (Endnotes collective). For instance, Sven Beckert has shown in his global history of the cotton industry that the restructuring of the global supply and manufacturing chain for cotton in the 1860s and 1870s entailed a de-industrialization within cotton-growing countries (312–39).

Beyond acknowledging de-industrialization as a historically recurrent phenomenon, we can interrogate how many of the terms associated with precarious labour today – un- and under-employment, informal and intermittent employment – pose themselves as counterpoints to an imagined standard of wage labour associated with mid-century Fordism: that of sustained high- or full employment.[10] Michael Denning reminds us, however, that 'unemployment precedes employment, and the informal economy precedes the formal, both historically and conceptually', and the categories by which we measure our economic status are inventions of the modern state: (un)employment, formal versus informal, waged versus unwaged (81). Our reliance on such categories for thinking about labour thus restricts, in Denning's view, how we are able to understand labour in the first place, by 'constitut[ing] a normal subject: the wage earner' (85). Denning's point is crucial if we are to work around a restrictive periodizing posture like that of the de-industrialization thesis; a narrowed frame of reference for labour impedes our ability to recognize the more abiding conditions of labour under capitalism, for, as Denning puts it, 'capitalism begins not with the offer of work, but with the imperative to earn a living' (80).

Karl Marx's well-known notion of an 'industrial reserve army' – or the idea that positions outside of waged employment are indexed to capitalist accumulation –

is not unique to Marx; the structural status of those marginal to formal waged labour was recognized by many nineteenth-century political economists, who variously acknowledged that the production of the so-called 'surplus populations' of capital is not a deviation from a standard or norm, but 'a condition for the existence of the capitalist mode of production' that 'creates a mass of human material always ready for exploitation by capital in the interests of capital's own valorization requirements' (Marx, 784). Unemployment is as much a part of capitalist labour markets as employment, and the unemployed remain 'ready for exploitation' as they are dispossessed of their land and of other means of making a living outside of the markets for labour and commodity exchange.[11] This is Marx's notion of how the worker is 'free [. . .] in the double sense' (273): she is free to sell her labour as a commodity and free *from* any other wealth that she holds or could sell. Marx exposes the worker's dependency as a necessary condition of the labour market *as such*, and I'll discuss shortly how *Sorry to Bother You* brings this condition into relief. Such 'double freedom' thus cautions us against fetishizing any particular wage-earning moment or the wage itself. As Denning urges: 'We must insist that "proletarian" is not a synonym for "wage labourer" but for dispossession, expropriation and radical dependence on the market' (81). The de-industrialization thesis that we've been examining here, on the other hand, is part of the 'normalization of employment and unemployment' that 'renders much of capitalism's multitude [. . .] unrecognizable' (85).

For it is capital itself that makes all wage labour precarious, and as such it is imperative that we view labour today in a much longer-range historical arc and as a product of capital's fundamental conditions. This is a response both to well-intentioned commentators on precarious labour like Guy Standing, whose work consistently posits contemporary labour and class conditions against a mid-century 'standard' of long-term, salary- and benefits-bearing work, and to those with more nefarious racial and nationalist positions, since both positions emerge from a focus on specific arrangements of wage-earning.[12] Decentring the wage, on the other hand, allows us to escape the trap of simple comparative, reactionary analysis that generates the de-industrialization thesis and that obscures the kinds of solidarity and systemic thinking that are needed to confront our shared precarity. 'Sun' has shown us the aesthetic and generic enticements of such a shortened scope (make big things again!), even as it embraces more recent dispositions towards wage labour. In the last section of this chapter, I'll turn to how *Sorry to Bother You* deploys very different generic forms to generate an alternative thesis about precarious labour today that does not rely on such problematic anachronisms, but which instead affords a systemic view of our labouring conditions.

Sorry to Bother You, *but we're all dependent on the market*

Like 'Sun', *Sorry to Bother You* acknowledges both precarious service and manufacturing labour; Riley's film, however, posits the persistence of both and stresses their points of convergence. *Sorry* opens when Cash (Lakeith Stanfield) is hired to work at telemarketing firm Regal View, where he initially sells books over the phone (anachronistic indeed!). Yet when he begins to use his cultivated 'white voice' (more on which soon), he becomes a top seller and is promoted to 'Power Caller' status which has him selling, among other things, labour time to manufacturing firms. The manufacturing labour that Cash sells, however, is a dystopian answer to 'Sun's' nostalgic longing for the Fordist factory. Manufacturing work in the film is undertaken by the Worry Free Corporation, which offers those beleaguered and bankrupted by their insecurity in labour and property markets the option of signing *lifetime* contracts that trade fourteen hours of daily labour for housing in company dormitories, clothing in company uniforms and sustenance from company canteens. No cash wages are paid, and it is implied that workers are not free to leave the Worry Free premises; instead, workers 'wilfully' enter into indentured servitude in exchange for the basic needs of human life. On the one hand, then, *Sorry to Bother You* answers the implicitly white industrial nostalgia of a text like *La La Land* with a depiction of manufacturing labour as consistent with the 'employment through misery – [or] the willingness of paupers to do anything to survive' (Kunkel) that describes other sectors of the labour market. It also depicts Worry Free manufacturing workers as overwhelmingly white (whereas the Regal View workers are a more racially diverse crowd), as if to suggest that nostalgia for the 'wages of whiteness' can in fact lure whites into complicity with their own exploitation (a caution against the seductions of racial anachronism if ever there was one).

The film also posits a more structural and longer-range historical account of precarious labour today than that offered by the deindustrialization thesis. It begins this with an acknowledgement of total market dependency by depicting the two conditions of the worker's 'double freedom' in the extreme: Worry Free workers have 'freely' entered into binding lifetime wage contracts precisely because they have nothing else to sell to maintain their own survival. The second condition of such 'freedom' is dramatized by Cash's uncle Serge (Terry Crews), who is on the verge of home foreclosure and is considering contracting himself to Worry Free; uncle Serge's immanent foreclosure and bankruptcy would leave him literally 'free' of any other property or assets (and would leave Cash homeless, as he resides in Serge's garage). In keeping with the film's explicit recognition of the workers' condition, Worry Free CEO Steve Lift (Armie Hammer) boasts that his company's labour model is 'saving lives'. The film thus establishes total market dependency as the baseline condition for its narrative: even Cash's girlfriend Detroit (Tessa Thompson), who is a conceptual artist and anti–Worry Free activist, takes on part-time work at Regal View to make ends meet.

The film likewise acknowledges the requirement to instrumentalize the self. Following a staff meeting with Regal View management, Cash remarks to his telemarketing colleague Squeeze (Steve Yeun), that he finds it 'ridiculous that [they] have to be all excited' about their obviously awful jobs. Yet Cash soon learns to manipulate the expectation for creative affect at work when he successfully puts on 'white voice' – a nasal parody of white American intonation and idioms (voiced in the film by David Cross) – on his sales calls under the tutelage of veteran telemarketer Langston (Danny Glover). Langston instructs Cash that white voice ought to sound like you 'don't have a care in the world [...] you got your bills paid'. Langston's remark in part recognizes the uneven racial distribution of precarious circumstances; yet given that the film's central villain is the Worry Free Corporation that exploits the market-dependent and desperate, he also sagely acknowledges that escape from such dependency and precarity – actually being 'Worry Free' – is a pervasive yet unattainable fantasy. The film literalizes Cash's entrepreneurial creation of identity with 'white voice' by locating Cash in his telemarketing setup – desk, phone, headset and all – directly in the homes of the potential customers he's calling. The magical realist scenes in which Cash is heaved into the environs of his customers literalize the norms of affective performance in the workplace; and given Cash's wild success using his white voice, the film literalizes how the creative production of human affect is monetized.

It is specifically through such magical realist features, then, that *Sorry* forges its account of the conditions of labour today. For instance, the film enacts Cash's supposedly meritocratic rise to 'Power Caller' with a ride in an ornate elevator that requires a pages-long passcode to operate; his navigation of the corridors of power is an actual stagger along a hallway of multicoloured doors in the basement of Worry Free CEO Steve Lift's home; Cash's fate – and the direction of the rest of the film – is ultimately determined by the door he chooses. Critic Eileen Jones refers to the film's elevator and door scenarios as a kind of 'satire that hardly even exaggerates' (Jones); I'd suggest, moreover, that it is not primarily satire that renders the most precise access to our precarious conditions, but rather literalization that is made possible by magical realist and science fictional generic tropes. When Cash enters the 'olive door' rather than the 'jade door' to which he had been directed in Steve Lift's basement, the film swerves into science fictional territory as he encounters a group of imprisoned 'Equisapiens' – men that have been turned half horse. Cash's horror at his science fictional discovery is met, however, with another of the film's characteristically absurd moments: Steve Lift coolly explains that the Equisapiens are part of an industrial engineering project to make workers stronger and thus more productive, and shows Cash a charming Claymation video explaining the project's aims. By pairing this outlandish, science fictional plot turn with Lift's casual managerial explanation, the film underscores its depiction of the literal ways in which human bodies and capacities are grossly manipulated for the labour markets, and how this is routinely rationalized and normalized by managerial discourse (indeed, no one really seems to care when Cash exposes the Equisapien project to the public, suggesting that such excessive forms of exploitation are largely considered acceptable). Again, where Eileen Jones claims that such science fictional elements are an 'attempt to suggest the kind of crude madness we live in every day' (Jones), a reading of *Sorry*'s generic effects insists that these are more than oblique 'suggestions' – they are, rather, realistic depictions. The Equisapiens' transformation is distinct from Cash's 'white voice' only in degree, but not in kind.

Parallel to Cash's adventures in the power calling suite and in Steve Lift's power basement, his colleagues on the entry-level floor at Regal View telemarketing have organized a union and walked out on strike. The film's depiction of the strike likewise relies upon exaggerated generic tropes – namely, absurdist literalism – and I'd argue that it is the depiction of the strike itself that focalizes and ultimately organizes (pun intended) the realist function and structural labour imaginary of the film as a whole. Sustained attention to labour organizing and to strikes in particular is rare in US films, with major films like *Norma Rae* (1979), *Matewan* (1987) and *Silkwood* (1983) being notable exceptions. *Sorry*'s kitschy, low-budget depiction of the Regal View telemarketer's strike is notable both because it shows a strike in the first place and precisely in its departure from the dramatic motifs – and largely white casting – of other labour films. Again, it is the generic mode of the strike's depiction that is significant here: it allows the film to comment upon structural conditions of labour specifically *because* its absurdist, surrealist mode demands a departure from individual characterization, a focus which renders labour strife as a personal, exceptional matter rather than a shared condition.

The strike registers as absurd in part because it is filmed on a small, cramped set. A few dozen strikers in matching t-shirts crowd around the front entrance to the Regal View facility; the shot remains tight, and it seems that a wider view of the street or other adjacent locations is beyond this production's means. As Cash enters the building with the Power Callers (in a direct commentary on the ways in which capitalism promises meritocratic rise to obscure workers' common interests, it seems that these elite employees are not themselves on strike), he is struck on the head by a cola can thrown by a picketer who shouts, 'Smile, Bitch!' This incident is caught on film and goes viral, with children constructing Halloween costumes depicting Cash's injury and the cola company hiring the picketer to star in their commercials; Cash also wears a bloody bandage on his head for most of the remainder of the film. *Sorry* thus deploys its absurdist humour onto the matter of the strike itself, diffusing more predictable tropes of individual suffering and conflict with what I'd call here a collectivist depiction. That is, by magnifying Cash's pain during the strike to comic effect, the film comments upon and defuses tropes of individual suffering; the workers who strive to emulate management (like, for a time, Cash) are humiliated rather than brought into psychological focus. The picketers' chant is profane, but efficient: 'Fuck You, Regal View!' articulates nothing besides the workers' anger towards their employer, thus focusing the film's depiction on exploitation itself. Furthermore, the absurd repetition of the picket line scenes (the picketers strategize to keep the scabs out; riot police brutally retaliate) is dramatized through the appearance of the Oakland High football team, who support the picketers with football plays. Again, the picket line is a depiction not of a teleological striving towards better conditions, but of the mundane routines of exploitative labour and management-state brutality.

The breaking point of the strike comes when the Equisapiens are drafted to the picketers' cause and use their engineered strength to overpower the police. Lead organizer Squeeze thanks them, emphasizing their shared conditions under Regal View and Worry Free: 'Same struggle, same fight'. Again, it is in this science fictional interlude that *Sorry* is able to literalize not only its depiction of labour conditions (here, as workers' bodies are subject to state violence when they don't comply with the labour markets), but also, as the solidarity between telemarketers and Equisapiens indicates, the film's structural labour imaginary which is rooted in the shared market dependency of both groups of (and, hence, all) workers – here, low-waged service workers and the Equisapiens, who Steve Lift calls the 'future of [manufacturing] labour'.

The film's vision of market dependency is thus literalized through its generic forms and indeed through its narrative, as the end of the film sees Cash and his crew return to wage labour at Regal View, albeit under improved conditions given the success of their unionization campaign. As a result, *Sorry* generates a structural account of the conditions that subtend all work under capitalism and stands as a corrective to the anachronistic hair-splitting and problematic hard periodization of a text like *La La Land*. Indeed, while 'Another Day of Sun' relies upon Fordist nostalgia and the de-industrialization thesis upon which it rests, *Sorry* in fact inspires a rereading of that song for the actual labour conditions that it exposes, rather than the ones that it contrives. Beyond 'Sun's' fetishization of a 'better' time for labour, we can also read this song another way: in depicting both contemporary forms of labour – immaterial, affective, creative, flexible, insecure – and an older 'industrial' imaginary, 'Sun' might allow us to realize both types of work *as work*, and as deriving from the same underlying conditions. That is, 'Sun' effectively positions the labour referenced in its formal and generic anachronism (industrial work under mid-century Fordism) and that which is implied by its thematic content (contemporary immaterial and flexible labour) as parts of the same whole. And in fact, it is the song's very formal gestures (which are creative and immaterial outputs) that are themselves the 'content' of the labour that is realigned historically with industrial production. In other words, if the 'output' that generates the industrial throwback (the big musical number) is itself a 'product' of creative and thus immaterial labour, then can industrial and immaterial work be so easily distinguished at all? Might the film recognize 'immaterial/affective/creative' and 'industrial' labour as products of one and the same forms of accumulation, since both render workers dependent on the market for survival – much like *Sorry*'s Regal View telemarketers and the Worry Free assembly line workers?

'Another Day of Sun' reminds us of the tendency to read our present against an arbitrary standard of mid-century 'security' – a tendency that is enacted time and again in both popular works and more specialized, scholarly analyses – when in fact labour under capital is always precarious. Especially when reading 'Sun' alongside *Sorry*, we are reminded of how we often validate certain features of precarious labour: insecurity as dynamism and flexibility; individual responsibilization as empowerment; subsumption as commitment and creative license. We thus see two ways in which our thinking about precarious labour today is determined by the immediate Fordist past: either as an escape from its alienating structures and protocols or as a loss of its security and the grandeur of its outputs. Both senses constrain our labour imaginaries to an enforced relationship to an arbitrary point in the past, and are promoted in this case by the seeming optimism of 'Sun's' musical form. Yet either of these two narratives of contemporary labour obscure the fundamental conditions of precarity that are consistent across capitalism's history. It might at first seem unlikely that an acknowledgement of such historical and structural conditions is made possible by the fantastic forms that we encounter in *Sorry to Bother You*. Yet in conclusion I contend that it is precisely the film's outlandish, imaginative forms that permit its departure from the conventional accounts of our economic situation – accounts that, given the increasingly desperate straits of workers worldwide, clearly no longer serve us.

Notes

1. *La La Land* was nominated for Best Picture, which it was briefly and erroneously 'awarded' due to a presenter's mistake at the ceremony. The 2016 Academy Award for Best Picture eventually and actually went to the film *Moonlight* (dir. Barry Jenkins); for those familiar with this award controversy, the relevance of its racial valences to the present discussion ought to be clear.
2. Here I am using the term 'Fordism' as a shorthand to designate the structuring of labour and markets in (mostly) high-GDP countries between the end of the Second World War and the end of the Bretton Woods gold standard in 1973. This period is generally marked by steady economic growth and output, relatively stable labour relations, state technocratic intervention in the economy and robust social welfare safety nets in most high-GDP countries. Analysts have pointed out that the conditions of Fordism are a result of very specific state and geopolitical interventions, including the deliberate stabilizing effects of the Bretton Woods international monetary system, rather than a naturally occurring high water mark of capitalist history (see, for instance, the Endnotes collective's 'Misery and Debt').
3. In a compelling reading of Fordist nostalgia, Matthias Nilges points out that while many post-Fordist imaginaries would seem egalitarian and populist on their surface, 'resistance to post-Fordism is indeed capable of producing desiring structures that paradoxically lead subjects to willingly subject themselves to Fordist exploitation, seeking enjoyment in the restoration of a paternalistic leader' (52). Nilges claims that such paternalistic desires are a function of longing for the *actually hierarchical* organization of manufacturing labour.
4. According to the Bureau of Labor Statistics, Los Angeles County is the most populous county in the United States, and houses the most manufacturing jobs by far, with 340,515 as of September 2018. Cook County, Illinois, comes in second with 185,352.
5. Immaterial labour is a concept developed in recent decades by neo-Marxists to identify the capacities required, and subjectivities entailed, by commodified service, caring, knowledge and communications-based work. 'Affective labour' is often categorized as a type of immaterial labour, yet the former term emerges from feminist thought from roughly the 1970s onwards that resists the marginalization of women's work as unproductive. Affective labour is typically classed as kinds of service work that involve personal interaction – traditionally in-person, but I'd point out, perhaps increasingly remote – and, as Michael Hardt puts it, involve the 'creation and manipulation of affects' (96).
6. Bernes writes: 'When it comes to cultural artifacts, approaches from the side of consumption or the marketplace also foreground the reader, critic, or interpreter who encounters the cultural object as already complete, already constituted by mute,

invisible labors that can be disclosed only through a post hoc hermeneutic. With the migration of manufacturing from industrializing or recently industrialized countries, this is a stance more and more residents in deindustrialized counties must take to the commodities they consume, produced as they are through globally distributed processes that remain necessarily opaque' (32).

7   I refer here to Sianne Ngai's notion of the 'zany', which she claims is an aesthetic response to the 'ever more elastic relations to work and personality'. Ngai's category captures the predicament of the contemporary subject of immaterial and affective labor 'who is nothing but a series of adjustments and adaptations to one situation after another' (174).

8   While the share of manufacturing jobs in total employment shows a sharp decline in high-GDP economies, it has also been relatively flat in most lower-GDP economies (Gruss et al.).

9   For a global picture of manufacturing productivity, see Gruss et al. See also Desilver.

10 For a critical assessment of the notion of 'full employment' from the mid-century to the present, see Kunkel.

11 For an analysis of how surplus laboring populations have arisen since the Second World War, see Benanav.

12 This is not, of course, to conflate Standing's description of the contemporary precariat with the positions of white exceptionalists. Standing's well-known thesis on the precariat does rely, however, on a comparison with the Fordist moment that preceded our own.

Works cited

Altman, Rick. 'The American Musical: Paradigmatic Structure and Mediatory Function'. *Genre: The Musical*, edited by Rick Altman. Routledge, 1981, pp. 197–207.

Beckert, Sven. *Empire of Cotton: A Global History*. Alfred A. Knopf, 2015.

Benanav, Aaron. *A Global History of Unemployment: Surplus Populations in the World Economy, 1949–2010*. UCLA Doctoral Dissertation, 2014, https://escholarship.org/uc/item/7r14v2bq.

Bernes, Jasper. *The Work of Art in the Age of Deindustrialization*. Stanford University Press, 2017.

Brody, Richard. 'The Empty Exertions of *La La Land*'. *The New Yorker*, 8 December 2016, https://www.newyorker.com/culture/richard-brody/the-empty-exertions-of-la-la-land.

Brouillette, Sarah. *Literature and the Creative Economy*. Stanford University Press, 2014.

Denning, Michael. 'Wageless Life'. *New Left Review*, vol. 66, November/December 2010, pp. 70–97.

Desilver, Drew. 'Most Americans Unaware that as U.S. Manufacturing Jobs Have Disappeared, Output Has Grown'. *Pew Research Center*, 25 July 2017. http://www.pewresearch.org/fact-tank/2017/07/25/most-americans-unaware-that-as-u-s-manufacturing-jobs-have-disappeared-output-has-grown/.

Dyer, Richard. 'Entertainment and Utopia'. Altman, ed. pp. 175–89.

Endnotes Collective. 'Misery and Debt: On the Logic and History of Surplus Populations and Surplus Capital'. *Endnotes*, vol. 2, April 2010, https://endnotes.org.uk/issues/2/en/endnotes-misery-and-debt.

Feuer, Jane. *The Hollywood Musical*. Indiana UP, 1982.

Flippen, Alan. 'When Union Membership Was Rising'. *The New York Times*, 29 May 2014, https://www.nytimes.com/2014/05/30/upshot/union-membership-has-declined-since-the-1970s.html.
Goddard, Michael and Benjamin Halligan. 'Cinema, the Post-Fordist Worker, and Immaterial Labour: From Post-Hollywood to the European Art Film'. *Framework: The Journal of Cinema and Media*, vol. 53, no. 1, Spring 2012, pp. 172–89.
Gruss, Bertrand et al. 'Manufacturing Jobs: Implications for Productivity and Inequality'. The International Monetary Fund / The Brookings Institution, 2018, https://www.brookings.edu/wp-content/uploads/2018/04/weo_apr2018_ch31.pdf.
Hardt, Michael. 'Affective Labor'. *boundary 2*, vol. 26, no. 2, 1999, pp. 89–100.
Jones, Eileen. '"Crazy" Anticapitalism'. *Jacobin*, 21 July 2018, https://www.jacobinmag.com/2018/07/sorry-to-bother-you-boots-riley-review.
Kunkel, Benjamin. 'Full Employment'. *n+1*, vol. 9, Spring 2010, https://nplusonemag.com/issue-9/politics/full-employment/.
La Berge, Leigh Claire. 'Decommodified Labor: Conceptualizing Work After the Wage'. *Lateral*, vol. 7, no. 1, Spring 2018, http://csalateral.org/issue/7-1/decommodified-labor-work-after-wage-la-berge/
La La Land. Directed by Damien Chazelle. Lionsgate Films, 2016.
Marx, Karl. *Capital*, Vol. 1 (1867). Translated by Ben Fowkes. Penguin Classics, 1990.
Nelson, Geoff. 'The Unbearable Whiteness of *La La Land*'. *Paste Magazine*, 6 January 2017, https://www.pastemagazine.com/articles/2017/01/the-unbearable-whiteness-of-la-la-land.html.
Ngai, Sianne. *Our Aesthetic Categories: Zany, Cute, Interesting*. Harvard University Press, 2012.
Nilges, Matthias. 'The Anti-Anti-Oedipus: Representing Post-Fordist Subjectivity'. *Mediations*, vol. 23, no. 2, Spring 2008, p. 27–69.
Scott, A. O. '"Sorry to Bother You," but Can I Interest You in a Wildly Dystopian Satire?' *The New York Times*, 2 July 2018, https://www.nytimes.com/2018/07/02/movies/sorry-to-bother-you-review-lakeith-stanfield.html.
Singh, Nikhil Pal and Thuy Linh Tu, 'Morbid Capitalism'. *n+1*, vol. 30, Winter 2018, pp. 101–16.
Sorry to Bother You. Directed by Boots Riley. Annapurna Pictures, 2018.
Standing, Guy. *The Precariat: The New Dangerous Class*. Bloomsbury, 2011.
United States Department of Labor Bureau of Labor Statistics. *Quarterly Report of Employment and Wages*, March 2019.
Weeks, Kathi. *The Problem with Work: Feminism, Marxism, Antiwork Politics and Postwork Imaginaries*. Duke University Press, 2011.

Chapter 8

SUBSTANCELESS SUBJECTIVITY

FROM PROLETARIANIZATION TO PRECARIZATION IN BRITISH EXPERIMENTAL FICTION

Benjamin Kohlmann

Recent explorations of precarity, in political theory as much as in literary and cultural studies, have tended to fold the question of precarity into the larger question of ontological precariousness. Judith Butler's work on the vulnerability of human life offers an exemplary exposition of this approach. Drawing in part on work by Giorgio Agamben (on bare life) and Michel Foucault (on the governability of human bodies) as well as on her own studies about the grievability of human life, Butler reminds us that experiences of economic precarity result from a particular social distribution of ontological precariousness as 'certain populations suffer from failing social and economic networks of support, and become differentially exposed to injury, violence, and death' (Butler *Frames of War*, 25–6). As such, precarity denotes the 'dimension of politics that addresses the organization and protection of bodily needs. Precarity exposes our sociality, the fragile and necessary dimensions of our interdependency' (Puar 170). Numerous scholars have built on Butler's reconceptualization of precarity. For example, Isabell Lorey notes that the socio-economic condition of precarity can be understood as the local intensification of positions of ontological precariousness. According to Lorey, precarity is produced when

> [t]he precariousness shared with others is hierarchized and judged, and precarious lives are segmented. This segmentation produces, at the same moment, the differential distribution of symbolic and material insecurities, in other words precarity. Precarity as the hierarchized difference in insecurity arises from the segmentation, the categorization, of shared precariousness. (21)

This reframing of precarity in terms of the unequal social allocation of precariousness builds centrally on neo-phenomenological work by thinkers such as Emmanuel Lévinas and Jean-Luc Nancy who have identified the condition of 'being-with' – that is, the necessary coexistence of human beings and the existential situation of openness, insecurity and vulnerability that results from it – as the most fundamental condition of human life.

In what follows, I do not seek to shed new light on the philosophical genealogy behind these arguments, or to explore the specific socio-economic conjuncture that has made the recent redescription of socio-economic precarity in terms of ontological precariousness possible. Instead, I consider the politico-artistic implications of this reconceptualization by sketching out an artistic tradition that is centrally concerned with foregrounding collective experiences of economic deprivation and dispossession. The tradition of literary production which I identify here could be called proletarian modernism – a mode of formally experimental and politically committed writing that extends from the politicized modernism of the later interwar years to the present. As I will suggest, the 'proletarian modernism' label can help us identify modes of writing that foreground processes of socio-economic exploitation and political disenfranchisement whose systematicity is well captured by the term 'proletarianization'. However, instead of returning us to the basic ontological condition of bare life, proletarian modernism focuses on processes of proletarianization in order to probe the possibility of a more fully collectivist politics.

The phrase 'substanceless subjectivity' in the title of my chapter is intended to index the constitutive tensions which accompany this project – tensions which increased as the field available for collective agency became increasingly fragmented in the wake of neoliberalization from the 1980s onwards. The idea of 'substanceless subjectivity' is introduced here as an exploratory heuristic, and I will use it as an entry point into the debates I associate with the tradition of 'proletarian modernism'. The phrase 'substanceless subjectivity' receives an extended gloss in Slavoj Žižek's book *Tarrying with the Negative* (1993), where it is attributed to Karl Marx. Commenting on Marx's *Grundrisse* (1857–8), Žižek elaborates:

> After deploying his grandiose conception of the proletariat as apogee as the historical process of 'alienation', of the gradual disengaging of the labor force from the domination of the 'organic', substantial process of production (the double freedom of the proletarian: he stands for the abstract subjectivity freed from all substantial organic ties, yet at the same time he is dispossessed and thus obliged to sell on the market his own labor force in order to survive, Marx conceives of the proletarian revolution as a 'materialist' version of the Hegelian reconciliation of subject and substance: it reestablishes the unity of the subject (labor force) with the objective conditions of the process of production, yet not under these objective conditions [. . .] but with collective subjectivity as the mediating force of this unity. (26)[1]

According to Žižek's account, Marx paradoxically presents the substancelessness of proletarian identity – its deracination from the 'substantial organic ties' of an older working-class sociability, and its reduction to mere labour power – as the very precondition of collective revolutionary agency: the very (cultural, social) substancelessness of the proletariat means that it can become a fully universal figure for the struggle against capitalist exploitation.

While Žižek's description of the 'substanceless' proletariat successfully captures the gist of Marx's discussion of revolutionary agency in *Grundrisse*, I have not been able to find the precise passage alluded to by Žižek in Marx's text. Instead, a combination of the terms referenced by Žižek appears in a chapter entitled 'Chapter on Capital', which focuses on the tightly integrated cycles of capitalist exploitation rather than on the possibility of future revolutionary agency. Here, in a subsection on 'Die Reproduktion und Akkumulation des Kapitals', Marx writes:

> Vom Standpunkt der Arbeit aus betrachtet erscheint [die lebendige Arbeit] als so in dem Productionsprozeß thätig, daß sie ihre Verwirklichung in objektiven Bedingungen zugleich als fremde Realität von sich abstößt und daher sich selbst als substanzloses, bloß bedürftiges Arbeitsvermögen gegenüber dieser ihr entfremdeten, nicht ihr, sondern andern gehörigen Realität setzt. (*Ökonomische Manuskripte* 363)

> Living labour therefore now appears from its own standpoint as acting within the production process in such a way that, as it realizes itself in the objective conditions, it simultaneously repulses this realization from itself as an alien reality, and hence posits itself as insubstantial [*substanzlos*], as mere penurious labour capacity in face of this reality alienated from it [...] ; that it posits its own reality not as a being for others, and hence also as mere other-being, or being of another opposite itself. (*Grundrisse* 454)

A few pages on, Marx elaborates:

> Daß [der Kapitalist] bereits als Kapital der lebendigen Arbeit gegenüberstand, erscheint als einzige Bedingung dafür, daß er sich nicht nur als Kapital erhält, sondern als wachsendes Kapital wachsend fremde Arbeit ohne Äquivalent *aneignet* oder seine Macht, seine Existenz als Kapital gegenüber dem lebendigen Arbeitsvermögen ausweitet und anderseits das lebendige Arbeitsvermögen in seiner subjektiven, substanzlosen Dürftigkeit als lebendiges Arbeitsvermögen stets von neuem setzt. (*Ökonomische Manuskripte* 366)

> The fact that [the capitalist] has previously confronted living labour as capital appears as the only condition required in order that he may not only maintain himself as capital, but also, as a growing capital, increasingly appropriate alien labour without equivalent; or, that he may extend his power, his existence as capital opposite living labour capacity, and on the other side constantly posit living labour capacity anew in its subjective, insubstantial penury [*substanzlosen Dürftigkeit*] as living labour capacity. (*Grundrisse* 457)

The difference between Žižek's account of proletarian substancelessness as the precondition of revolutionary agency and the content of these passages from *Grundrisse* is striking. Whereas Žižek invokes the phrase 'substanceless subjectivity' in order to describe the *structural position* of the proletariat in the labour process (i.e. the structural precondition of its emergence as a collective force), Marx's passages from the 'Chapter on Capital' aim at something that more properly resembles a *phenomenology* of proletarian existence. By emphasizing the 'subjektive, substanzlose Dürftigkeit' experienced by workers, Marx gives us an inside view of the process of capitalist exploitation by which living labour is incessantly expropriated and transformed into something alien to the worker himself or herself. This process, Marx points out, is most immediately experienced by the worker as a state of unmitigated deprivation or material-affective deficiency (*Dürftigkeit*), rather than as an opportunity for future collective action.[2]

In what follows, I am not interested in reclaiming a doctrinally pure, or allegedly orthodox, use of the phrase 'substanceless subjectivity'. Instead, I want to suggest that it is precisely the multivalence of the phrase – as a category of structural analysis *and* as a register of phenomenological experience; as a category of revolutionary action *and* as a mode of existence irreparably integrated into the cycles of capitalist exploitation – that can be useful for an exploration of the proletarian modernist tradition. As I want to suggest, proletarian modernists share an interest in the category of the proletariat as a figure of revolutionary action, yet while some texts foreground the possibility of a fully collectivist politics by emphasizing the proletariat's privileged position as a revolutionary class, others – especially texts written in the wake of neoliberalization from the 1980s onwards – focus on experiences of economic exploitation and political disenfranchisement that undermine visions of revolutionary agency. Building on some further exploratory remarks on proletarian modernism in the next section, this chapter will then turn to two texts associated with the proletarian modernist tradition in order to explore these developments: John Sommerfield's *May Day* (1936), a novel that closes with a vision of the proletarian revolution in Britain, and *GB84* (2004), David Peace's fictional engagement with the 1984 miners' strike and the human toll of deindustrialization in Thatcherite Britain. The two novels encapsulate the ambivalence of the term 'substanceless subjectivity': while *May Day* mobilizes the proletariat's substancelessness (i.e. its functional centrality in the capitalist economy) in the name of a revolutionary politics, Peace's novel presents us with seemingly irredeemable experiences of exploitation and disenfranchisement, a non-revolutionary vision of 'mere' substancelessness that looks back with considerable nostalgia to earlier moments of collective proletarian agency. I conclude by suggesting that *GB84*'s vision of the profound crisis of proletarian agency in the wake of Thatcherite neoliberalization looks ahead to the newer social formation that has been labelled 'the precariat'.

Proletarian modernism and fictions of proletarianization

Unlike high modernism, which is conventionally associated with the moment of intensely experimental artistic production in the 1910s and 1920s, we can think of proletarian modernism as a product of the radical culture of the long 1930s. The label of the 'long 1930s' is intended to signal an experiment in reperiodization: by reframing the 1930s as an elongated literary-historical unit, we can begin to identify questions that were raised with particular urgency during this decade, including the possibility of collective action and of a genuinely radical politics, while also tracing their resonances well beyond the period's conventional temporal boundaries. The task, then, is not simply to make the 1930s longer but to use the decade as a reference point for a partial remapping of twentieth- and twenty-first-century literary and artistic production. Recent artworks that can be associated with the tradition of proletarian modernism explore the historical aftermath of the large-scale eclipse of collectivist projects from the 1980s onwards, and they sometimes experiment with reactivating seemingly defunct political signifiers (including the signifier of the 'proletariat') in order to mobilize energies for collective action.[3] To claim that the tradition of proletarian modernism extends into our own present, then, is not to assert the unbroken continuity of a mode of communist politics. Instead, this operation draws attention to the fact that the processes of exploitation and 'proletarianization' which proletarian modernism describes with such poignancy and precision have become more rather than less widespread since the 1930s. As Jodi Dean has recently observed,

> we need to detach 'proletarian' from the factory, so that we can understand *proletarianization* as a process that deprives humans of their 'substance' and reduces them to providers of labour. [. . .] Neoliberalism (with its declining investment in production and diversion of capital into finance) amplifies [this] process. [P]roletarianization operates through precarization: it is capitalism's production and consumption of the workers it needs. (107–8; orig. emphasis)

When proletarian modernism is described in this way, it becomes clear that there has been a certain revival of the proletarian modernist tradition in recent literature and art. This body of work, which is both politically engaged and aesthetically experimental, includes texts and artworks as diverse as John Berger's *King: A Street Story* (1999), Bruce Gilden's photographs of foreclosed homes in Detroit (2008–11), Zadie Smith's *NW* (2012), Jim Crace's *Harvest* (2013) and Ali Smith's *Autumn* (2016), as well as Michael Glawogger's brilliant and shocking films about exploitative labour in developing countries from the early 2000s.

There has been no shortage of accounts of the long life of modernism, many of which have been formulated under the aegis of the so-called New Modernist Studies.[4] These accounts have been concerned with the consolidation and transformation of a set of experimental modes of writing across the twentieth century, but they have generally failed to comment on the progressive collectivist projects to which these experimental styles were put. By contrast, the political legacy of the formally experimental writing of the interwar years is foregrounded in a set of essays by Raymond Williams, which include his influential 1987 lecture 'When Was Modernism?'. In these texts, Williams discusses the ways in which the aesthetic logic of modernism, with its insistent emphasis on formal innovation and newness, prefigured the post-1945 capitalist settlement, the institutional consolidation of capitalist markets with their own unrelenting imperative to 'make things new'. Williams identifies what he calls 'the two faces of "Modernism"', that is,

> those innovative forms which destabilized the fixed forms of an earlier period of bourgeois society, but which were then in their turn stabilized as the most reductive versions of human existence in the whole of cultural history. The originally precarious and often desperate images – typically of fragmentation, loss of identity, loss of the very grounds of human communication – have been transferred from the dynamic compositions of artists who had been, in majority, literally exiles, having little or no common ground with the societies in which they were stranded, to become, at an effective surface, a 'modernist' and 'post-modernist' establishment. This, near the centres of corporate power, takes human inadequacy, [. . .] the confusion and substitution of individuals in temporary relationships, as self-evident routine data. ('Culture and Technology' 130)

What Williams describes here is the co-optation of modernism into the capitalist status quo, a process whereby the politically radical charge of modernist formal experimentation – its keen rendering of 'precarious images' as well as its ability to talk about social 'fragmentation' and 'loss of identity' – has become nearly invisible. Williams's 1987 lecture challenges this muting of modernism's radical charge by attempting to disaggregate modernism from capitalism:

> The innovations of what is called Modernism have become the fixed forms of our present moment. If we are to break out of the non-historical fixity of post-modernism, we must search out and counterpose an alternative tradition taken from the neglected works left in the wide margin of the century. ('When Was Modernism?' 135)

On Williams's account, the political valences of modernism – the political *content* of modernism's experimental *forms* – have ceased to be intelligible to us. To counter this historical drift, Williams recommends a form of recuperative retrospection, a rescue operation of sorts that would seek to identify a vital but neglected 'alternative tradition' of modernist writing that is no longer visible from our own historical vantage point. According to Williams, such a rereading would address itself 'not to an inhuman rewriting of the past [i.e. to the reduction of modernism to a set of purely formal protocols] but, for all our sakes, to a *future* in which community may be imagined again' (ibid; orig. emphasis).

Williams himself does not specify what such an alternative modernist tradition would look like, or which texts it might comprise. In what follows, I will turn to two strike novels which can help us flesh out Williams's suggestive claims: I will first discuss Sommerfield's *May Day*, a text which offers a complex engagement with Virginia Woolf's high modernist novels of the 1920s, before turning to Peace's novel *GB84*. These texts attempt to imagine social interdependence not primarily under the sign of ontological precariousness or in terms of the weak ties of cohabitation, but as the possible precondition of a more fully collectivist politics.[5] As such, Sommerfield's and Peace's novels are representative of an alternative tradition of proletarian modernism that has been left abandoned 'in the wide margin of the century'. Before I turn to these two works, it is worth noting, if only briefly and in passing, that proletarian modernism lost its critical visibility in large part due to the processes of deindustrialization that culminated in the 1980s and that are described in Peace's novel, that is, at the very moment when Williams diagnosed the eclipse of modernism's radical, political élan. Indeed, Peace's novel can be read as self-reflectively registering the crisis and imminent demise of the radical political energies of the proletarian modernist tradition, offering a sobering view of economic devolution and collapse rather than envisioning the possibility of future collective action.

'The spiderwebs of capitalism': Proletarian modernism in John Sommerfield's May Day

Sommerfield's novel *May Day* describes three days in the lives of several dozen characters, culminating in a general strike and the beginning of the proletarian revolution on May Day itself. The novel uses a peripatetic narrative in the manner of Virginia Woolf's *Mrs Dalloway* to describe continuities and divisions between the wealthiest and poorest citizens of London, ranging from industrialists and the city's *jeunesse dorée* to an unemployed seaman who ends up getting involved in the general strike. Sommerfield's novel shows that despite class differences the characters are connected in manifold ways: through shared thoughts, through linked perceptions of the world around them and through what the novel calls the 'invisible spiderwebs' (Sommerfield 160) of capitalist social relations.

May Day's debt to *Mrs Dalloway* includes Sommerfield's interweaving of multiple voices as well as the deployment of narrative devices which engineer changes in perspective, similar to *Mrs Dalloway*'s skywriting aeroplane. As a communist, Sommerfield repurposes these narrative effects to create the impression of an emerging social collectivity, of a democratically organized present in which (to quote Williams) 'community may be imagined again'. However, Sommerfield also registers the constraints which this aesthetic mode imposes on the novel's communist vision. At various points, *May Day* shifts into a Woolfian idiom which presents the constitution of social collectives as the result of a communally experienced 'rhythm' or 'energy'. As *May Day* approaches its climax, Sommerfield writes:

> At thousands of street corners little groups clustered, they were held together by a strong and indescribable force. They would meet tomorrow, on the job, in the factory, at the garage [. . .] but now they hated to part. Their minds had been relaxed, they had been able to feel free human beings. (184)

It is easy to see the appeal which Woolf's style held for Sommerfield. It allowed him to present the experience of collectivity as a vital connection, as a type of electric current that is quickly transmitted beyond the site of its generation and that helps to galvanize collective action. However, from the perspective of a committed communist like Sommerfield, this view of collective agency is also problematic because it presents the experience of collectivity as a somatic connection: the revolutionary current is generated spontaneously by the motion of bodies in public spaces; it is not the result of conscious collective action on the part of a mature proletariat. Sommerfield clearly struggled to harness the Woolfian vision of an embryonic social collectivity to what he found to be the very different ideological demands of communist doctrine. As the novel builds towards its climax, the proletarian revolution in Britain, Sommerfield's narrator surveys the buzz of London life: 'Only the mathematics of class struggle can make order and design out of this seething chaos of matter in motion. [...] Today things are artificially simplified. There is a line, on one side are the proletariat, organized into a militant class by life itself, on the other are the forces of the [capitalist] State' (203). However, in *May Day* the clear-cut quality of such line drawing and side-taking is complemented by the articulation of collective experiences that are grounded not in the mathematics of class struggle but in 'embodied experiences, sensations, and emotions' (Purdon n.p.).

Sommerfield had another purpose in adopting Woolf's novelistic mode, namely to map the decentred interconnectedness of social relations under capitalism. In *May Day*, radio tunes are overheard, and newspaper items are read, simultaneously by a multitude of different characters, thus creating connections between individuals belonging to separate social classes (employers, workers and aristocrats). For example, the private feelings of discontent experienced by the factory worker Ivy Cutford, as she listens to a song on the radio, are shown to have their roots in the miserable working conditions of the factory where the same song is playing to Ivy's co-workers, even though they are too exhausted to pay attention to the tune. Similarly, through another series of linked scenes, Sommerfield hints that the casual indifference with which Ivy's employer sexually exploits the girls working in his factory mirrors the wage slavery on which the factory as a whole operates. To give these analogies additional political edge, Sommerfield interlaces his narrative with references to the larger economic context. For example, there is the case of the young and precariously employed Mabel who goes to work in Ivy's factory. While she is chatting with her friends about going to the pictures, Mabel pays little attention to her work: she slips on the floor, and when her hair gets caught on the conveyor belt, she is dragged downwards and ends up scalped. As another character explains, Mabel's death is not simply the result of her lack of attention; instead, responsibility for her death needs to be placed squarely at the feet of the capitalists whose only aim is the generation of surplus value at the expense of the safety of the workers: 'You know what really causes accidents is speed-up and cramped working conditions. If factory girls were put on a wage basis that didn't drive them to death there'd soon be an end to all the bloody accidents' (164).

Sarah Cole has recently reminded us that modernist texts, including the novels of Virginia Woolf, are particularly skilful at depicting states of physical vulnerability and human interdependency, what Raymond Williams calls modernism's 'precarious and often desperate images [. . .] of fragmentation and loss of identity'.⁶ Proletarian modernists such as Sommerfield transform this modernist concern with the universal anthropological condition of precariousness into an exploration of structures of socio-economic dependency, of economic precarity. If the use of free indirect discourse had allowed Virginia Woolf to explore networks of human interdependency, Sommerfield retools Woolf's modernist techniques in order to explore the systemic factors that drive socio-economic proletarianization. To put this another way: in Sommerfield's proletarian modernist novel, subjectivity appears substanceless to the degree that the representation of socio-economic relations takes precedence over a Woolfian interest in the rendering of psychological interiority; and this substancelessness in turn makes it possible for the radical current to be transmitted without any significant resistance from one proletarianized subject position to the next.

Yet while Woolf's literary idiom enabled Sommerfield to experiment with the novelistic mapping of capitalist relations and to imagine the emergence of new social collectives, *May Day* ultimately resists identifying the Woolfian aesthetic on which it models itself with the political vision of a genuinely classless society. Sommerfield achieves this through a formal manoeuvre that appears striking in the context of the novel's modernist allegiances. While *May Day* borrows a number of formal features from *Mrs Dalloway*, the novel does not generally adopt Woolf's technique of free indirect discourse but rather resorts to an omniscient narrator who is located outside the novel's story-world. It would be wrong to see Sommerfield's use of this narrator-function as the sign of a flawed, or 'bad', modernism (Mao and Walkowitz *Bad Modernisms*). Instead, Sommerfield's stylistic choice should be understood as a generative critique of modernism, as an attempt to reinscribe modernism itself as part of a longer and more capacious tradition of realist writing. Forcing us into a position outside the seemingly de-hierarchized aesthetic field projected by Woolf's modernist art, Sommerfield suggests that this critical distancing of Woolf's aesthetic of ontological precariousness is necessary so that a proletarian appropriation of it becomes possible and so that Sommerfield's Marxist analysis of socio-economic relations can be anchored in an authoritative narrative voice. Similar observations could be made about other works of the long 1930s that try to articulate the emergence of a collectivist politics by retooling modernist forms: this canon of proletarian modernist works includes books such as James Hanley's polyphonic family saga *The Furys* (1935) and Jack Lindsay's modernist historical novel *1649: A Novel of a Year* (1938). These works and the alternative canon of proletarian texts which they exemplify have suffered critical neglect because their conjunction of formal experimentation and political purpose resists aesthetic valorization along more canonically modernist lines.

Proletarian modernism and the making of the precariat in David Peace's GB84

Sommerfield's Popular Front novel was republished for the first time in the summer of 1984, at the height of the British miners' strike. In a new postscript, written in

1984, Sommerfield recorded his hope that 'whatever the book was then [in 1936], it is worth reading now, I hope, in relation to our own times' (244). If Sommerfield hoped that his novel might help to ignite the spark of the proletarian revolution in 1980s Britain, David Peace's strike-novel *GB84* (2004) has a more modest aim. It suggests that the events of 1984 can speak to the novel's readership in the early 2000s precisely because the neoliberal model of governance intensifies the historical patterns of proletarianization, economic deprivation, and socio-cultural dispossession that had culminated so dramatically in the miners' strike of 1984-5.

GB84 fictionalizes the events of 1984–5 when Margaret Thatcher's government defeated a strike action by the National Union of Mineworkers, the 'militant vanguard of the British trade-union movement' (Hart 573). Much of the novel is centred on events unfolding in the northern English county of Yorkshire, and the Orwellian echoes of Peace's title – *GB84* rather than *1984* – are clearly intended to call up the dystopian vision of a repressive Thatcherite state that deployed the full brutality of army and police as well as the secret service's counter-insurgency methods against the striking miners and their union. As one character, the miner Peter, notes: 'the full weight of the state is being brought to bear upon us in an attempt to try to break this strike. On the picket lines, riot police in full battle gear, on horse-back and on foot, accompanied by police dogs, have been unleashed in violent attacks upon our members' (Peace 168).

Peace's novel consists of fifty-three chapters, one for each week of the strike. Peace calls his book 'a novel based upon fact' ('Author's Note', n.p.), but the text splits its narratives in a manner which turns it into a form of experimental montage rather than a more conventionally realist fiction. The main chapters of *GB84* consist of several third-person narratives focalized through different characters. Most prominent among these focalizer figures are Neil Fontaine, the assistant to Stephen Sweet, Thatcher's right-hand man during the strike; and Terry Winters, modelled on Roger Windsor, the hapless chief executive of the National Union of Mineworkers (NUM). Set against these third-person narratives, which show us the political scheming behind the strike's collapse, we are given two first-person narratives, set in two compact columns that occupy the left-hand page before the start of each main chapter. These first-person narratives offer fictionalized accounts which Peace adapted from his own interviews with former coal miners and which build on his research into the oral histories of the strike. The two stream-of-consciousness-like voices belong to two men, the striking miner Martin and the NUM shop steward Peter, and they offer an inside view of the struggle which acts as a counterweight to the high politics and backroom intrigue that dominate in the third-person narratives. The opposition between the two blocks of text – the two parallel columns of first-person narration, as well as the contrast between first-person narration and third-person narration – visualizes the unrelenting logic of confrontation and social antagonism that drove the historical events of 1984–5, what one character calls England's '[c]ivil fucking war' (202): the police against the miners, and the miners against the scabs.

Crucially, however, the novel's first-person narratives are not limited to accounts in the first-person singular. Threaded through these intimate, personal narratives by Martin and Peter are fragments of a collective voice marked by the first-person plural 'we'. This shared voice heightens the significance of the strike by calling up the lives and experiences of countless past generations of workers: '*The dead brood under Britain*,' the first-person narrative begins on page one, '*We whisper. We echo. The emanation of Giant Albion*' (2). The tightly printed columns of text which comprise the narratives of the miners create a visual echo that further emphasizes the narrative function of these individual and collective voices: Martin's and Peter's first-person narratives are consolidated into a more robust communal voice; but we are also reminded, visually, of the intense historical pressures by which individual voices are condensed – over time, coal-like – into a more solid collective bloc. In *GB84*, this sedimented collective voice takes on an antiphonal, choral quality, and it emphasizes the workers' historical solidarity through centuries of exploitation.

This blending of voices creates a narrative temporality which runs aslant to the chronological unfolding of events in the novel's third-person narrative. This alternative temporality could be called revolutionary deep time: Peace's novel imaginatively reaches across centuries, connecting the strike of 1984–5 to temporally remote moments of social and political resistance in a way that transposes it into a transhistorical realm. In its most hopeful aspects, *GB84*'s use of a collective voice suggests that the period of profound socio-economic crisis that marked the mid-1980s can be meaningfully connected to earlier moments of political resistance. Peace indicates that what the novel calls 'Giant Albion' (2) – the sleeping giant mentioned in Geoffrey of Monmouth's *Historia Regum Britanniae* and William Blake's Romantic mythology, the embodiment of the British people – had raised its head at various points in history: during the fourteenth-century Peasants' Revolt, during the English Civil War of the seventeenth century, during the Chartist revolts of the mid-nineteenth century and during the General Strike of 1926 – and that it did so once again when the Yorkshire miners resisted the restructuring of the industrial economy and the razing of their communities under Thatcher: '*The soil is cold. The wounds old*', the novel's collective voice notes poignantly (248; orig. emphasis). This mythical temporality, this vision of revolutionary deep time, is dramatically set against the novel's stark descriptions of economic precarity and poverty in the Yorkshire mining communities. However, rather than limiting its description to these naturalistic descriptions of historically specific suffering, *GB84* crucially deindividualizes the first-person narrative voice, depriving it of its specific historical substance as a means of dissolving singular subjectivity into a collective, transhistorical voice.

The doubling of narratives that I have been describing – the way in which these storylines mirror and echo each other – is central to the design of Peace's novel, and it reflects his view of the political struggle. Indeed, the strike of 1984 itself doubles as return of the socialist struggles of the interwar years. At many points, the novel looks back to the Hunger Marches of the interwar years and to the battles between Yorkshire miners and police later: '*It's 1926 all over again*,' the chauffeur Neil Fontaine observes at one point, looking back to the year of the General Strike in Britain (158; orig. emphasis). *GB84* places different revolutionary moments on a single developmental arc, connecting the Russian Revolution to the workers' movement of the 1930s, to the miners' strikes in the 1980s, and to the novel's neoliberal present of the early 2000s. Peace's text thus articulates the hope that these distinct historical moments will turn out to be so many linked stages in a single, ongoing struggle between capitalists and precariously employed industrial labourers.

In *GB84*, this belief in the continuity of historical struggles is associated most clearly with the historical figure of Arthur Scargill, the president of the NUM. Throughout the strike, the union president has Dmitri Shostakovich's 1939 'Leningrad' Symphony playing on loop in his office, and he frequently lectures his audiences on the Popular Front politics of the 1930s. For the president, the strike of 1984 is part of a long revolutionary tradition. 'The *history* of the Miner,' he muses at one point: 'The *tradition* of the Miner. The legacies of their fathers and their fathers' fathers. [...] This union will be in the vanguard of that battle, as it has been in every struggle, as it has been in every victory' (7, 16; orig. emphasis). *GB84* traces how this vision of a popular radical tradition enters a profound historical crisis in 1980s Britain. In the novel, the struggle between capital and labour devolves into a play of strategic trade-offs between political representatives. Scargill's appeal to the miners as the Leninist 'Shock Troops of Socialism' is intended to rally support for the NUM, but in view of the political realities of 1980s Britain, his own socialism begins to look like a romantic aberrance: 'The President shouted, "*Vive la Révolution!*" The President loved Paris. *Revolutionary City*. Second only to sacred Leningrad. *Holy City*. The President loved the bread. The cheese. The good coffee. The red wine. The President carried Zola everywhere. *Germinal*' (95; orig. emphasis). Scargill's failure to secure financial backing from the Soviet Union brings home to him the historical belatedness of his own revolutionary internationalism. Similarly, the miners' strike action appears as an increasingly anachronistic form of resistance in the face of the historical restructuring of the economy and labour, as well as in the face of the governmental regime of economic precarity that will take the place of industrial employment.

Like Sommerfield's novel, *GB84* experiments with the representation of communal voices and shared experiences of economic precarity in order to gesture towards the possibility of collective revolutionary action. However, the intertwining of the different narrative strands in *GB84* also draws attention to the way in which such revolutionary action is stifled by the spiderwebs of capitalism. By placing Peter's and Martin's stories alongside the narrative about the NUM's negotiations with the government, Peace shows us that the NUM's trade-offs – its decision to assent to the privatization of uneconomic collieries – end up exacerbating the suffering of the miners' families, pushing them to the extreme edge of economic precarity. The union's capitulation to the law of the Thatcherite capitalist state seals the union's political defeat but, as the narratives of Martin and Peter poignantly illustrate, it also precipitates the disintegration of the industrial working class and the rise of a new age of neoliberal financial capitalism.

GB84 charts the decline of the industry-based economy during what the novel calls 'Year Zero' (462), the midpoint of Thatcher's ascendancy and the terminal point – or catastrophic Ground Zero – of the workers' movement. The novel focuses on the crisis of industrial labour, but it also traces the collapse of a collective way of life, the 'real subsumption' of a shared social world under the totalizing logic of capital.[7] Peace asks us to see society, and the fragmented text of the novel itself, as structured not by the perspective of any specific class, and notably not by the perspective of the proletariat as the subject-object of history, but by the totality of capital. What I have identified as *GB84*'s formally experimental use of montage – its strategic loosening of plot conventions and narrative coherence in order to map the distribution of economic precarity – can thus be read as mirroring the fragmentation of the social realm and of productive processes dictated by capitalism. To put this another way: *GB84*'s narrative withholds the authoritative, unified class perspective of the proletariat – a perspective that is associated in *May Day* with the point of view of the heterodiegetic narrator – and instead echoes the looser, decentred connectivity of social relations that obtains under capitalism.[8]

May Day and *GB84* share an interest in the networks of exploitation that characterize capitalist societies. However, while Sommerfield's novel expects that a collective political subjectivity will emerge from the dispersed structures of industrial capitalism, *GB84* records the incipient demise of the proletariat as a figure of revolutionary action. And yet, *GB84*'s particular attention to the 'deep time' of the miners' strike also indicates that for Peace, the artistic act of recreating the labour struggles of 1984 in 2004 is not simply a matter of historical record, or the nostalgic memorialization of a time when such labour struggles seemed somehow more meaningful. Instead, the destruction of the industry-based economy during the highpoint of Thatcher's political ascendancy starts to come into focus as the prehistory of the novel's own present, the moment of New Labourite financial capitalism. Building on a set of terms proposed by the political scientist Samuel A. Chambers, we could say that *GB84* charts the demise of the proletariat as a collective figure of political action and its wholesale replacement by 'the specific form of *homo politicus neoliberalis*'. As Chambers points out, the latter term is intended to signal that neoliberalization and the concomitant rise of financial capitalism do not entail a complete dismantling of the sphere of the political but rather give rise to the emergence of a distinctive 'series of historical processes and practices that lead to the production of a [new] form of political subjectivity' (723).

By exploring the large-scale demise of organized industrial labour in the mid-1980s, then, *GB84* presents us with the prehistory of our current social, economic and political crisis. It presents us not with an optimistic aesthetic vision of a collective political subject whose power is rooted in shared conditions of economic exploitation, but with the emergence of an economically disenfranchised precariat whose voice has become synonymous, for many contemporary commentators, with the shrill sounds of right-wing populism. The emergence of this precariat is only hinted at in *GB84*, but we can recognize without much difficulty the contours of a new social class pervasively exposed to economic precarity.[9] Peace leaves his readers in no doubt that this precariat will find it difficult to mobilize collective political agency, and that its political subjectivity will appear disconcertingly substanceless when compared to that central protagonist of Marxist historiography, the proletariat as the subject-object of history. 'The precariat', as Chambers explains, is a 'potential subjectivity irreducible to the [atomized neoliberal] entrepreneur, but it remains problematic because it names less a viable future subject and more a victim of globalization and/or neoliberalism' (739).

GB84 looks ahead to the emergence of a new and amorphous social class, the precariat, which recruits its members from a number of older classes, including but not limited to the working class. As the economist and social scientist Guy Standing observed in 2009, the precariat 'has yet to solidify as a class-for-itself': 'People are not born in it and are unlikely to identify themselves as members with a glow of pride. This is a contrast with the traditional industrial working class. [. . .] The precariat is not yet at that stage, even if a few in its ranks display a defiant pride, in their parades, blogs and comradely interactions' (22). Standing is careful to distinguish the 'old proletariat' from the new precariat on the grounds that while the working life of the former was characterized by 'long-term, stable, fixed-hour jobs with established routes of advancement, subject to unionisation and collective agreements', members of the precariat typically have 'no enterprise benefits to give income security and no contributions-based social protection' making them 'dependent on an enfeebled community system of social support' (6, 44–5). Despite these important differences, however, Standing has proposed that the category of proletarianization continues to be of value if we want to name the intensified processes of political invisibilization and socio-cultural 'insubstantialization' that have characterized the most recent wave of capitalist restructuring (36–7).

GB84 is a late exponent of the proletarian modernist tradition I have been discussing here, and as such the novel speaks to recent forms of socio-economic proletarianization. On the one hand, the novel crucially problematizes the NUM leadership's sentimental fetishization of radical history, and it questions the future feasibility of the proletariat as a figure of collective resistance. Yet on the other, Peace clearly expects that his elegiac description of the miners' strike – his artistic rendering of lives increasingly exposed to economic precarity – will be able to speak to the novel's own readership in 2004. If we want to understand this ambition, we should recall once more Jodi Dean's strategic attempt to resignify the term 'proletarianization', an attempt which anticipates Standing's reactivation of the term by a few years: 'we need to detach "proletarian" from the factory, so that we can understand *proletarianization* as a process that deprives humans of their "substance" and reduces them to providers of labour. [. . .] [P]roletarianization operates through precarization: it is capitalism's production and consumption of the workers it needs' (107–8; orig. emphasis). These comments foreground the potential significance of the proletarian modernist tradition for our contemporary moment. They suggest that it is a mistake to reduce this cultural tradition to texts and artworks which celebrate a fixed class identity – although this particular critical misreading has beset the study of proletarian writing for many decades. The proletarian modernist tradition is richer than such narrow accounts suggest, and it can notably prompt us to pay attention to literary fiction's particular skill at mapping the structures of economic proletarianization that invariably support the reproduction of capitalism.

Conclusion

Comprising a distinctive strand of formally experimental and politically committed writing, proletarian modernism constitutes an important line of twentieth-century and early twenty-first-century artistic production. As I have described it here, the neglected tradition of proletarian modernism has drawn its politico-artistic energies from several sources. Proletarian modernists of the interwar period such as John Sommerfield, Jack Lindsay and James Hanley took inspiration from a Marxist vision of history that attempted to locate revolutionary agency in the privileged structural position of the working class: according to this view, the proletariat's 'substanceless subjectivity' – its reduction to abstract labour power in the capitalist system of exploitation – simultaneously ensured its functioning as a universal category of anti-capitalist struggle. By contrast, revolutionary expectation takes a backseat in more recent texts such as David Peace's *GB84*, which pay more attention to the harrowing experiences of exploitation and vulnerabilization that give rise to phenomenologies of substancelessness in the first place. As I have indicated, the case of *GB84* suggests that we should think of proletarian modernism as a literary and artistic tradition that is not just interested in representing a fixed class position but in exploring processes of proletarianization more generally. When it is understood in this wider sense, proletarian modernism is not a thing of the past. Indeed, to note the continued urgency of this alternative tradition today is to observe that processes of proletarianization have not disappeared but have become more pervasive – it is to note that we are still, or again, living in the long 1930s.

Notes

1 For the phrase 'substanceless subjectivity', see Žižek 27.
2 Guillaume le Blanc, whose book *Vie ordinaires, vie précaires* (2007) offers a more extensive account of the phenomenology of substanceless subjectivity, observes that 'la précarité commence comme une décomposition de la normalité même. Elle détache ce qui a été péniblement attaché dans la longue et incertaine construction sociale de soi. [. . .] L'expérience de la précarité [est] une précarisation de l'expérience' ('precariousness begins as a breaking-apart of normality itself. It disassembles what has been painstakingly put together through the long and uncertain social construction of the self. [. . .] The experience of precariousness [is] a precarization of experience') (14; my translation).
3 For an influential account of the historical evacuation of the signifier of the 'proletariat' in the 1970s and 1980s, see Gorz. For an exploration of the long life of proletarian modernism beyond the interwar years, see Kohlmann.
4 Douglas Mao and Rebecca L. Walkowitz's 'The New Modernist Studies' offers a now-classical survey of the recent expansion of the field of modernist studies (Mao and Walkowitz 'The New Modernist Studies').
5 On 'cohabitation', see Butler 'Precarious Life'.
6 For Cole's Butlerian discussion of an 'ethics of mutuality' in modernism, see esp. Cole 20–1.

7   'Real subsumption' is Marx's term for the complete restructuring of labour, and for the seemingly autonomous 'self-valorization and realization of capital', under the conditions of advanced financial capitalism. By contrast, Marx's term 'formal subsumption' signifies an earlier moment of economic development during which the means of production become monopolized but in which the labour process itself continues much as before (*Capital* 1019–39).
8   To the extent that the narrative grammar of Peace's novel is governed by the logic of capital, the text can be seen to echo the syntactic slippage that we find in in the sentence from Marx's *Grundrisse* which I cited towards the beginning of this chapter. In Marx's sentence, the agency of individual exploiters ('the capitalists') is refigured as the impersonal, self-valorizing momentum of capital itself: the aim of 'the capitalist', Marx writes, is 'not only maintain himself as capital, but also, as a growing capital'.
9   For a discussion of the specific class character of the precariat, see Standing.

Works cited

Butler, Judith. *Frames of War: When Is Life Grievable?* Verso, 2010.
Butler, Judith. 'Precarious Life, Vulnerability, and the Ethics of Cohabitation'. *The Journal of Speculative Philosophy*, vol. 26, no. 2, 2012, pp. 134–51.
Chambers, Samuel A. 'Undoing Neoliberalism: *Homo Œconomicus*, *Homo Politicus*, and the *Zōon Politikon*'. *Critical Inquiry*, vol. 44, no. 4, 2018, pp. 706–32.
Cole, Sarah. *At the Violet Hour: Modernism and Violence in England and Ireland*. Oxford University Press, 2012.
Dean, Jodi. *The Communist Horizon*. Verso, 2012.
Gorz, André. *Farewell to the Working Class*. Pluto, 1994.
Hart, Matthew. 'The Third English Civil War: David Peace's "Occult" History of Thatcherism'. *Contemporary Literature*, vol. 49, no. 4, 2008, pp. 573–96.
Kohlmann, Benjamin. 'Proletarian Modernism: Film, Literature, Theory'. *PMLA*, vol. 134, no. 5, 2019, pp. 1056–75.
Le Blanc. *Vie ordinaires, vie précaires*. Editions du seuil, 2007.
Lévinas, Emmanuel. 'Ethics as First Philosophy'. *The Levinas Reader*, edited by Seán Hand. Blackwell, 1989, pp. 75–87.
Lorey, Isabell. *State of Insecurity: The Government of the Precarious*. Verso, 2015.
Mao, Douglas, and Rebecca L. Walkowitz, eds *Bad Modernisms*. Duke University Press, 2006.
Mao, Douglas, and Rebecca L. Walkowitz. 'The New Modernist Studies'. *PMLA*, vol. 123, no. 3, 2008, pp. 737–48.
Marx, Karl. *Capital*. Vol. 1. Edited by Ernest Mandel. Penguin, 1976.
Marx, Karl. *Grundrisse: Foundations of the Critique of Political Economy*. Penguin, 1993.
Marx, Karl. *Ökonomische Manuskripte 1857/8*. Dietz, 2006.
Nancy, Jean-Luc. *Being Singular Plural*. Stanford University Press, 2000.
Peace, David. *GB84*. Faber and Faber, 2004.
Puar, Jasbir. 'Precarity Talk: A Virtual Roundtable with Lauren Berlant, Judith Butler, Bojana Cvejić, Isabell Lorey, Jasbir Puar, and Ana Vukanović'. *TDR: The Drama Review*, vol. 56, no. 4, 2012, pp. 163–77.
Purdon, James. 'The Early Fiction of John Sommerfield'. *Oxford Handbooks* Online, www.oxfordhandbooks.com. Accessed 20 December 2019.

Sommerfield, John. *May Day*. London Books Classics, 2012.
Standing, Guy. *The Precariat: The New Dangerous Class*. Bloomsbury, 2011.
Williams, Raymond. 'Culture and Technology'. *The Politics of Modernism: Against the New Conformists*. Verso, 2006, pp. 119–40.
Williams, Raymond. 'When Was Modernism?'. *The Politics of Modernism: Against the New Conformists*. Verso, 2006, pp. 31–5.
Žižek, Slavoj. *Tarrying with the Negative: Kant, Hegel, and the Critique of Ideology*. Duke University Press, 1993.

Chapter 9

THE FUTURE IS A GHOST

PRECARITY, ANTICIPATION AND RETROSPECTION IN ANNELIESE MACKINTOSH'S 'LIMITED DREAMERS' AND LEE ROURKE'S *VULGAR THINGS*

Emily J. Hogg

Precarity disrupts the experience of time's passing. According to Pierre Bourdieu, 'Casualization profoundly affects the person who suffers it: by making the whole future uncertain, it prevents all rational anticipation', amounting to a 'destructuring of existence' (82). Through casualized work, he argues, existence is 'deprived among other things of its temporal structures' producing 'the ensuing deterioration of the whole relationship to the world, time and space' (82). This chapter addresses the temporal destructuring that Bourdieu associates with precarity: the sense that temporal co-ordinates have been lost, the future is difficult to imagine, and the possibility of anticipation is foreclosed. Drawing on the work of Lauren Berlant, Anna Tsing and Mark Fisher, I argue that this difficulty with anticipation is inextricably bound up with retrospection: that, in precarity's structure of feeling, the problem of the unimaginable future is related to difficulties making sense of the past, in particular – in a British context – the past of industrial capitalism and the post-war welfare state. Issues of anticipation, retrospection and – crucially – the relationship between anticipation and retrospection are also highly significant in recent accounts of fiction's temporality (notably in the work of Mark Currie), and this chapter brings these bodies of theoretical work together. The aim of the chapter is to suggest that narrative fiction might serve as a resource for negotiating precarity's temporal anxieties because of the way that narratives depend upon, manipulate and connect readerly anticipation and retrospection.

To read a narrative is, necessarily, to be involved in processes of looking forward and looking back. Though anticipating in fiction is not precisely the same as anticipating in life, the philosopher Paul Ricoeur suggests a method for thinking about the relationship between temporalities in narrative fiction and in the world without suggesting that they are identical, or that one directly produces the other in a straightforward way. Through elaborating a three-part model of mimesis, he shows that narratives rely on ideas about causality that are rooted in real social existence, that they alter and play with these ideas in their textual forms, and that, through engagements with these textual forms, readers might have their perceptions about temporality shifted in ways that they then feed back into the world. Time in narrative therefore influences extra-narrative time and vice versa, in a continuous cycle. In this way, Ricoeur argues, reading narratives can help to mediate problems or impasses concerning temporality that are impossible to solve through analysis or abstract speculation alone.

This chapter uses an account of narrative's relationship with temporal experience that is inspired by Ricoeur and by contemporary narrative theorists who engage with his work, to show how two contemporary narrative fictions might help to mediate the anxieties about time identified in precarity theory. I use Anneliese Mackintosh's short story 'Limited Dreamers' (2014) to show how the anticipation/retrospection problem I associate with precarity can be clarified and expanded through its representation in literature. I then consider whether literature can work to challenge, as well as to represent, the difficulties of precarious time. Examining the way anticipation and retrospection work in Lee Rourke's 2014 novel *Vulgar Things*, I argue that the novel's temporal structures can work to modify readers' understandings of anticipation and retrospection in the precarious world beyond the text.

Precarious time

The inability to imagine or plan the future is a characteristic element of precarious experience. This is the case on a very concrete level. For example, zero-hour contracts mean that workers do not know in advance how many hours they will work and be paid for in a given month – if any – which makes it difficult to plan the day-to-day, as well as to plan for the long term. Guy Standing argues that precarious workers are 'under time stress' because they are required to take on increasing numbers of activities, and the temporal boundaries between work and leisure have become blurred. This leads to a scattering of energy, the seeming necessity of making intense effort which does not connect with future goals or aspirations (224). In a flexible labour market, he argues, workers must try to make themselves as employable as possible by continually upgrading their skills in their free time, selling themselves on social media and/or undertaking multiple jobs at once to avoid the risk of unemployment. Standing argues that this 'lifestyle' amounts to 'multitasking without control over a narrative of time use' (224). Workers intensify their efforts, knowing that their employment is always at risk, but this pervasive insecurity means that they are multitasking without 'seeing the future' or 'building on the past'; they lack a 'sense of occupational development' (224).

This resonates with what Lauren Berlant has described as the 'ongoing now' of precarity (196). Standing and Berlant have very different accounts of what precarity is: for Standing, the precariat is emerging as a new social class, with distinctive relations of production, distribution and relations to the state, whereas for Berlant precarity is an affective experience of insecurity that saturates the existing class hierarchy without dissolving it. Nonetheless, both theorists suggest that precarity is often experienced as an inability to either envisage the future or see one's actions as building towards it. Instead, it is, as Berlant describes it, an 'enduring present that is at once overpresent and enigmatic' (196). But Berlant also shows how this sense of the 'enduring present' is connected with the question of retrospection. She argues that what characterizes the present moment is that 'there has been a mass dissolution of a disavowal. The promise of the good life no longer masks the living precarity of this historical present' (196). That is, she argues that in the past, especially in the mid-to-late twentieth century, and especially in the Global North, it was possible to believe in and aspire to economic security. Work hard and the symbols of middle-class prosperity could be attained; social mobility was feasible; a reliable relationship between effort and material reward was assumed. Similarly, Anna Tsing writes that in the mid-twentieth century, 'dreams of modernization and progress [. . .] offered a vision of stability': 'Modernization was supposed to fill the world – both communist and capitalist – with jobs, and not just any jobs, but "standard employment" with stable wages and benefits' (3).

This imagined future, of course, did not come to pass: 'Such jobs are now quite rare; most people depend on much more irregular livelihoods' (Tsing 3). Today, 'it seems that all our lives are precarious – even when, for the moment, our pockets are lined [. . .] now many of us, north and south, confront the condition of trouble without end' (Tsing 1). But even at the height of their significance, these ideas were often more fantasy than reality for many people. What is lost in the present, Berlant and Tsing emphasize, is not so much the actual Fordist past (which for many was not exactly the era of security and prosperity that more sepia-tinted narratives suggest), but rather a way of picturing the future that mattered: a mode of anticipation that seemed realistic. Tsing and Berlant suggest that the 'promise of the good life' (Berlant 196) or dreams of modernization and progress (Tsing 3) could, in the past, mask precarity and the reality of insecure living; today, it is impossible to have such faith and belief in the promised future. What have been lost are the ideas and dreams about the future that once mattered, and – perhaps – the idea that anticipation is actually possible and potentially fruitful. In the mid-twentieth century, Tsing writes, 'The direction of the future was well known; but is it now?' (3). The dreams of modernization were the 'handrails, which once made us think we knew, collectively, where we were going' (Tsing 2). The collective mood of contemporary precarity, characterized by employment insecurity, the rollback of the welfare state and impending environmental catastrophe, is more like the sickening realization that we really had no idea where we were heading, or have become lost somewhere on the way. The difficulty of precarity as Tsing and Berlant conceptualize it, then, is not only the wild unpredictability of the future, but also the feeling of having lost the dreams about the future that were once resonant and meaningful in the past.

This affective experience constantly requires individuals to try and work out what is going on, and what they need to do – it constantly requires 'finding one's footing in new manners of being in it' (Berlant 196) – but the intense effort of orienting oneself means that all attention is directed to the mysterious and unsettling now, and none is left for looking forward. According to Bourdieu, this is how the precaritization of work functions as a mode of domination in more general terms. He argues that the insecurity of employment produces a 'generalized and permanent state of insecurity aimed at forcing workers into submission, into the acceptance of exploitation' (85). It does this through closing off the possibility of imagining the future: casualization, he says, prevents 'the basic belief and hope in the future that one needs in order to rebel, especially collectively' (82).

Precarious time and culture

Mark Fisher makes a similar – though not identical – series of claims about the relationship between retrospection and anticipation in precarity. He argues that 'the future has been eroded over the last thirty years' (13), and, in line with Berlant's account of the 'ongoing present', for Fisher the 'general condition' of the contemporary moment is one in which 'life continues, but time has somehow stopped' (6). Importantly for the purposes of this chapter, he traces this 'slow cancellation of the future' (the phrase is Franco 'Bifo' Berardi's (quoted Fisher 6)) through cultural forms and tendencies, showing how the seeming impossibility of imagining the future produces, in culture, a tendency towards retrospection. His writing provides one way of thinking about the temporalities of neoliberal capitalism, especially the anxieties of retrospection and anticipation, as they are registered in cultural texts.

He explains that the period since the 1970s in Britain has 'been a time of massive, traumatic change' as the 'shift into so-called Post-Fordism – with globalization, ubiquitous computerization and the casualisation of labour – resulted in a complete transformation in the way that work and leisure were organised' (8–9). However, despite, or even because of, these intense and dramatic changes, culture has not kept pace. In cultural forms, he argues, we do not witness an ongoing experimental and fast-moving development to mirror that which has occurred in forms of work and technology. Instead, he observes widespread conservatism, repetitiveness, and a general lack of innovation and invention. Most prominent ideas about the 'futuristic' in art and culture, he points out, would be familiar to futuristic dreamers in the 1970s and 1980s.

The inability to register the new and the disappearance of the sense of pushing into the future are registered in culture in two distinct ways, both of which involve a preoccupation with the past. In much popular culture, he suggests, there is a repetitively retro feel. It circles around the same structures and modes of expression again and again. Listen to the singer Adele's music, he suggests, and there is nothing about it that sounds contemporary – indeed, it is 'saturated with a vague but persistent feeling of the past, without recalling any specific moment' (14). What is being evoked is not the actual past in its specificity, but rather a more general pastness, in which everything is retro, and everything becomes blended together.

This endless looking back is, Fisher argues, not an engagement with the real past or its struggles. To deal with the cancellation of the future, we need another attitude to past time. 'What should haunt us is not the *no longer* of actually existing social democracy, but the *not yet* of the futures [. . .] which never materialised. These spectres – the spectres of lost futures – reproach the formal nostalgia of the capitalist realist world' (27). In the past, he argues, cultural forms helped us to imagine a better world. In their constant innovation and radicalism, they were pushing towards the new, and embodied a courageous and imaginative sense of anticipation. They helped audiences to dream that the future could be better than the past. For Fisher, then, as for Tsing, the sense of the impossibility of the future is linked with the loss of the dreams that mattered in the past. The crucial difference between these thinkers is that Tsing's argument is ultimately about learning to live without the illusory support of ideas of modern progress. The dreams Fisher refers to are socialist and radical, and underlying his argument is a sense that we need to develop new ways of imagining equitable futures. For example, he argues that a second, more positive response to the cancellation of the future can be found in a body of work that Fisher, adapting a term from Jacques Derrida, describes as 'hauntological'. This is cultural production in which there is 'an implicit acknowledgement' that 'not only has the future not arrived, it no longer seems possible' but which nonetheless 'constitutes a refusal to give up on the desire for the future' (21). However, despite the differences between Tsing and Fisher concerning the political usefulness of the past's dreams of the future, what is notable is that this way of conceptualizing the temporality of precarity recurs in the different theorizations. Precarious time, as it emerges in the work of these theorists, is a difficulty with imagining the future that prompts a sense of loss and longing for the forms of anticipation that were prevalent in the past.

'Limited Dreamers'

This way of experiencing time is something we can approach not only in theoretical terms, but also through literary texts. Anneliese Mackintosh's short story 'Limited Dreamers', published in her 2014 collection *Any Other Mouth*, is a text which registers and reflects this temporal experience, while also expanding and clarifying it. In theoretical terms, we have seen that the endless now, the impossibility of the future, and the sense of loss regarding the possibility of dreaming about the future is a characteristic of precarity. In 'Limited Dreamers', this temporal experience is rendered visible in a new way – not in the abstract or conceptual sense, but through the representation of characters' lives, feelings and interactions.

The short story is about two women who meet while undertaking insecure, precarious employment: they had 'worked at the Council for a very short time, brought in via a temping agency, dismissed at a week's notice' (Mackintosh 213). They are precarious characters in a more existential sense too: the story names them Banana and Schmidt, but these are described as pseudonyms, related to their real names but a little different. 'Both girls had unusual names. One was a kind of fruit. The other was German' (213). This leads the narrator to suggest the pseudonyms – 'let's call her Banana', 'let's call her Schmidt' (216) – self-consciously emphasizing the artificiality and fictionality of the narration and producing a sense of fragility. The names are provisional placeholders, suggesting that the women's identities are, likewise, not wholly solid.

Now that they have been dismissed from their work, they decide to meet 'to talk about signing on [i.e. claiming unemployment benefits], working tax credit, housing benefits: things which scared them both' (213). The story describes this meeting, focusing on this single incident in one day in their lives, with some flashbacks. Nothing in the story progresses beyond this day, and the women do not actually get around to discussing the practical issues they intend to discuss – their financial plans, now that they have been made unemployed. The list of topics is repeated twice more in the narrative, but the characters do not actually discuss them. 'And they talked about everything, *everything*, but signing on, working tax credits, housing benefits, or how they were going to function in the real world after today was over' (215). At the end of the story, they agree that 'the next time they met they would discuss signing on, working tax credits, and housing benefits' (218). The point at which they actually discuss their future functioning 'in the real world' is deferred again and again. This repetition suggests an inability to move forward: the characters seem, within the story's limited temporal frame, to be unable to picture or really grapple with the future. They do not know how they will 'function in the real world after today', and they do not do anything to make this functioning easier.

This inability to picture the future recurs in other places in the story too. During the meeting at the bar, Schmidt makes a 'brainstorm in purple pen [. . .] entitled *What I Want From Life*' (216). But the long-range goals and aims suggested by the title of the brainstorm prove elusive: 'She had only got as far as "a dressing gown".' Schmidt wonders 'what she was going to fill the rest of her life with. It felt like she'd already got to wherever she was heading, and she couldn't think of anything she wanted to happen next, except for that damn dressing gown' (216). She thinks about 'how long two decades might feel, and the fact that once she hit fifty she'd be as good as dead' (216). She finds it difficult to imagine future time; what helps to clarify the point is looking back: she remembers a 'day at Brownies two decades ago – so *that's* how long two decades feels' (216).

Although the women are adults – the narrative notes that one of them is thirty and the other is married – the narrative repeatedly describes them as 'girls' (213). This is an oft-criticized way of patronizing women, but in the story, it is used differently. It suggests the ongoing significance of the past for them – their longing for prior experience. Throughout the story, the 'girls' are associated with objects and behaviours connected with childhood. They go to a bar where they sit next to 'an abandoned scooter and toy gun' (217). Behind one of them is a skip, and she jokes that she looks like Stig of the Dump, the beloved children's book character. At another bar they draw with felt tips, one of them 'colouring so hard she was making a hole in the page' (216). The narrative states that 'they were glad they had felt-tips' because:

> There was no guilt in stationery. Stationery was pre-words. It was pre-love letters and terrible drawings of your own hand. It was pre- let's-write-our-initials-on-our-books-and-CDs, and pre- I've-underlined-every-number-on-this-phone-bill-

that-I-have-a-problem-with. It was pre- why-I'm-breaking-up-with-you-notes and pre- bullet-point-lists-of-everything-you-ever-did-to-hurt-me. (214)

This evocation of the past has no positive content. The felt-tip pens are appealing because they are reminiscent of an abstract 'before'. What matters is the way they evoke a time *before* other things happened – they are simply 'pre'.

Theorizations of precarity stress its ongoing present, its lack of future and its longing for the dreams of the future that were believable in the past. In the story, we find a representation of characters who seem to live in the expanded present, and who seem to be stuck in it, without being able to progress towards the future. This impression is heightened by the story's limited, somewhat claustrophobic time frame: it takes place across only one day and describes fairly small-scale inconsequential encounters. Moreover, the story also adds to the account of precarious time I have been advancing. As in the theoretical accounts of Tsing, Berlant and Fisher, in the story precarity is associated both with a sense of the impossibility of anticipation, and with an insistent retrospection. But in 'Limited Dreamers', there is a depiction of the character and quality of this precarious backward glance. The past is longed for simply because it was before – before things turned out the way they did, before assorted disappointments in romantic relationships, in work, in adulthood. There is no nostalgia for a specific past here, but rather a type of content-less retrospection. With the present unstable and insecure, and the future impossible to predict, it is the past which becomes the characters' focus, not for any characteristic of its own, but simply because of its perceived difference from the present.

Reading 'Limited Dreamers' alongside theoretical accounts produces a coherent picture of precarious time. The characters are stuck in the present and find it impossible to think about the future. This produces a tendency towards retrospection. Tsing and Berlant suggest that this is because in the past it felt more possible to imagine the future. The short story adds to this account, showing that – for its characters – retrospection in a situation of precarity has little to do with what the past was actually like. The characters look to the past simply because it came before their present. The past that is referred to is a sort of abstract 'before'. Drawing from both theory and literature, we can thus begin to construct an account of precarity's temporality: precarity produces an inability to look forward in time, and a related dedication to looking back. The affective power of retrospection here is about the past's distinctiveness from the present, either because, in the past, anticipation was possible (as the theory suggests) or simply because the past is understood to be an abstract 'before', before the problems and limitations of real existence (as the story indicates).

Ricoeur and the refiguration of time

I now turn to consider whether literature might also challenge or reorganize this way of thinking about the past, present and future, through the theory of Paul

Ricoeur. Ricoeur elaborates a three-part model of mimesis, which shows how textual narrative is both shaped by and shapes experiences of time beyond the text. Mark Currie explains that, in Ricoeur's analysis,

> the organization of events in a narrative fiction modifies the understanding that a reader may have of real time, and this changed understanding in effect comes to be part of the world of action which subsequent narrative fictions may then reflect [...] the temporality of fiction both reflects and produces the temporality of, for want of a better word, 'life': a kind of spiralling movement in which the fictional representation of time and the lived experience of time constantly modify each other. (Currie, *About Time* 94)

This 'spiralling' is accomplished through the three-part mimesis.

The first part of Ricoeur's model of mimesis (mimesis$_1$) is 'prefiguration'. This describes the way that the same structures of causality are operative in narrative as in the ordinary day-to-day social world. We understand the way events produce other events in narrative because we understand basic action in the real world – for the most part, we can comprehend why people act in the way they do on a day-to-day level. We bring to the text our competence in making causal connections. At the same time, our day-to-day actions might be considered stories waiting to be told, because narrative does not provide, but rather reiterates and transforms, the causal chains through which we make meaning in the social world. The term 'prefiguration' suggests the rootedness in the world of the logic and action that underlies narrativity. Mimesis$_2$ is narrative emplotment, the narrative organization of the text itself. This can be termed 'configuration'. Emplotment or configuration is the way that narratives order their own events. Mimesis$_3$ – or refiguration – is neatly summarized by William Dowling. It is 'the alteration brought about in individual consciousness by narrative experience' (16). To read a narrative is, Ricoeur argues, to participate in a temporal experience. Narrative depends upon causal chains, on the idea of knowledge that unfolds over time. Through reading a narrative we have a temporal experience which can shift our sense of time beyond the experience of reading itself.

By mimesis, then, Ricoeur means the way that a narrative takes up and arranges notions of action and causality that exist beyond it, providing readers with potentially novel experiences of temporality, which they then take with them back into the extra-textual domain. One of Ricoeur's examples – which both helps to clarify the threefold model and suggests some of the difficulties inherent in translating this model to the context of precarity – concerns the meaning of time itself. Through its three-part mimesis, Ricoeur argues that narrative can help us deal with a series of significant aporias in the philosophical discussion of the nature of time. Philosophy gets stuck on a number of points, Ricoeur states, but if philosophizing only takes us so far, then narrative might be able to make the aporias 'work for us' (4). Narrative does not necessarily provide a solution but rather it helps us to live in the aporias, to live with them, as a fundamental aspect of human experience. One such aporia is a question which, as Ricoeur shows, can be traced through the history of Western philosophy: Is time external or internal to human consciousness? Aristotle and Kant advance a notion of 'cosmological time', he argues: they see time as objective, physical and independent of human consciousness. The phenomenological approach to time, exemplified for Ricoeur by Augustine, Husserl and Heidegger, suggests that time exists solely in human perception and the operations of the mind.

Through detailed readings of all five philosophers, Ricoeur shows that it is has been impossible to define cosmological time without reference to phenomenological time, and impossible to define phenomenological time without reference to cosmological time. Aristotle and Kant are forced to draw on terms and concepts which properly belong to a theory of time as perceived or subjective, while Augustine, Husserl and Heidegger cannot describe the perception of time without presuming some external reality. 'The aporia of temporality', Ricoeur writes, 'lies precisely in the difficulty in holding on to both ends of this chain, the time of the soul and that of the world' (14). It might be argued that the two approaches to time need simply to be combined, but Ricoeur argues that 'a psychological theory and a cosmological theory mutually occlude each other to the very extent they imply each other'(14). It seems both impossible and necessary to think the phenomenological and the physical aspects of time together.

This is where narrative becomes crucial to Ricoeur. For him, narrative mediates between the two conceptions of time, bringing these experiences of time together. Many literary texts represent or discuss time. But narrative is also a temporal experience, in and of itself, involving the reader in the progression through time, from incomplete to more complete knowledge, and through the connections between different narrative events, which produce each other in causal chains. As many theorists have noted, narrative possesses a peculiar temporal structure. It 'is generally retrospective', Mark Currie writes, 'in the sense that the teller is looking back on events and relating them in the past tense' (Currie, *About Time* 29). However, 'a reader or listener experiences these events for the first time, as quasi-present' (Currie, *About Time* 29–30). Or, as Peter Brooks puts it, the present in the novel 'is a curious present that we know to be past in relation to a future we know already to be in place, already in wait for us to reach it' (23). Reading feels like experiencing the present and anticipating the future – but readers always know that, if the events are presented to us as narrative, they are in some sense already past, already being perceived retrospectively. There has to be some gap between events and their narration, however small. However immediate the narrative feels to the reader, it is always already past to the narrator or narrating consciousness. Brooks calls this dynamic 'the anticipation of retrospection' (23).[1]

It is this quality of narration that enables it to mediate problems in the theorization of time, in Ricoeur's account. While the reader is in the process of reading, she does not have the overview of the story as a whole. She experiences events one after another, and can only guess how events relate, or where they will lead. This is akin to internal, subjective time. Yet she is also simultaneously aware that if the story presents itself for reading, then someone does have the overview: that what feels like immediate, present experience has already been understood and shaped into a narrative, and that the story has already been perceived as whole. These two ways of experiencing time are constantly working together in the process of reading; they are inseparable, and both shape the reading experience. At the end of the narrative, the reader perceives the significance of the events which feature in the narrative and understands why these particular events have been chosen and represented. The feeling of present experience comes together with the sense of overarching God's eye perspective. This is one of the ways that emplotment mediates the aporias of time 'by both reflecting and resolving, in its own temporal structures, the paradox of temporality' (Goldthorpe 86). It enables readers to experience phenomenological and cosmological time together – something both necessary and impossible in abstract philosophical speculation.

Ricoeur's claims depend on the universality of the problems of time he identifies. It is because the paradox of the cosmological and phenomenological understandings of time is a foundational problem for Western understandings of time itself that he can picture narrative as a mediator in general terms. All readers whose experiences are shaped by conventional Western conceptions of time can be assumed, Ricoeur thinks, to experience narrative's mediating functions in similar ways; narrative's strange temporality resolves a difficulty which is inherent to those conceptions. The problem of precarious time is, clearly, not an equivalent difficulty. As Tsing, Fisher and Berlant describe it, it is historically and geographically circumscribed: the feeling that 'The direction of the future was well known; but is it now?' (Tsing 3) is a specifically late-capitalist affect, related to historically contingent developments. Moreover, it is not clear that this temporal anxiety is even held in common by *everyone* living in this particular conjuncture – the super-rich, the securely employed and those marginalized because of race, ethnicity, gender or citizenship from ever belonging in the Fordist vision of security – may not share in the temporal structure of vanished future and longed-for past that I have associated with precarity.

However, in the tradition of hermeneutics from which Ricoeur wrote, it is possible to make a smaller-scale and more modest claim, inspired by the structure of Ricoeur's ideas. Instead of suggesting that all readers approaching Lee Rourke's novel *Vulgar Things* will, necessarily, find a mediation of precarious anxiety about time, I argue that if we choose to approach the novel with this issue in mind, then we can interpret it as a text which can reframe readerly perceptions of anticipation and retrospection in precarity. That is, in understanding the text as a possible source of refiguration of ideas about time in the extra-textual world, I see this possibility to depend on the interaction between the novel's structure and the reader's approach. In the next section, I show how the text creates a particular temporal experience of anticipation and retrospection. Because the seeming disappearance of the future and affective pull of the past are central to the experience of precarious time, the reader's immersion in the novel's temporality might help to refigure and readjust her sense of time in precarity, just as Ricoeur sees narrative as a refiguration of broader and more general temporal experiences. This potential is there in the text, as I suggest in the following: it exists in the way that the reader, as Ricoeur shows, inevitably becomes involved in a temporal experience, through reading. Whether the text actually enables a refiguration of *precarious* time, however, depends on the way individual readers approach it – although the novel's setting and plot may well bring the issue of precarity to mind.

Vulgar Things

Lee Rourke's 2014 novel *Vulgar Things* is about a man called Jon. At the beginning of the novel he works, unhappily, for an academic journal publisher. 'I look at what my life, until now, has amounted to: a boring job, a failed marriage, a small flat I can barely afford' (1). The event which sets the plot in motion – as in Mackintosh's short story – is sudden unemployment. Jon is fired from his job. This tips him into a new temporal experience. He drifts around Soho, in London, getting drunk: 'I bathe in the dislocation from my usual routine, allowing the nowness of my predicament to cover me' (7). He feels 'behind-time, having no idea at this moment what time it is or what I am really doing' (8). The next day, he gets a phone call from his brother informing him that their uncle has died by suicide and asking him to clear out the uncle's caravan, in Canvey Island, Essex. At the caravan, Jon finds out that his uncle has bequeathed him all of his life's savings – £100,000. He becomes obsessed with a woman he meets fleetingly on a pier. And he discovers a series of recordings that the uncle, Rey, had made over many years on video cassette, Betamax and DVD. They are all part of a sprawling and somewhat inscrutable project in which Uncle Rey records himself speaking to camera, talking about the meaning of Virgil's *Aeneid*, and also discussing Petrarch. There is also a manuscript, which is apparently part of the same project. Through watching the videos, Jon learns that his uncle is actually his biological father and that he had kidnapped his mother and held her captive in the caravan. For years, when Jon was a child, Rey had followed him and his family around, making secret video recordings of them.

Time is an explicit theme in the novel, and there is a repeated sense that Jon's sense of time has become disrupted and confused. All of the videos in Rey's caravan are hand-labelled with the year they were made, and watching them produces for Jon a sense of temporal disorientation. 'His voice, his voice is so real, like sitting beside me, talking to me. Only he isn't, he's dead and these words are from 1982, another time, another existence' (41). After only a few days in Canvey, his former employment begins to feel distant: 'London seems like a fading memory to me, like a fading dream. I'm happy to have escaped their clutches, even if it might only be for the duration of the task at hand' (91). Visiting an arcade in Southend he says, 'it's a mess, like the world has short-circuited and there's not much time left, so everything is accelerated: everything is happening too quickly for me to assimilate what is actually taking place' (75). Looking at up at the sky, he feels 'It all seems so fragile, too unstable, as if some fall or crash in the universe is imminent' (93). At times, everything in Canvey Island seems resistant to time: 'It hasn't changed since I was last here. Why should it? There's nothing to dictate that sort of thing out here. I'm sure the two men sitting at the bar are the same two men who were sitting at the bar when I was last in here' (22). At other times, the changes seem overwhelming. Looking back at the coastline where the cottages used to be 'occupied by fishermen and farmers', Jon says that 'it kind of sickens me, not that I'm in any way nostalgic for a past I've never known. But I feel like I need to accelerate away from it, Southend, the past, the present, a possible future' (56).

There is one important moment in the text which is explicitly reminiscent of the anticipation-retrospection difficulty I have identified in relation to precarity. Jon finds a DVD labelled 'Jon #1 1976-1984' (130). On the DVD are various videos of Jon himself as a child. Several of these have been taken without Jon's or his parents' knowledge. Jon watches the DVD and then it seems to stop playing and the screen goes dark. Jon, who is very emotional at what he observes, tries to compose himself. Then, after a long pause, another video begins, featuring Jon and Uncle Rey.

> inside a caravan
> This caravan
> [...]
> The boy: 'I've forgotten...'
> The voice: 'You know... the message to your future self... the message we made up for you to listen to when you're older...'
> [...]
> The boy: 'There is no future me... He's a ghost. (130)

Jon watches the younger version of himself saying that his future self does not exist. At this moment in the novel, the newly unemployed Jon is imagined to embody, in his very person, precarious temporality and its insecurities, the sense that the future failed to come into being and yet has a weird quasi-presence nonetheless. According to Mark Fisher, we should be haunted by the 'the spectres of lost futures' (27). Here we find Jon experiencing, on a personal level, a microcosm of what, according to Fisher, we should all be experiencing on the social, collective level: the awareness that the future has disappeared and is non-existent, but, at the same time, exists as a haunting presence, a feeling of loss that emerges from the past.

However, if narratives not only represent time, but also constitute an experience *of* time, we can consider the extent to which the characters' experiences of time, and the thematization of time in the novel, match the reader's temporal experience. In *Vulgar Things*, there is a significant difference between the way time works for the reader and for Jon. Jon's experience of time is unsettled and confusing. When he watches his younger self on tape, he experiences precarity's characteristic temporality: the impossibility of the future bound up with the recollection of the past. By contrast, for the reader, the novel's future is not impossible or difficult to envisage. It is often entirely predictable.

Early in the novel, Jon drops a key, the key to the safety deposit box in which Rey has left his life savings for Jon, and it lands the manuscript of Rey's long work. This is a heavily overdetermined moment: the manuscript, as the reader likely anticipates, will indeed be the 'key' to interpreting Rey's life, and the manuscript will reveal the reason for Rey's generous bequest. Consider too the tapes and DVDs that Rey has made. Not only are they labelled, they are also given a number in a sequence and a date. Jon does not need to scrabble around to put them in order or work out how they relate to one another. They are helpfully situated in chronology. Moreover, in Rey's caravan no technology is outdated. He has the means to play video cassettes, Betamax tapes – and the new equivalents. As readers we know from the outset that Rey has created this chronologically ordered work, and that the technology exists in the caravan so that Jon can watch it. On the thematic level, this connects the novel with the type of music that Fisher describes as hauntological, which is 'preoccupied with the way in which technology materialised memory – hence a fascination with television, vinyl records, audiotape, and with the sounds of those records breaking down' (21). Hauntological music, Fisher writes, makes 'use of crackle, the surface noise made by vinyl. Crackle makes us aware that we are listening to a time that is out of joint; it won't allow us to fall into the illusion of presence' (21). The representation of the accumulation of technologies in Rey's caravan could be interpreted in a similar way. Obsolete and outdated technologies do not disappear; in the caravan, they simply accumulate. Instead of the smooth, swiftly forgotten replacement of CDs with MP3s, and videos with DVDs, engaging with Rey's text involves switching between multiple different technological devices. The materiality of the recording of Rey's memories is emphasized. On the level of plot, however, I think it works somewhat differently. Jon arrives at the caravan. He finds the videos, Betamax cassettes, and DVDs, along with all the technology he needs to watch them. Everything is arranged and pre-prepared – the technology exists in the caravan so that Jon can watch the videos and try to make sense of them, which is exactly what he does.

The most striking way in which the reader's accurate anticipation becomes crucial in the novel is through its second major plot strand. Jon becomes obsessed with a woman he meets one day. He believes that she needs him to rescue her. In his narration, he details multiple encounters with her. However, for the reader it is always abundantly clear that he is actually describing multiple different women. It is possible to imagine a novel where this would be a source of suspense and mystery for the reader, but here the women are described as having different haircuts and accents and appearances on the different occasions he encounters them.

> As I get closer I notice that although her hair is still blonde, it's now shorter again, and seems to be styled differently than it was the last couple of times I'd seen her. How did she have the time not only to change her clothes but the style of her hair in the short amount of time it has taken me to walk to the end of the pier. (187)

Moreover, it is absolutely clear that none of the women are remotely interested in Jon, which they make very obvious, and that his dreams of rescuing one of them are always, for the reader, wildly misguided. Jon is running multiple different women together in his mind, creating one composite idealized image without care or interest for the differences between the women. One or more of the women – it is not wholly clear – are migrant sex workers, who are precariously employed by violent men. By the end of the novel, there has been a police raid and the women are taken away. Jon and the reader have entirely different experiences of anticipation in relation to the women. Jon thinks that there is one woman and he needs to rescue her so that he can start a new life somewhere else. The reader sees the yawning gap between this idea and the novel's reality.

Jon is obsessed with a romantic fantasy with its roots deep in the literary tradition of male objectification of women. His uncle Rey's text frequently refers to Petrarch's Laura, and Jon calls his imagined woman Laura too. He therefore misses what is actually more important and interesting about the women he seems to be observing so closely, but in fact is not really looking at or understanding at all. What Jon and the women share is not love, but rather their precarious position as contemporary workers – Jon is unemployed and drifting, the women are scared both of the immigration authorities and their employers. There can, in the novel, be no connection or interaction between them on this basis, however, because Jon does not clearly see or understand them.

Reading the novel is, therefore, an experience of having predictions of the future proved right. Key elements of the plot – the fact that Rey is Jon's biological father, and the differences between the various women Jon interprets as one woman – are clear to the reader long before they are clear to Jon. Reading the novel is not about waiting with a certain excitement for the text's narrating consciousness to draw the threads of the story together, but rather the sensation of already knowing in advance what is going to happen, and then being proved right. If we approach this aspect of novel's plot with the question of precarious time in mind, the temporal experience it creates for its readers has a potentially useful function. One of the things the novel does is provide a temporal experience of a future which comes into being almost exactly as predicted. What the reader anticipates turns out to be what actually happens – and it is a depressing and disappointing experience. No bonds of solidarity are formed between Jon and the women he is obsessed with, and they remain simply images of romantic obsession rather than people in their own right. No one familiar with the Petrarchan tradition of the representation of women that the novel references can be surprised by this outcome.

This attitude, this way of feeling about anticipation that is produced by the interaction with the text, is something that readers might use beyond the text itself, to reframe or give another perspective on, the anxiety about the failure of the past's future to materialize which is associated with precarity today. Perhaps readers might put the book down with an affective inclination, even if it is only a fleeting moment or tendency, towards the surprising and the unpredictable. Perhaps experiencing the inevitability of the plot is a temporal experience that might lay the groundwork for a turn away from anticipation in the sense of predicting the realistic future, towards anticipation in the sense of excitement. The actual effect of any single text depends on questions of circulation and issues of individual interpretation. But because reading is in itself a temporal experience, it provides readers different affective experiences of time which might – in small, subtle ways – work to shift their responses to the difficulties of time in precarity.

Conclusion

In both 'Limited Dreamers' and *Vulgar Things* we find evocations of precarious temporality. Both texts feature characters who have recently lost their jobs and whose identities are presented as provisional and uncertain. In 'Limited Dreamers,' the newly unemployed characters experience the flexible neoliberal labour market in action – even in the local government sector that was once relatively reliable – and their names are tenuous placeholders. In *Vulgar Things*, Jon loses his job and sees himself as a child on video undermining his identity and seeming to doubt his very existence: 'There is no future me . . . He's a ghost' (130). The novel's emphasis on the felt impossibility or non-existence of the future is echoed in the short story, where Schmidt cannot 'think of anything she wanted to happen next, except for that damn dressing gown' (216).

Theoretical accounts of precarious time, like Berlant's, Fisher's and Tsing's, emphasize the sense of stall in the present, the retrospective glance that focuses on the past's hope for the future (as opposed to the actual facts of the past), and the feeling that the future has disappeared. In these texts, we find just this kind of experience of time rendered as subjective experience for the characters. For both Jon and Banana, the possibility of the future is put radically into question; Jon's 'future self' is described as a haunting revenant from the past, and the future is similarly impossible for Banana, who is drawn to objects from childhood – not for childhood memories themselves, but rather because the past was before the multiple disappointments of her current existence.

In this sense, we find in the texts a valuable picture of time as it can be experienced in precarity; a vivid imagining of the disappearing future, and the longing for the sense of expectation about the future that can only now be associated with past time. But narrative time in *Vulgar Things* – the way the text draws its readers into a new experience of temporality – also works to challenge this way of approaching and thinking about time. In *Vulgar Things*, what the reader expects comes to pass, and the novel's conclusion is anticlimactic because it is expected and known in advance. The 'anticipation of retrospection' at work here, then, is one in which anticipation is accurate, and final retrospection adds little that was not already known. For Bourdieu, casualization makes 'the whole future uncertain' and 'prevents all rational anticipation' (82). What we find in *Vulgar Things* is an experience – on a very small and limited scale – of reliable anticipation. But it is one that is dissatisfying and limiting. Reading the novel encourages a desire for surprise and a longing for the unexpected and unpredicted, and, in this way, it can reframe readers' attitudes towards the value of certainty and predictability in the world beyond the text.

Note

1   For full discussions of the complexities of anticipation and retrospection in relation to reading contemporary fiction, see Currie's *The Unexpected* and *About Time*, and Wylot.

Works cited

Berlant, Lauren. *Cruel Optimism*. Duke University Press, 2011.
Bourdieu, Pierre. *Acts of Resistance: Against the New Myths of Our Time*. Translated by Richard Nice. Polity, 1998.
Brooks, Peter. *Reading for the Plot: Design and Intention in Narrative*. Harvard University Press, 1984.
Currie, Mark. *About Time: Narrative, Fiction and the Philosophy of Time*. Edinburgh University Press, 2006.
Currie, Mark. *The Unexpected: Narrative Temporality and the Philosophy of Surprise*. Edinburgh University Press, 2013.
Dowling, William. *Ricoeur on Time and Narrative: An Introduction*. University of Notre Dame Press, 2011.
Fisher, Mark. *Ghosts of My Life: Writings on Depression, Hauntology and Lost Futures*. Zero Books, 2014.
Goldthorpe, Rhiannon. 'Ricoeur, Proust, and the Aporias of Time'. *On Paul Ricoeur: Narrative and Interpretation*, edited by David Wood. Routledge, 2002, pp. 84–101.
Mackintosh, Anneliese. 'Limited Dreamers'. *Any Other Mouth*. Freight Books, 2014, pp. 213–18.
Nankov, Nikita. 'The Narrative of Ricoeur's Time and Narrative'. *The Comparatist*, 2014, pp. 227–49.
Ricoeur, Paul. *Time and Narrative*, vol. 3. Translated by Kathleen Blamey and David Pellauer. Chicago University Press, 1988.
Rourke, Lee. *Vulgar Things*. Fourth Estate, 2014.
Standing, Guy. *The Precariat: The New Dangerous Class*. Bloomsbury, 2014.
Tsing, Anna Lowenhaupt. *The Mushroom at the End of the World: On the Possibility of Life in Capitalist Ruins*. Princeton University Press, 2015.
Wylot, David. *Reading Contingency: The Accident in Contemporary Fiction*. Routledge, 2020.

Chapter 10

MAKE IT NOW

POETRY, PRECARITY AND SECURITY IN JORIE GRAHAM AND GHAYATH ALMADHOUN

Walt Hunter

The experience of time in a poem has helped readers identify and delight in specific types and subgenres of poetry, from the crafted spontaneity of a song to the progressive development of a sonnet. It is common enough to discover poems, across many traditions and histories, that use aesthetic strategies to acknowledge, celebrate, lament or resist the time-boundedness of human lives. Take, for example, Edmund Spenser's 'Epithalamion' (1595): written for Spenser's wedding day, the poem inscribes human time in the very number of its long lines (365, for the days of the year) and in the number of its stanzas (twenty-four, for the hours of the day). Closer to the present, certain experimental US poems investigate how a poem might approach the temporality of daily experience. Bernadette Mayer's *Midwinter Day* (1982) narrates the course of a single day with a combination of diaristic prose-poetry, descriptions of dreams and lullabies. Other poems search for or attempt to enact immersive temporal structures outside of daily human life, lingering 'at the still point of the turning world', as T.S. Eliot puts it in *Four Quartets* (1941) (15). The roundel with its repeating lines, the sestina and its lexical repetitions, and the ballad and its refrains are three patterns of poetry that complicate or undermine their own inevitable linear progression in time. In another category, there are poems that refresh sensations of surprise and astonishment with their sudden beginnings, their interrupting voices and, in general, their uncanny proximity to human speech. From George Herbert's anxious calls – 'I struck the board and cry'd, No More [. . .]' – to H.D.'s vatic apostrophes – 'Whirl up, sea – ' poems can erupt into time through urgent, quickly elapsing utterances (159, 55). Finally, poems can open passages through historical time by employing words taken from discrepant strata of the language: jos charles's *feeld* (2018) is a book of trans love lyrics told in a recreated Middle English, while M. NourbeSe Philip's *Zong!* (2008) tears apart the legalese of a 1783 court case, *Gregson v. Gilbert*, to listen to the haunted syllables of the slaves whose drowning the case condones. Understanding the nature of time in a poem calls attention to its uses in the rituals and catastrophes of personal and collective life, as well as to the ties between a poem and other poems, or between poetry and other kinds of writing. There is, in other words, an elaborate set of contact points between poetic time and historical time, often mediated through the 'poor passing facts' (Lowell 229) of individual figures.

Many claims about poetic time, however, have been curiously denuded of the material circumstances from which these poems emerge, aspects of which can be described using the ethical and political term 'precarity'. This chapter considers one special poetic desire – the intention to stop time altogether, at least for a moment – by looking at two poems that respond directly to the precariousness of life under present forms of historical capitalism. These poems search for forms in which the so-called timeless act of poetic discourse is set not only against the passing of time, but also against the politics of security and safety. My interest in time, poetry and precarious life is continuous with the investigations of several other scholars, poets and theorists who take poetic and philosophical abstractions like 'inspiration' and 'subjectivity' and bring them, as it were, down to earth. In a recent volume called *Poetics and Precarity*, poet and critic Nathaniel Mackey has spoken about breath, black life and precarity.[1] Sarah Dowling has discussed the form of the die-in and the prevalence of the precarious material body in poems by Bhanu Kapil.[2] The nature of time under precarious urgencies – which often have a hurry-up-and-wait type of logic – offers a way to think about contemporary poems that attempt to isolate and dilate a single moment.[3]

Precarity is a loosely defined concept that can refer to the uneven distribution of citizenship, rights, security and welfare for workers both in the Global North and the South, as well as to the constant threat of being stripped of them. Precarity may well be the 'norm' of historical capitalism, mitigated somewhat by the brief period of post-war liberalism. Today, Isabell Lorey suggests that amounts of precarity are managed by governments to keep populations at a minimal 'threshold' of survival (2). The temporality of precariousness has a frozen quality: the feeling, for instance, of being forever in debt, perpetually in asylum or detention. For those on the so-called zero-hour contracts, labour is precarious because the employer stipulates no minimum hours. In return, the employee is not required to work a set number of hours every week. In an infamous version of intermittent employment in the 1990s, Burger King tried to pay its workers only for the time spent actually serving customers (Adams, Freedland and Prassl 4). In political regimes of precarity, the smallest units of time are monetizable: interest on student debt is charged by the day, if not by even smaller units; wages are paid according to minute-by-minute availability of the worker and demand from the consumer. Other recent work on precarity has looked beyond its Eurocentric origins in EuroMayDay protests to conditions of partial citizenship held by refugees.[4] Precarity, in this research, involves the possibility of deportation or repatriation, as a consequence of the temporary contract and of differential inclusion in social welfare and citizenship (Platt et al. 124).

Precarity has, in general, an odd relation to time: while it suggests fragility, it really implies a permanent fragility, or a state of tense expectation without a clear horizon, since maintaining that 'looming threat' is what keeps capital moving and profits growing (Platt et al. 122). Susan Banki writes that 'precarity suggests the *potential* for exploitation and abuse, but not its certain presence. Thus precarious work is not the fact of consistent unemployment, but the looming threat, and perhaps frequent fact, of it' (450). Syrian refugees in Turkey, for instance, are allotted some of the citizenship rights that Turkish citizens have, but occupy an unstable position between citizen and non-citizen, 'neither refugee nor guest' (Baban, Ilcan and Rygiel 53). In the case of construction and domestic workers who travel abroad to Singapore to generate remittances, short-term contracts and restrictive visa policies combine to put the worker at heightened risk. Debt finances the recruitment, training and the reservation of a spot in the labour market (Platt et al. 122). The cultivation of precarity, its careful trimming and daily maintenance, is the joint activity of finance (through debt) and the state (through visa and citizenship policies). It is the work of keeping the right amount of terror and anxiety on the horizon of daily life.

The poems in this chapter by the US poet Jorie Graham and the Syrian-Palestinian-Swedish poet Ghayath Almadhoun rearrange time in certain ways that are not possible in the world. In Graham's 'Ashes' and Almadhoun's 'The Details', the poet stills time into a single moment of perception. Their poetry opens up a temporal space of attention to images, details and the rapturous intuition of a shared fragility. Yet these poems do not appear as monuments or memorials, compensatory fantasies of immortality, of permanence or of poetic artifactuality. Instead, they find a way to gather together and to archive the overwhelming presentness of experience as it passes. I choose these two poems because, first, they recall and revise two nineteenth-century English definitions of a poetic present: Robert Browning's 'good minute' and Dante Gabriel Rossetti's 'moment's monument', which I review later in the chapter. I follow some trails from those earlier poems into the twentieth century before turning to Graham and Almadhoun. Second, these poems deserve close attention because they are clearly embedded in the precarious time of the present, not in a philosophical or transcendent wish for immortality. Their luminous, terrifying 'now' confronts the moment's monetization, the produced fragility of daily life, the labour contract that expires from day to day. In their stricken immediacy, the poems meditate on the relation between multiple types of precariousness – while also being critical or suspicious of casual affiliations between incommensurate dangers.

By pairing the poems, I explore two different political situations in which the stopping of poetic time coincides with the precariousness of contemporary life. My argument confronts, without attempting to answer in definitive terms, the charged question of how to pair disparate poetic texts and traditions: Almadhoun's 'The Details' is translated from Arabic, while Graham's 'Ashes' is written in English. I close the chapter with Almadhoun's poem because it analyses the global connections between the Syrian War and the American empire, and because it contains an explicit critique of the complicity between European culture and Syrian occupation. Graham's poem, meanwhile, thinks towards a global horizon by situating its speaker's perception in the planetary scale of climate change, among other transnational phenomena. I rely, in a sense, on the poets' joint acknowledgement that their writing sits outside any one national culture or tradition. While acknowledging their discrepant contexts and lineages, I emphasize that both these poems translate some of the material conditions of precarious lives into a poetic grappling with time, one that exposes and dwells within the sudden accelerations and frozen moments that structure precarious existences.

One of the generative fictions of poetry has been that it might intercede against precarity – that it might stop time in the name of an impossible immortality. A condition of existential risk, of radical exposure to loss, is one kind of temporal precariousness, an 'excruciating pain' that seems built into poetic speech of the lyrical kind. The idea that a poem might be a 'lyric cry against time' does justice to a common feeling that poetry takes up a melancholic or rageful position against the inevitable passage of time (Cameron 21). In Sharon Cameron's account, one of the few extended treatments of time in English-writing poetry, Emily Dickinson is compelled by a vision of life as a 'landslide of lost things'. Cameron writes, 'the excruciating pain to which her poems give faithful testimony left Dickinson with a radically dislocated sense of time, and sometimes with the illusion of its cessation' (45). In response to an overwhelming sense of loss, poetic imaginations of the past have devised methods of 'securing' or shoring up spots of time.

To trace part of the history of this poetic tendency, I am prompted to turn back first to the nineteenth century by Jorie Graham herself, who begins her collection *Fast* (2017) with an epigraph from Robert Browning: '*Then the good minute goes.//Already how am I so far/Out of that minute?*' Certain late-nineteenth century English poems by Browning and by his contemporary Dante Gabriel Rossetti are peculiarly taken with poetry's failing attempts to occupy time. These poems make time an explicit problem for poetic representation and come up with various solutions, or else narrate their failure. Browning's 'Two in the Campagna', from *Men and Women* (1855), stages a tension between the poetic 'now' and the progress in time that is inherent to narrative. The 'good minute' of a moment of love is impossible to capture in a poem, Browning finds, because to write about it is already to situate it in the past:

X.

No. I yearn upward, touch you close,
Then stand away. I kiss your cheek,
Catch your soul's warmth – I pluck the rose
And love it more than tongue can speak –
Then the good minute goes.

XI.

Already how am I so far
Out of that minute? Must I go
Still like the thistle-ball, no bar,
Onward, whenever light winds blow,
Fixed by no friendly star? (266)

The poem seems to join its readers in real time as it narrates a scene between the two lovers and then stares astonished at how quickly it passes. Browning captures the distance between feeling and the recognition of feeling, but the 'I' is also the writer who cannot make experience present in poetry.

Browning's essential tragedy – 'Already how am I so far/Out of that minute?' – is built into a line of poetry in English from the earliest Marian lyrics through Shakespeare's sonnets to Dante Gabriel Rossetti's 'Sonnet on the Sonnet', the first poem in *The House of Life* (final version 1881). Rossetti's ars poetica begins with a proposition that connects poetic form, time, and built space:

> A Sonnet is a moment's monument –
> Memorial from the Soul's eternity
> To one dead deathless hour. Look that it be,
> Whether for lustral rite or dire portent,
> Of its own intricate fulness reverent:
> Carve it in ivory or in ebony,
> As Day or Night prevail; and let Time see
> Its flowering crest impearled and orient. (127)

Rossetti theorizes a relation between time and poetry: the sonnet's intricacy of constructed form is an emblem of eternity. The sonnet opposes time aesthetically, standing out in contrast to day or night, formally extravagant ('impearled') and exoticized ('orient').

The 'moment's monument' and the 'good minute' are two primarily thematic elements for Browning and Rossetti, both of whom are driven to longer, narrative forms of poetry. Browning gapes at the distance between poetry and the emotion recollected; Rossetti makes poetry the antagonist to time. In some ways, however, these laments for lost time reveal how gendered or localized such conceptions of a poetic 'now' have been in the past. The potential for permanence can be a source of extreme anxiety rather than the object of desire. In the poem 'Medusa' (1923) by Louise Bogan, a woman approaches a house and is frozen to the spot by the mythological creature:

> This is a dead scene forever now.
> Nothing will ever stir.
> The end will never brighten it more than this,
> Nor the rain blur. (4)

Replacing the memorial to the moment – a monument that is, after all, historically gendered and placed under the male gaze – is an allegory of a frozen life from which there is no escape. In another example, Louise Glück's 'The Garden' (1993), the writing of the poem takes place under severe duress. The poet begins her description of a couple planting a garden with 'I couldn't do it again./I can hardly bear to look at it' (16). The vision of the poem takes place against the will of the poet, either as an involuntary memory, in Gluck's poem, or an inescapable condition, in Bogan's. The task of these poems is to end time, not to prolong it – to find a spell to make the scene vanish. In this sense, the contrasting will of the poem to representation and the will of the poem to the abolition of the conditions it represents pull the poem into a taut shape. The stilling of the poem is not compensatory, but rather mimetic of a claustrophobic life, and the drama of the poem is its fight to set time into motion again.

In poetic criticism from Northrop Frye to Jonathan Culler, the rejection, negation or suspension of time helps to define what kind of a thing a poem is. But it is hard to find an example of what might replace narrative – though Franco 'Bifo' Berardi has noted the place of poetic rhythms and refrains in the transformation of social life and Jacques Rancière has found in Keats' inaction an intimation of political equality (132, 248). Typically, however, the names for this non-narrativity tend towards the religious and the metaphysical: 'eternity', in Rossetti's Pre-Raphaelite imagination, 'immortality', in Cameron's account of Dickinson's lyric time, the 'dead scene' in Bogan's poem.[5] In some contemporary poetry, the unattainable term might be 'security', though that word does not appear directly in the poems. The pressure is not between human time and the religious or transcendental terms of eternity and immortality but rather between the present as valued now and the present as 'securitized', in both senses of that word: an investment and an immunity. There are certainly poems that seek to build compensatory structures, construct memorials and monuments of eternity, and purchase insurance for the future through the harvesting of the present. But there are also poems that, instead, hold at bay the desire for security and hold open the 'now' of precarity, defined in the most capacious terms as 'living with the unforeseeable, with contingency' (Lorey 2).[6] These poems and fictions of duration create an aesthetic link to the state of suspended life registered in some political forms of precariousness. The 'meditative space' of the poem, to borrow Claudia Rankine's term, generates a special kind of contemplative urgency in which consciousness is raised to a pitch that is both exhilarating and exhausting (Rankine and Hoover, n.p.).

In the epigraph to Graham's *Fast*, Browning's words set the stage for a series of meditations about time and death. The double meaning of the title *Fast* conflates two kinds of precarity: hunger and speed. Here is the material body under pressure (to echo Sarah Dowling), starving or sped up or both. A third meaning suggests itself: fastness, or security. To make fast: to make secure, to protect. Graham begins the book with a poem called 'Ashes', which itself conjures the eschatological time of 'ashes to ashes, dust to dust'. Here is the first section of the poem, which challenges the reader to make sense of a number of different registers and scales at once:

> Manacled to a whelm. Asked the plants to give me my small identity. No, the planets.
> The arcing runners, their orbit entrails waving, and a worm on a leaf, mold, bells, a
> bower – everything transitioning – unfolding – emptying into a bit more life cell by
>   cell in wind like this
>   sound of scribbling on
>   paper. I think

> I am falling. I remember the earth. Loam sits
> quietly, beneath me, waiting to make of us what it can [. . .] (3)

'Ashes' asks a question and explores its ramifications through dense lines that alternate between the very small and the very large. The question is something like, 'what am I, when everything is changing around me constantly – including me?' I take this to be what 'manacled to a whelm' means: the word 'whelm' means 'surge' and stands in for a notion of precariousness in this poem. Then the speaker looks down: the plants. And up: the planets. What does she resemble? Both are distinct, but both are in movement, manacled to a whelm as well.

Then quite suddenly the poem breaks through to a simile. The 'whelm' of planetary motion and of plant growth is like the movement of the pen making the poem. The poet participates in the 'whelm' by making sounds that are part of it, the 'scribbling' of the pen. Focusing on the pen, and the moment of the poem's own construction, the poet loses a sense of the context and has a feeling of falling. Then she recalls the earth again. 'Ashes' asks an essential human question: How am I part of what is around me, since we are both falling apart? The poet under medical treatment can die; the universe can die as well. Like the planets and the plants, she leaves traces too; what she does while writing contributes to the total sensory impression that tells her she is here, that is, in some sense, the aesthetic accompaniment to her constant movement. Precarity, being manacled to a whelm, registers as aesthetic experience and is identified with literary production itself. 'Ashes' comes close to making the reader present in the moment of its composition – the sound of the scribbling on paper that produces the words one is reading. The poem does this in part by eschewing verbs and generating participle after participle, twenty-one different words that end in '-ing'. The result is a poem that seems to occupy a perpetual present. The poem tries as long as it can to be part of the world, like the plants and planets. More specifically, Graham's poem wants us to experience the aesthetic pleasure of the 'whelm', not only a commentary on it.

But the exhilaration of change gives way to the experience of degradation and depreciation, what the poem calls 'thinning', as the body of the speaker thins under treatment. And this 'thinning' calls to mind, in the poem's expansive sense of common precarity, the melting of glaciers:

> [. . .] the question of place hanging over me
> year after year – me thinning but almost still here in spirit, far in, far back, behind,
> privy to insect, bird, fish – are there nothing but victims –
> that I could become glass – that after that we would become glacial
> melt – moraine revealing wheatgrass, knotgrass, a prehistoric frozen mother's
>   caress – or a finger
>   about to touch
> a quiet skin, to run along its dust [. . .] (3)

The most difficult part of the poem to follow is this leap between scales of precarity. The poet imagines a 'prehistoric frozen mother's/caress', an image that prompts her to wonder 'on whom'. Touch is, of course, one aesthetic sense that a poem simply cannot provide. The dream of the poem, to join its own aesthetic production with the 'whelm' and the 'thinning' of the planet, vanishes with the return to the actual world, at which point the poem ends:

> Now listen for the pines, the bloom, its glittering, the wild hacking of sea, bend in each stream, eddy of bend – listen – hear all skins raveling, unending – hear one skin clamp down upon what is no longer
> missing.
> *Here you are*, says a voice in the light, the trapped light. Be happy. (3)

The poem begins with movement, with a vertiginous scepticism of personality and existence, and with a fragment of a sentence. It comes to an end in presence, in otherness and in an address from a voice: here you are! But the security of the poem's conclusion – 'be happy' – is also the closure of its dream; what's lost, in the fastness, is the fast scribbling, the green growth, the melting of the glacier, the moment of birth, the movement of the sea, all the grand sensorium of the present, of precarity writ very large. Graham dramatizes the limits of what might be called co-precarity – the cancerous body and the melting glacier – by tuning her poem to the aesthetic dimension of the whelm. The poem can only go so far, however, in its thought experiment. It cannot ultimately capture, in scribbling, the human interdependency that the austerely thinning realms of the plants, planets and glaciers lacks. In this sense, the poem's shuttling between the precarious body and the dying universe is too much reality for it to take. There was the temptation of falling, of immersing the self in the whelm, even a delight in the sensuality of what amounts to total destruction, but this impulse gives way to the relief at being discovered as a distinct body, still here.

The next poem imagines a very different kind of destruction and constant exposure to risk – not the planetary time of glaciers melting and the universe dying, but the human-made time of American and European wars. Ghayath Almadhoun's title, *Adrenalin*, calls back the acceleration that propels Graham's *Fast*. Part of the conceptual challenge for both books is to develop a meditative style that is adequate to the adrenalized body of precarious life, the experience of the 'whelm'. Moving from Graham, born in Italy, educated in France, and currently a professor at Harvard, to Almadhoun, a Palestinian-Syrian-Swedish refugee, involves resituating the poetry in the destruction of the Syrian War. Almadhoun was born in the Palestinian refugee camp Yarmouk, from which 5,000 Palestinians were recently displaced (Najjar n.p.). The setting for Almadhoun's poetry – this collection was written in 2012 – includes the longer legacies of European colonialism in the Middle East. In this context, the emblem for security from precarity is 'Fortress Europe', the lethal combination of official migration quotas and black market traders who regulate the flow of displaced persons through the Mediterranean and beyond.

'The Details', a long poem from *Adrenalin*, takes place in the expanse of a single minute, the minute in which a bullet enters a body and kills a Syrian. Almadhoun begins with a series of italicized questions about the death that puncture the platitudes circulated by Western media:

Is it friendly fire?
How can it be
When I've never made friends with fire in my life? (23)

The poem's language moves between an ironic distance and a deadly serious proximity: 'I was exploring the difference between revolution and war when a bullet passed through my body' (24). This moment of death fills with details:

> The moment the soul begins to escape through the little gate the bullet has opened, things become clearer, the theory of relativity turns into something self-evident, mathematical equations that used to be vague become a simple matter, the names of classmates we've forgotten come back to us, life is suddenly illuminated in perfect detail, the childhood bedroom, mother's milk, the first trembling orgasm, the streets of the camp, the portrait of Yasser Arafat, the smell of coffee with cardamom inside the house, the sound of the morning call to prayer, Maradona in Mexico in 1986, and you. (26)

The tone of the poem moves quickly from irony ('the theory of relativity turns into something self-evident') to a cascade of personal memories: the refugee camp, coffee, the call to prayer, a famous world cup goal by Diego Maradona and, possibly, a lover, or else the reader: 'you'. The overcharging of the moment with details is one of the moves the poem keeps repeating.

Almadhoun's poem searches for a language adequate to the limit experience of time that it inhabits, but keeps encountering the bad faith of poetic representation: 'It was the most beautiful war I've been in in my life, full of metaphors and poetic images, I remember how I used to sweat adrenalin and piss black smoke' (25). Here, the poetic 'now' becomes both a spur for the poem's beauty and a problem for its politics: 'When I became a member of the Union of the Dead, my dreams improved' (26). The question Almadhoun poses is something like this: Does poetry, at least the poetry of 'metaphors and poetic images', offer a problematic consolation? The words 'clearer', 'self-evident', 'simple', 'perfect detail' and 'improved', as well as the rush of memory and of sensuality – all of this material fills the minute of death with a fantasy of repair that must be tested against the atrocity upon which the poem is constructed.

And that is precisely how 'The Details' ends – not only with the scepticism of poetic language, but also with an ambivalent series of exhortations. The final section of the poem, a catalogue of European hypocrisy, can be read as a call to reality or description and away from the decoys of poetic language. Right before this final section, Almadhoun writes, 'come, let's give up poetry, exchange the songs of summer for gauze dressings and harvest poems for surgical thread' (26).

Then Almadhoun juxtaposes the artefacts of European culture and the histories of destruction that surround them:

> Throw away the Renaissance and bring on the inquisition,
> Throw away European civilization and bring on the Kristallnacht [. . .]
> Throw away Van Gogh's starry sky and bring on the severed ear,
> Throw away Picasso's Guernica and bring on the real Guernica with its smell of fresh blood.
> We need these things now, we need them to begin the celebration. (27)

Almadhoun's poem moves us, step by step, towards what it calls 'the celebration'. It begins with the remote talk about 'friendly fire', as though in a news broadcast; it continues by trying to write a poem in the minute of death, a death the poet himself escaped; and it concludes with a plea to pay attention to the precarity that has been produced by securing Fortress Europe.

Both Graham and Almadhoun employ thought experiments that drive their poems forward: Graham imagines her depleted body as a thinning glacier, then finds herself called back from the terrifying consequences of that relation. Almadhoun imagines himself as a Syrian in Damascus who has just been shot by a sniper. Although neither poet occupies a secure position, both attempt to see what relation their own precariousness has to a larger scale of insecurity. The motive or impulse behind these two poems could be stated in the following way. The sense of personal instability or danger sends the poet out in the world, imaginatively, to see who or what might be there. Graham is drawn to the aesthetic details of things in flux, and Almadhoun to the ashes of a city under sniper fire, a city from which he managed to escape. The poem is not an emblem of security, nor of the exercise of control or flight to safety. Instead, their poems risk inhabiting even greater scenes of precarity. Security is not only impossible, but undesirable, since the immunity for some is so often purchased with the precarity of the many. Even as they take back the present moment, imaginatively thwarting its inevitable passing, Graham and Almadhoun refuse the weaponized dream of immunity. They seek their images of precarious lives, human and non-human, in the space between uneven exposure to danger, finding in the relation between scales of insecurity both the ashes and the details. Rather than providing a substitute for the fleeting present, these poems provide a supplement: they exist in a time, or at a speed, that is a reminder of the lived experiences from which they emerge and to which they give form.

Today the desire for immortality appears not as much in the quasi-religious terms of Browning, Dickinson or Rossetti as in violent claims to security, from the white nationalism that powers the construction of border walls to the upward redistribution of wealth through the future-oriented logic of financial derivatives. When a worker's risk is understood as an investment, a migrant's debt is underscored as the only route to survival, and, in general, the value of the present is brutally extracted in order to secure the future, then the obsession with 'now' in various contemporary poems takes on a political charge. The poetic time of the present comprises the emergent precarities of social insecurity, of intermittent work contracts, of financial speculation and of personal exposure to risk, racialized violence and affliction. These are what constitute the temporal unmaking of the present. The meditative openings of poetic time, the preservation of the aesthetic density of ordinary experience and the capacious archiving of the present offer an alternative vision to the racist politics of security, for which the 'immortality' of global elites is created by manipulating the precariousness of others.

Notes

1 Mackey writes that Black music 'insists that we can, for a time at least, breathe, that what we do with breath, from which, to belabor the obvious, animacy, agency and all possibility of action arise, matters most' (18).
2 Dowling argues for a 'shift in critical emphasis: from the psychological precarity of the "I" and the economic precarity of the worker, to the physical precarity of the body as matter and as flesh' (156).
3 Neferti X.M. Tadiar writes, 'if financial reason has moved into the person, becoming a practical form of life, the time frame of its philosophy, *whereby the future is already seen as the present*, shapes and defines the new temporal protocols and conditions of lived life' (21; italics mine).
4 Brett Neilson and Ned Rossiter are somewhat less inclined to want to use the term outside its European provenance: 'the discourse of precarity does not translate on a global scale as a descriptor of contemporary labor precisely because of its connection as a political-analytical concept and mobilizing device within predominantly European-based social movements responding to the erosion of the welfare state' (54–5).
5 Attempts to specify the time of poetry often require some leaps of faith. Grossman describes the beginning of the poem as prompted by the 'dislocation [. . .] of the relationship of a subject and an object' and the closure of a poem as the addition of 'some new cognitive element [. . .] to the relationship of subject and object'. In Grossman's terms, the beginning of the poem is analogous to 'Creation', the end of the poem to 'apocalypse' (218). For Grossman, the time frame in which the poem takes place is closer to the temporality of scripture than to other forms of narrative time, including the epic. Lewis suggests that '[the] saying of only one thing at a time, without reservations, modifying parentheses, mental complications of any kind, is the lyric's chief term of reference' (5). I am less interested in Lewis's 'one thing' than in the severely circumscribed time of its articulation. In one of the most compelling accounts of poetry and time, Helen Vendler has written of the 'binocular vision' of poets contemplating death and yet maintaining their attention on the life that continues around them: 'he feels that both are equally true, and must be simultaneously held in a binocular frame in which neither can obliterate or dominate the other' (4). See also Culler on the 'special temporality' of the apostrophe (149).
6 Lorey draws out the difference between regimes based on security and regimes that profit from insecurity: 'contrary to the old rule of a domination that demands obedience in exchange for protection, neoliberal governing proceeds primarily through social insecurity, through regulating the minimum of assurance while simultaneously increasing instability' (2).

Works cited

Adams-Prassl, Abi, Mark R. Freedland and Jeremias Adams-Prassl. 'The "Zero-Hours Contract": Regulating Casual Work or Legitimating Precarity?' Oxford Legal Studies Research Paper No.11/2015, 2015, pp. 1–21.
Almadhoun, Ghayath. *Adrenalin*. Translated by Catherine Cobham. Action Books, 2017.
Baban, Feyzi, Suzan Ilcan and Kim Rygiel. 'Syrian Refugees in Turkey: Pathways to Precarity, Differential Inclusion, and Negotiated Citizenship Rights'. *Journal of Ethnic and Migration Studies*, vol. 43, 2017, pp. 41–57.
Banki, Susan. 'Precarity of Place: A Complement to the Growing Precariat Literature'. *Global Discourse*, vol. 3, no. 3–4, 2013, pp. 450–63.
Berardi, Franco. 'Bifo'. *The Uprising: On Poetry and Finance*. Semiotext(e), 2012.
Bogan, Louise. *The Blue Estuaries*. Farrar, Straus and Giroux, 1995.
Browning, Robert. *Robert Browning's Poetry*. Edited by James F. Loucks and Andrew M. Stauffer. W.W. Norton & Company, 2007.
Cameron, Sharon. *Lyric Time: Dickinson and the Limits of Genre*. Johns Hopkins University Press, 1979.
charles, jos. *feeld*. Milkweed, 2018.
Culler, Jonathan. *The Pursuit of Signs*. Routledge, 1981.
Dowling, Sarah. 'Supine, Prone, Precarious'. *Poetics and Precarity*, edited by Myung Mi Kim and Cristanne Miller. State University of New York, 2018, pp. 145–60.
Eliot, T.S. *Four Quartets*. Faber and Faber, 1972.
Glück, Louise. *The Wild Iris*. The Ecco Press, 1992.
Graham, Jorie. *Fast*. The Ecco Press, 2017.
Greer, Ian. 'Welfare Reform, Precarity, and the Re-commodification of Labour'. *Work, Employment and Society*, vol. 30, no. 1, 2016, pp. 162–73.
Grossman, Allen, with Mark Halliday. *The Sighted Singer: Two Works on Poetry for Writers and Readers*. Johns Hopkins University Press, 1992.
Han, Clara. 'Precarity, Precariousness, and Vulnerability'. *Annual Review of Anthropology*, vol. 47, no. 1, 2018, pp. 331–43.
H.D. *Collected Poems 1912–1944*. Edited by Louis L. Martz. New Directions, 1983.
Herbert, George. *The Temple and a Priest to the Temple*. J.M. Dent & Co., 1902.
Langbaum, Robert. *The Poetry of Experience*. Norton, 1957.
Lerner, Ben. 'The Future Continuous: Ashbery's Lyric Mediacy'. *boundary2*, vol. 37, no. 1, 2010, pp. 201–13.
Lewis, C. Day. *The Lyric Impulse*. Harvard University Press, 1965.
Lorey, Isabell. *State of Insecurity: Government of the Precarious*. Translated by Aileen Derieg. Verso, 2015.
Lowell, Robert. *New Selected Poems*. Edited by Katie Peterson. Farrar, Straus and Giroux, 2017.
Mackey, Nathaniel. 'Breath and Precarity: The Inaugural Robert Creeley Lecture in Poetry and Poetics'. In *Poetics and Precarity*, edited by Myung Mi Kim and Cristanne Miller. State University of New York, 2018, pp. 1–30.
Najjar, Farah. 'Syria's Yarmouk Camp: From a "War on Stomachs" to "Annihiliation."' *Al Jazeera*, 24 April 2018, https://www.aljazeera.com/news/2018/04/syria-yarmouk-camp-war-stomachs-annihilation-180423212111918.html
Neilson, Brett and Ned Rossiter. 'Precarity as a Political Concept, or, Fordism as Exception'. *Theory, Culture & Society*, vol. 25, no. 7–8, 2008, pp. 51–73.

Ng, Brian. 'Milton, Ashbery, Time'. *Medium*, 10 December 2016, https://medium.com/@nwk/milton-ashbery-time-67a88cab9d20

Pater, Walter. *The Renaissance*. Random House, 1873.

Philip, M. NourbeSe. *Zong!* Wesleyan University Press, 2008.

Platt, Maria, et al. 'Debt, Precarity and Gender: Male and Female Temporary Labour Migrants in Singapore'. *Journal of Ethnic and Migration Studies*, vol. 43, 2017, pp. 119–36.

Rancière, Jacques. 'The Politics of the Spider'. *Studies in Romanticism*, vol. 50, no. 2, 2011, pp. 239–50.

Rankine, Claudia and Elizabeth Hoover. 'Poet Claudia Rankine on Wounds We Should Not Forget'. *Sampsonia Way*, 12 November 2010, https://www.sampsoniaway.org/literary-voices/2010/11/12/poet-claudia-rankine-on-wounds-we-shouldnt-forget/

Rossetti, Dante Gabriel. *Collected Poetry and Prose*. Edited by Jerome McGann. Yale University Press, 2009.

Ruefle, Mary. *Madness, Rack, and Honey: Collected Lectures*. Wave, 2012.

Tadiar, Neferti X. M. 'Life-Times of Disposability within Global Neoliberalism'. *Social Text*, vol. 31, no. 2, 2013, pp. 19–48.

Valéry, Paul. *The Art of Poetry*. Translated by Denise Folliot. Vintage Books, 1958.

Vendler, Helen. *Last Looks, Last Books: Stevens, Plath, Lowell, Bishop, Merrill*. Harvard University Press, 2010.

Chapter 11

FINDING TIME IN COMMON

SPECULATIVE FICTION AND THE PRECARIAT
IN ROBINSON'S *NEW YORK 2140*

Bryan Yazell

Set a century into the future, Kim Stanley Robinson's *New York 2140* imagines a scenario in which the precariat rally together and transform the political landscape. But neither the precariat nor the conditions for their radicalization are inventions of speculative fiction. Instead, what the novel provides is a future case when these parts finally cohere together to spark the collective action so sorely lacking in the present. *New York 2140* takes place well after rising sea tides have displaced countless coastal populations, which have fled from drowned areas and resettled in the land that remains above water. Through collective work, this vulnerable population has built homes under the harshest conditions; for capitalists, on the other hand, 'refugee capital' represents yet another opportunity to profit from precarious labour (206). After all, financial institutions in both our present and this imagined future depend on precarious workers going into debt, taking out loans and trying to spend their way into a stable life. In short, precarization continues unabated in the novel's future world. The radical break from this familiar precarity cycle comes, however, in the form of a simple declaration: 'we're all wet, we're all in the precariat, we're all pissed off' (400). Charlotte, a civil servant, decides she has had enough of this exploitation and – more importantly – recognizes the need to rally and organize the precariat together around shared actions such as mass demonstrations and boycotts of debt and mortgage payments. In relatively short order, this plan actually produces the results it seeks. Charlotte is elected to Congress on a radical-left platform, the financial market is brought to heel, and the US government – facing a furious and organized precariat – puts the taxpayer first when the banks inevitably ask for a bailout. Solidarity among the precariat in the future makes all these things achievable, but this simple premise is also the most elusive for readers in the present.

As the explicit reference to the precariat suggests, Robinson demonstrates how speculative fiction theorizes both precarity and anti-precarity politics. Throughout his career, Robinson has drawn from the pages of critical theory on the way to becoming one of the most acclaimed speculative authors today.[1] Within *New York*

2140, for example, references to the precariat appear alongside quotations from cultural theoreticians such as Fredric Jameson and Gilles Deleuze. What emerges from this encounter between genre and theory in the novel is a keen awareness of the complex role temporality plays in shaping the precariat's potential for solidarity. In this case, I refer to precarity and the precariat in the sense developed most prominently by the economist Guy Standing. Standing uses the precariat to denote those in a perpetual state of economic insecurity, which includes everyone from displaced migrants, indebted students, and workers locked in a perpetual cycle of temporary contracts (*New* 6). Standing is distinct from other theorists of precarity owing to his sense of the precariat as a 'class-in-the-making', a group that – despite its obvious internal differences in terms of education or specific labour practices – must acknowledge its shared interests and make its presence felt to agitate for a 'politics of paradise' (*New* vii).

For those among the ranks of the precariat, however, this quasi-utopian agenda hits a wall in the very act of imagining utopia. According to Standing, exposure to precarity encourages one to think in terms of returning to a time of perceived security. Members of the populist right, for example, may recognize the problem of chronic job insecurity today, but their political agenda involves returning to a time when whiteness connoted strict social privilege, a vision that is inherently exclusive rather than inclusive in its imagined bonds of solidarity. As is explained at length in the following text, temporality is something that divides rather than unites different groups of the precariat; feeling fundamentally insecure in the present, they tend to look to the past or future for a sense of stability. In view of this problem, *New York 2140* reworks the concept of the commons, which typically connotes shared public spaces, to better account for time as well as space as assets to be shared in common. New York's semi-submerged areas gather precarious life in ways that, according to the speculative framing of the novel, extrapolate from and amplify precarity as it exists today. The flooded metropolis thus provides readers with an imagined space for seeing precarity's future and, most pressing for Robinson, its embeddedness in the present. To elaborate on this last point in particular, this chapter connects utopian fiction criticism from Ursula K. Le Guin to sources like Standing and David Harvey, who press for reclaiming time from the so-called precarity trap, which monopolizes one's time and thereby one's capacity for dreaming alternatives to precarity. Showcasing precarity's longevity in the future, the novel makes apparent time's unequal distribution in the present among the precariat. If time appears to be on the side of widening inequality, then radical action in the present is more rather than less pressing.

The ways in which speculative writing such as Robinson's assists in the project of imagining temporality in common are at the centre of the pages that follow. The goals of this chapter are twofold: to develop the notion of temporality underlying writings on the precariat and to emphasize more generally speculative fiction's value as a resource for theorizing precarity and anti-precarity politics.[2] Although the idea that science fiction and related genres often depict precarious life – whether it be in the post-apocalyptic desert or in an lonely space station – may come as little surprise to experts in this field, it is rarely mentioned in connection with what critics call the literature of precarity. Instead, scholars have tended to focus on narratives that realistically depict contemporary scenes of precarious labour – such as the office or the housing estate – or otherwise reflect the experience of precarity for, among others, the temporary worker, the indebted postgraduate and the immigrant.[3] Such accounts help explain how literature addresses precarity as it crosses traditional lines of class and national affiliation. But the relative absence of speculative fiction from these critical accounts warrants correction, since it risks rearticulating the conventional sense either that the genre retreats from serious issues of the world or that its popularity with audiences comes at the cost of overly reductive depictions of serious topics like racial difference or political strife. As Tom Moylan points out, speculative fiction 'does not necessarily mean a debilitating escape *from* reality because it can also lead to an empowering escape *to* a very different way of thinking about, and possibly of being in, the world' (xvii). The present chapter stresses the social relevance of speculative fiction by placing it into close proximity with theorizations of precarity, an issue that cuts to the core of everyday life for populations around the globe.

Precarious time

Before unpacking speculative fiction's capacity for addressing precarity, it is necessary first to consider the overarching theorization of the precariat in relation to political action. While avoiding Standing's reference to class-based politics, political theorist Isabell Lorey nonetheless emphasizes the essential state of precariousness that defines our social life. Precariousness defines who we are, since we are all embedded in social and ecological networks that act upon us while we act upon them. In simple terms, living in society entails a level of unavoidable vulnerability. The problem, Lorey continues, is that an array of legal, economic and political institutions distribute this vulnerability unevenly, so that certain people feel their precarity more acutely – which manifests, for example, in the form of unstable employment or inaccessible healthcare – while the wealthiest effectively know very little of insecurity at all (Lorey 12). In view of this inequality, Judith Butler outlines an anti-precarity politics that essentially galvanizes the various precarious groups into a coalition that, while not collapsing this inherently diverse population into a single voice or identity, nonetheless might 'reorient politics on the Left' in response to entrenched neoliberalism (Butler 28).

There remains substantial disagreement over the nature of solidarity among the precariat between theorists like Butler and Lorey on one end and Standing on the other. Standing conceives of the precariat as a 'class-in-the-making', which may yet become a 'class-for-itself' in the more conventional Marxist sense of class (*New* 7). In contrast, Butler and Lorey are more interested in forging alliances between the disparate groups within the precariat around common interests. The distinction here is important, and for the purposes of this chapter I use the term 'solidarity' in the sense inspired by Raymond Williams's description of building the 'good community': action that draws together 'all and any who can contribute to the advance in consciousness which is the common need' (320). For Williams, addressing the 'common need' requires a coalition of people that cuts across traditional class lines – since the common, after all, is inherently open to everyone. Williams imagines a 'common culture' resulting from this work, one that does not constrain its members to predetermined practices but instead is open to all and thereby always changing to reflect the input of its collective membership. Moreover, this form of solidarity around common needs must act in the present since 'we can only, now, listen to and consider whatever may be offered and take up what we can' (320). To be sure, Williams writes well before the semantic codification of precarity and the precariat along the lines of what Standing, Butler and Lorey describe. Nonetheless, theorists of precarity agree that such acts of common purpose are necessary in order to redress growing socio-economic inequality in contemporary society.

But not all members of the precariat share the same sense of the world that they want to create. According to Standing, a primary obstacle to generating solidarity among the precariat is lingering disagreement over not only who matters, but *when*. Indeed, different conceptualizations of time are key to his presentation of the 'three varieties of the precariat': reactionary 'atavists', who 'tend to relate their sense of deprivation and frustration to a lost past, real or imagined'; the 'nostalgics', 'who have a strong sense of relative deprivation by virtue of having no *present*, no home'; and the 'progressives', the highly educated group who 'experience in their irregular labour [...] a sense of relative deprivation and status frustration, because they have no sense of future' ('Precariat' 7–8). By describing the precariat as a class-in-the-making, Standing is interested in fostering solidarity among this group in the most practical sense: voting for their interests to support mutually beneficial policies such as a universal living wage as well as punitive taxes on absentee property owners. But political participation alone is not enough to enact this reform agenda, since any particular group within the precariat that is aware of their insecurity is likely to have a dramatically different sense of when security was (or will be) lost, and consequently what direction they would like the political system to move in order to redress this loss. In short, this problem is better understood as a disagreement not between the left and the right so much as between the past and the future. Standing's classification of the precariat suggests that the political is fundamentally linked to the temporal, so to address this temporal disunity will likely generate a more politically unified precariat.

If time is a problem for the precariat, then speculative fiction clarifies how solidarity might be found in the present via better recognition of a shared temporality. For the genre's scholars, it is a common refrain that speculative texts are less about the future than they are about the present. In fact, Rebekah Sheldon argues that speculative fiction should be understood as a type of historical fiction due to its reliance on past precedents for imagining future and present phenomena (207). In general terms, speculative narratives understand that our perception of time – our sense of history and our fears, concerns or hopes for the future – informs how we feel about ongoing events. To subject this underlying temporality to scrutiny in turn invites refreshed or reoriented social imaginaries in the present. In other words, we should avoid the temptation to look to the future as the time when things will happen and instead focus on how these futuristic scenarios reflect our understanding of today. Echoing this sentiment, speculative author Ursula K. Le Guin warns against looking for utopia only in the future. 'It seems that the utopian imagination is trapped', she observes, 'like capitalism and industrialism and the human population, in a one-way future consisting only of growth' (85). To break this monopoly on the imagination, she argues, authors must generate a radical or utopian imaginary that is at once grounded in the past and producible in the present. She concludes: 'If utopia is a place that does not exist, then surely (as Lao Tzu would say) the way to get there is by the way that is not a way. And in the same vein, the nature of the utopia I am trying to describe is such that if it is to come, it must exist already' (93). Le Guin's utopian thinking is more about recovering the ways of seeing the world that are rooted in history than it is about exploring entirely new, unexplored subjects. Speculative narratives in this tradition do not look to the future to invent a way out of the intractable morass of neoliberalism or colonialism; instead, they put into perspective the long stretch of history that, running through the present, contains the conditions for making the utopian turn a reality. For Le Guin and her literary inheritors like Robinson,[4] utopian thinking must produce a 'habitable present', a sense of time that empowers radical thought by embracing diverse voices and the disorderly present (87). The conditions for utopian thinking along these lines have existed at different points in time; the question for speculative authors should therefore be, why not then? And why not now?

Le Guin's theorization of utopia in speculative writing situates how the genre not only represents the scale of precarity, but can also promote an anti-precarity imaginary.[5] Standing claims that solidarity can only come after the various groups constituting the precariat recognize themselves as vulnerable while also agreeing that this vulnerability is shared in common with others ostensibly unlike themselves. The problem, as noted earlier, is that these groups understand their insecurity in relation to time in dramatically different ways, which results in contrasting political programs. The utopian orientation to speculative writing works with this same understanding of time in mind. Le Guin's utopian thinking helps to clarify the points of connection between speculative fiction, precarity and time. To produce a more radical imaginary, Le Guin states, speculative fiction must invite its readers to find a temporality in common – that is to say, a habitable present that operates on the basis of shared embeddedness in the social. Her formulation understands the intersection of time and space as the basis for inspiring more utopian thinking and, potentially, a more equitable society.

The connection of time and space in Le Guin's habitable present extends beyond utopian narratives. David Harvey likewise calls for expanding conventional understandings of the commons, which tend to focus on public spaces, to better account for its temporal dimensions. Too many arguments about the commons, Harvey writes, focus on reclaiming public lands that have been subject to capitalist enclosure. To look only to these historical cases overlooks the various ways that the commons are produced and then subject to privatization before our very eyes. The battle over gentrification illustrates this last point. Through their collective work, residents raise the profile of their neighbourhood only for capital to seize upon it and subject it to enclosure – namely, by raising rents to translate an otherwise intangible value like community character into monetary value. In view of this example, Harvey concludes: 'The common is not, therefore, something extant once upon a time that has since been lost, but something that [. . .] is continuously being produced' (105). Taken together, Le Guin and Harvey bring into focus two essential points to elucidate how precariat solidarity might, in the form of the commons, find its footing. First, it is critical that the commons as a concept stretch beyond physical space and include shared assets like time. Second, the commons should be understood as something that both existed in the past and is also produced in the present. Ultimately, they each understand that finding time in common is a struggle because we are not accustomed to recognizing how we share precarious time with each other in the same way we might recognize sharing precarious spaces. The concept of the habitable present overlaps with Williams's good community and Harvey's commons to the extent all point to the present as the moment when the tools for building a more equitable society are already in place. The key for each is to find the means for tearing down the imaginative barriers that have us believe that time is something experienced alone rather than in common with others.

Such insights guide my interpretation of Robinson's *New York 2140*, a case study for speculative fiction's capacity to produce a vision of the habitable present in the context of precarity on the one hand and global warming on the other. In the novel, as is true in general, climate change and precarity are thoroughly linked phenomena. While climate change affects the entire globe, exposure to the worst effects is not evenly distributed. Moreover, as Stephanie LeMenager notes, extreme weather fundamentally calls 'attention to the profoundly ecological, interdependent state of humanity' (221). This state of catastrophic precariousness is especially evident in Robinson's novel, which is set well after climate change has already dramatically altered the face of the planet. While this chapter treats *New York 2140* as an example of the speculative genre, it is important to note its relation to climate fiction (or cli-fi), a label denoting speculative fiction specifically concerned with the future consequences of anthropogenic climate change. The works emerging in this field offer valuable insights for scholars of precarity inasmuch as they all share an interest in addressing the global insecurity that climate change poses – along with the unequal distribution of this insecurity. Cli-fi texts like Robinson's, moreover, present scenarios in which extreme weather and the sense of precariousness it generates are not apocalyptic, one-time events but rather the new normal. This framing in turn moves away from understanding precarization as the result of any single event or crisis and rather as a slow, violent process that extends across time.[6] In short, *New York 2140*'s concern for precarious life is not anomalous but reflects cli-fi's shared interest in depicting the fundamental state of precariousness that follows anthropogenic climate change. By invoking the precariat in particular, Robinson's novel leads the way in highlighting how the emergent cli-fi genre can offer insight into not only environmental-related precarity but precarization as it unfolds across traditional class lines in the present.

New York 2140: *Showing and feeling precarity*

Robinson's novel takes up the problem of precarization and amplifies it, imagining spaces where precarious lives gather and proliferate squarely in the centre of social life. In Robinson's account, the New York City of the twenty-second century is a semi-submerged metropolis. In the intervening period from the present to this future, two successive 'pulses' or inflection points in the melting of the polar ice cap resulted in cataclysmic rises in the sea level, which thoroughly wrecked the coastlines around the globe and displaced the populations living there (34). But despite this widespread violence, New York City subsists as a major population hub largely because innovative residents over time have constructed a series of canals and skyward pedestrian bridges to turn the city into what they call a 'SuperVenice' (76). If the city is precarious as a whole, some neighbourhoods are markedly more vulnerable than others. Uptown is, for the time, safe from the water, while downtown consists of an 'intertidal zone' that is literally precarious: it is an interstitial place between the fully submerged (and uninhabitable) zone and the point in the city still fully above water, and which continues more or less as it did before the climate collapse. While the skyscrapers rise above scenes of disorder, the intertidal zone is thoroughly enmeshed in 'uncertainty and doubt' (126).

In presenting this precarious space, Robinson's novel extends a speculative fiction tradition of staging social critique by extrapolating 'from actually existing trends' (Davis 223). In other words, the text's imaginative setting works, so to speak, inasmuch as readers still recognize a compelling connection to the present. Darko Suvin's axiomatic account of science fiction is helpful here: settings such as the SuperVenice in the novel ask readers to consider points of overlap between these ostensibly foreign worlds and their own. The overlap must be believable insofar as it produces what Suvin describes as cognitive estrangement, a feasible plot device or setting – such as a world-changing scientific discovery or event – that challenges the readers' assumptions about their empirical surroundings and their social conventions (7–8). While speculative writings might deal with fantastical differences, Suvin reminds us, they must still be plausible at their core. As critics following Suvin have elaborated, this cognitive aspect tasks readers with evaluating the mimetic limits to the speculative narratives they encounter, thereby providing them with an imaginative frame of reference in order to 'reveal new social and intellectual possibilities' (Stableford 18). Thus, the interstitial societies in speculative fiction provide an estranging lens to see the world outside these narratives.

As the staging suggests, the primary struggle in *New York 2140* involves the precarious community in the intertidal zone defending their homes from wealthy interests who see it as a development opportunity. The squatters, refugees, radicals and other groups who settled in the ostensibly non-inhabitable space of the intertidal zone have successfully proven that a community can, in fact, thrive there. The ramshackle living spaces in the zone lend it a bohemian character that has made it a destination for tourists and, consequently, a desirable project for redevelopment. The enduring liminality of the intertidal zone, however, is a problem for capital. Franklin, a financier in the novel, explains the intertidal's ambiguous status explicitly: 'Who owns it? No one! Or everyone! It was neither private property nor governmental property, and therefore, some legal theorists ventured, it was perhaps some kind of return of the commons' (119). The cast of characters in the book reflects at once the diversity and the collective integrity that the novel elsewhere references in relation to the commons. As in the case with the precariat, the 'commons' is a term loaded with theoretical implications. At first glance, the references to the commons in *New York 2140* call to mind the very concept that Harvey wishes to move beyond: physical spaces that are open to all. All of the protagonists live in the same building, the Met Tower, which itself is semi-submerged in the intertidal. But their socio-economic status differs widely, from the finance trader Franklin, all the way down to Stefan and Roberto, a pair of children who squat in the unobserved spaces in and around the building. The antagonist in the novel is nothing less than capitalism itself, which – more than any single individual or corporate entity – is to blame for the precarious condition the characters find themselves in. As the novel makes clear, capital has essentially locked society in a repeating cycle of 'creative destruction' – a term popularized by the economist Joseph Schumpeter that the novel uses frequently – where markets push the economy and the environment alike to utter collapse, which in turn creates a 'great investment opportunity' for financial institutions that meanwhile promote 'more police state and more austerity' to cover their losses (144).

But the novel also pushes for a more encompassing sense of the commons, one that situates both space and time as shared components for forging solidarity. Robinson not only invites the reader to connect the futuristic SuperVenice to the rising wealth gap and sea levels observable today, it encourages us to think about forging bonds of solidarity in the present as well. In other words, the text addresses what Standing describes as the temporal disunity of the precariat as a class-in-the-making. Mutt, another resident of the Met, makes this last point especially clear: 'Have you ever noticed that our building is a kind of actor network that can do things? [. . .] we have all the right players here to change the world' (399–400). If the novel imagines a scenario where anti-precarity solidarity is possible, it must be acknowledged that none of the pieces to this plot are unimaginable or unattainable in the present. Rather, the novel is speculative in the way Le Guin describes her utopian fiction: it confronts us with a clear sense that if utopia – or, in more modest terms, radical social change – is ever to happen, its conditions are not inventions of the future but artefacts in the present. The text therefore imposes a sense of the present precarity crisis, one that climate change and neoliberalism together accelerate, even as it is set in the distant future.

Demarcating common ground within the context of the narrative, Robinson's speculative writing also invites readers to extend this sense of solidarity outside the narrative and into the real world. As Mutt's declaration above makes clear, *New York 2140* is committed to an understanding of the social that eschews any emphasis on individual actors – great leaders whose singular vision changes history – and instead focuses on assemblages (in the Deleuzian tradition) or actor-networks (in the Latourian one) that together, as equal co-agents, make things happen.[7] In other words, Robinson's novel is less interested in individual character development than in generating a picture of the social itself and the agents for social change.[8] One of the pleasures for readers of the genre is to become immersed in new social systems – as Suvin has explained, ones that are both like and unlike our own – and to learn via this immersion more about the various conventions and implicit rules that shape their own society. Having done so, readers might be better equipped to change these rules.

Working within this generic framework, Robinson promotes an understanding of social organization that is both inclusive in scale and amenable to radical action in the present. In response to Mutt's declaration that 'we have all the right players here to change the world', other characters in the novel clarify his comments by amplifying the inclusivity of the 'we' in his statement. As Charlotte, one of the novel's main characters, explains, 'there's something like two hundred major coastal cities, all just as drowned as New York [. . .] We all want justice and revenge' (400). The Met building and its inhabitants are just one example of countless others in New York and, more generally, the entire world. As noted earlier, Charlotte's call for 'justice and revenge' is not wishful thinking; it marks a moment when the precariat actually comes together to make progressive changes to the country. The novel's concluding pages thus note the passage of progressive legislation that addresses precarity by, among other things, taxing capital assets (a 'Piketty tax') and restricting capital flight by way of punitive taxation (602). If this recollection of the events in *New York 2140* gives short shrift to plot, it is because the novel itself is at pains to avoid any simplified explanation of what, precisely, makes things go right for the precariat this time around. The denizens of the intertidal had become 'radicalized by their experiences', the narrative notes (145). But then again, as it explains elsewhere, 'wherever there is a commons, there is enclosure' (210). The conditions for radical action in the novel are not new – at least, not in its essential depiction of capitalism and inequality – and yet, this time, change does come.

To return to the questions from the preceding pages, why does radical change happen in the year 2140, and why not now? For Robinson's part, these are precisely the questions we should be asking, since they emphasize the fundamental feasibility of precariat solidarity and radical action today. A character known as 'citizen', a meta-narrator within the text, makes this last point emphatically clear. Reflecting on the events of the novel, the citizen remarks that 'individuals, groups, civilization, and the planet itself all did these things, in actor networks of all kinds. Remember not to forget, if your head has not already exploded, the nonhuman actors in these actor networks' (603). In short, Robinson embeds a fundamentally flattened ontology in his narrative, to adapt the phrase from Manuel DeLanda,[9] made up of unique individuals that are fundamentally precarious in their status (51). The hyper-local geographic setting of New York City grounds the narrative in a space where individuals can come together for a common purpose, but this setting does not presume that it – or any specific character within this space – is more valuable than others in effective social action. As the citizen character puts it, the social is 'always more than what you see, bigger than what you know' (603).

The citizen's declaration also casts into relief not only Robinson's presentation of precarity but also the novel's own role in resisting precarization. This last point should not be oversimplified. The novel's depiction of a humming New York City is not meant to argue that humanity's adaptability or inventiveness will effectively save us from climate change's worst effects. Nor does it imply that, because precariousness is a fundamental aspect of social life, we should accept insecurity or structural violence as unavoidable by-products of our vulnerability. Rather, as Gerry Canavan explains, Robinson's novel encourages us to think of utopia as a project for the now, albeit one that has historically been suppressed by our own inability to take the seeds of utopian thinking to fruition. *New York 2140*, Canavan concludes, 'simply imagines people who are just like us, except they chose to seize hold of utopia, together, in their shared moment of danger' (Canavan). In other words, we need not observe the dramatic destruction in the text in order to appreciate how capitalism can accelerate and then weaponize the basic insecurity that characterizes – albeit to different degrees – all of our lives. Instead, the novel asks us to see in the SuperVenice scenario the 'shared moment of danger' in our present and to build on this acknowledgement a productive solidarity among the precariat.

The inhabitable now

It bears repeating that the utopian project in the novel is far from a fantasy scenario, but rather one that is applicable today in response to contemporary conditions of precarization. Indeed, finding time in common, as Robinson's narrative has done, is also critical in Standing's own platform for combating precarity. For instance, a key platform in his proposed agenda for combating precarity and empowering the precariat involves a universal basic income (*New* 171). In this case, Standing is referring to the time crunches associated with and exacerbating precarious employment: we see declining returns on our labour, so we must work more short-term or insecure jobs, which then prevent us from taking time to plan ahead and acquire more stable work (*New* 178). Standing relates this scenario to the idea of the 'precarity trap', a closed loop that prevents members of the precariat from reflecting or taking time in the present to find more stable outlets for their labour. Consequently, inequality in control over one's time is growing alongside the wealth inequality gap. In response to these developments, Standing calls for a better politics of time, one that frames time inequality as a matter suitable for regulatory policy and finds 'the language to do so' ('Tertiary Time' 19). Robinson's text demonstrates at least some of the ways speculative fiction, in its imaginative presentation of precarity running across the past, present and future, already helps delineate viable literary methods for promoting a politics of time.

Reclaiming time is elsewhere an important component to producing precariat solidarity. As Standing further notes, the drive to expand profits at any cost is responsible for precarization and also for global climate change. As this chapter has argued, precarity and climate change are twin phenomena that both involve the unequal distribution of harm: the small percentage of the population that reaps the greatest profits from the economy are also the least likely to experience the brunt of climate collapse so long as they 'can retreat to their islands in clear blue sea and their mountain retreats' (*New* 179). As in the case of the precarity trap, time appears to be on their side. Of course, both time and space need not be so unevenly distributed as to contribute to greater inequality, especially in the face of the common threat posed by catastrophic climate collapse. As *New York 2140* demonstrates, imagining solidarity among the precariat involves reclaiming time as a well as spaces in common. The intertidal zones are one example of how this common space becomes literal in the novel. To different degrees, both Standing and Robinson argue that occupying space in common will not alone generate better solidarity so long as time itself is an unequal commodity. To seize hold of utopia now, as Canavan claims, grounds otherwise disparate groups in the present and, in doing so, acknowledges their shared commitments not only to each other but also to the world they share in common against shared threats.[10]

Reading speculative fiction alongside theorists of precarity clarifies how temporality – especially in how one relates not only to the present but to the past and future – drives internal divisions within the precariat. As these sources argue, to recognize insecurity in one's neighbours as well as in oneself is a necessary, but not sufficient, condition for sparking solidarity. Rather, we must recognize this condition as fundamentally shared in a manner that affirms our mutual embeddedness in the same time and place. Le Guin's utopian concept of the habitable present is useful to this end, because it emphasizes the role that speculative fiction plays in bringing shared vulnerability into clearer view and places theorists like Lorey and Butler in dialogue with authors like Robinson. For Robinson as well as Le Guin, this utopian project can take place now because the actors, so to speak, are already assembled. Robinson's gambit ultimately lies in connecting worldwide, structural problems like climate change and precarization to the demarcated space of New York City in general and the community in the Met Tower in particular. If this specific setting limits the novel's capacity to represent the true breadth and diversity of the precariat, it nonetheless provides a striking example of what reclaiming both space and time together might look like. Charlotte and her allies in the Tower are, the text reminds us, just a few facets of larger collective action that is 'always more than what you see, bigger than what you know' (603). Ultimately, speculative fiction like Robinson's connects events over the span of centuries and collects people in specific spaces. In doing so, it helps to theorize precarity by reiterating the shared moment of danger that connects the present to the past and the future – and it resists precarization by encouraging us to imagine what a more habitable present might look like here and now.

Notes

1   In his *New Yorker* piece, Tim Kreider describes Robinson as 'one of the greatest living science-fiction writers' (Kreider). In their overview of climate change literature, Trexler and Johns-Putra note that Robinson is currently 'science fiction's most

important writer to deal explicitly with the problem of climate change' (Trexler and Johns-Putra 187).

2 There are numerous writings on the semantic distinctions between science fiction as opposed to speculative fiction. Margaret Atwood, for instance, argues that science fiction denotes stories involving technology, settings and subjects that are inaccessible in the present, whereas speculative fiction 'employs the means already more or less to hand, and takes place on Planet Earth' (Atwood 513). But this separation of the two terms has been subject to considerable critique as well, as P.L. Thomas explains in his introduction to *Science Fiction and Speculative Fiction*. In this chapter, I use 'speculative fiction' as an umbrella term to encompass all manner of future-looking speculative writing, such as science fiction, climate fiction (cli-fi) and utopian fiction. As *New York 2140* further demonstrates, elements of several generic categories exist in a single speculative narrative.

3 See, for example, studies in precarity literature from Liam Connell and Jennifer Lawn. I have elsewhere emphasized speculative fiction's relevancy to theoretical debates about precarity in 'The Politics of Precarity in William Gibson's Bridge Trilogy'.

4 Robinson was a student of Le Guin's and has since cited her direct influence on his own writing. See his article in *Scientific American* for more on this subject.

5 One may object to my linking of Le Guin's utopian imaginary to any relatively pragmatic political program. On this point, I agree with Ellen M. Rigsby, who addresses this same objection in her essay on Le Guin: 'It does not follow that one must abstain from talk about politics because one is trying to describe a way of governing in which the state has been abolished. Nor does it follow that a system must be wrung from the text for it to describe a politics' (168).

6 Different sources have elaborated upon the specific temporal dimensions to precarization along these lines. The most prominent account of precarity's unfolding violence in the context of neoliberalism is Lauren Berlant's 'slow death', which she develops in *Cruel Optimism*. Rob Nixon addresses the difficult task of addressing the long-term, geological temporality of climate change in *Slow Violence*.

7 See Müller and Schurr for a thorough overview of where these theoretical terms overlap and where they diverge. As they explain, both ANT and assemblage thinking 'have a relational view of the world, in which action results from linking together initially disparate elements' (217). At the same time, a key difference for social theoreticians lies in ANT's focus on 'the metaphysics of presence' as opposed to assemblage thinking's emphasis on 'a metaphysics of potentialities' (Müller and Schurr 219–20). To be sure, when *New York 2140* refers to the actor-network, it is less concerned with these distinctions and more with the fundamental sense that change occurs as the result of both human and non-human agents acting together.

8 Mark Jerng's account of genre literature in *Racial Worldmaking* stresses that this drive to think schematically about society is a defining feature of science fiction and speculative narratives (15).

9 Robinson's presentation of flat ontology appears elsewhere in his work. See Wark and Bryant for accounts of this philosophy in Robinson's *Mars Trilogy*, a series of novels published in the 1990s.

10 In *Down to Earth*, Bruno Latour discusses the paramount importance of articulating a world that is common to all in response to climate change denialism. His writings supplement the account of Standing and Robinson offered here by showcasing how the wealthiest class, which at once funds polluting industries while also planning personal escape routes from climate change, has essentially abandoned any pretense of residing on the same planet as the rest of the world's population.

Works cited

Atwood, Margaret. 'The Handmaid's Tale and Oryx and Crake in Context'. *PMLA*, vol. 119, no. 3, 2004, pp. 513-17.
Berlant, Lauren. *Cruel Optimism*. Duke University Press, 2011.
Bryant, Levi R. 'Flat Ontology and Flat Ethics'. *Larval Subjects*, 27 June 2010, https://larvalsubjects.wordpress.com/2010/06/27/flat-ontology-and-flat-ethics/.
Butler, Judith. *Frames of War: When Is Life Grievable?* Verso, 2009.
Canavan, Gerry. 'Utopia in the Time of Trump'. *Los Angeles Review of Books*, 11 March 2017, https://lareviewofbooks.org/article/utopia-in-the-time-of-trump/.
Connell, Liam. *Precarious Labour and the Contemporary Novel*. Palgrave Macmillan, 2017.
Davis, Mike. *City of Quartz : Excavating the Future in Los Angeles*. Verso, 1990.
DeLanda, Manuel. *Intensive Science and Virtual Philosophy*. Bloomsbury, 2005.
Harvey, David. 'The Future of the Commons'. *Radical History Review*, no. 109, Winter 2011, pp. 101-7.
Jerng, Mark. *Racial Worldmaking: The Power of Popular Fiction*. Fordham University Press, 2018.
Kreider, Tim. 'Our Greatest Political Novelist?' *The New Yorker*, 12 December 2013, https://www.newyorker.com/books/page-turner/our-greatest-political-novelist
Latour, Bruno. *Down to Earth: Politics in the New Climatic Regime*. Translated by Catherine Porter. Polity Press, 2018.
Lawn, Jennifer. 'Precarity: A Short Literary History, from Colonial Slum to Cosmopolitan Precariat'. *Interventions*, vol. 19, no. 7, 2017, pp. 1026-40.
Le Guin, Ursula K. 'A Non-Euclidean View of California as a Cold Place to Be'. *Dancing at the Edge of the World: Thoughts on Words, Women, Places*. Grove Press, 1989, pp. 80-100.
LeMenager, Stephanie. 'Climate Change and the Struggle for Genre'. *Anthropocene Reading: Literary History in Geologic Times*, edited by Tobias Menely and Jesse O. Taylor. The Pennsylvania State University Press, 2017, pp. 220-38.
Lorey, Isabell. *State of Insecurity: Government of the Precarious*. Verso, 2015.
Moylan, Tom. *Scraps of the Untained Sky: Science Fiction, Utopia, Dystopia*. Westview, 2000.
Müller, Martin and Carolin Schurr. 'Assemblage Thinking and Actor-Network Theory: Conjunctions, Disjunctions, Cross-Fertilisations'. *Transactions of the Institute of British Geographers*, vol. 41, no. 3, pp. 217-29.
Nixon, Rob. *Slow Violence and the Environmentalism of the Poor*. Harvard University Press, 2011.
Rigsby, Ellen M. 'Time and the Measure of the Political Animal'. *The New Utopian Politics of Ursula K. Le Guin's the Dispossessed*, edited by Laurence Davis and Peter Stillman. Lexington Books, 2005, pp. 167-80.
Robinson, Kim Stanley. *New York 2140*. Orbit, 2017.
Robinson, Kim Stanley. 'Ursula K. Le Guin, 1929-2018'. *Scientific American*, 25 January 2018, https://blogs.scientificamerican.com/observations/ursula-k-le-guin-1929-2018/.
Sheldon, Rebekah. 'After America'. *The Cambridge Companion to American Science Fiction*, edited by Gerry Canavan and Eric Carl Link. Cambridge University Press, 2015, pp. 206-19.
Stableford, Brian M. 'Alienation'. *Science Fact and Science Fiction: An Encyclopedia*. Routledge, 2006, pp. 16-19.
Standing, Guy. 'Tertiary Time: The Precariat's Dilemma'. *Public Culture*, vol. 25, no. 1, 2013, pp. 5-23.

Standing, Guy. 'The Precariat and Class Struggle'. *RCCS Annual Review*, no. 7, 2015, pp. 3–16.
Standing, Guy. *The Precariat: The New Dangerous Class*. Bloomsbury Academic, 2011.
Suvin, Darko. *Metamorphoses of Science Fiction : On the Poetics and History of a Literary Genre*. Yale University Press, 1979.
Thomas, P. L. 'Introduction: Challenging Science Fiction and Speculative Fiction'. *Science Fiction and Speculative Fiction: Challenging Genres*, edited by P. L. Thomas. Sense Publishers, 2013, pp. 1–14.
Trexler, Adam and Adeline Johns-Putra. 'Climate Change in Literature and Literary Criticism'. *WIREs Climate Change*, no. 2, 2011, pp. 185–200.
Wark, McKenzie. 'Molecular Red: Theory for the Anthropocene (on Alexander Bogdanov and Kim Stanley Robinson)'. *e-flux journal*, vol. 63, March 2015, pp. 1–13.
Williams, Raymond. *Culture and Society 1780–1950*. Penguin, 1985.
Yazell, Bryan. 'The Politics of Precarity in William Gibson's Bridge Trilogy'. *Studies in the Fantastic*, no. 6, 2019, pp. 39–69.

INDEX

Note: Page numbers followed by 'n' refer to notes.

Adan, Elizabeth   13–14
affective class   27–40
affect   1, 6, 14, 16–17, 20, 29–32, 34, 36–7, 39 n.2, 39 n.4, 42–4, 48, 52, 53, 53 n.2, 79, 80, 94, 104, 127, 133, 136–7, 161, 162, 166, 169, 173
  of class   34, 42–54
affective labour   6, 14, 129, 131, 132, 137, 139, 140 n.5, 141 n.7
Allegra, Indira   18, 75–87
Almadhoun, Ghayath   176–86
anger   62–8
anticipation   160–74
antiretrovirals (ARVs)   112–16
anxiety   1, 6, 14, 16, 17, 18, 19, 21, 27–40, 42–54, 60, 169, 173, 178, 180
  as affect of class   43–5
  existential anxiety   45
anxious reading   27–40
aporias   167, 169
'Ashes'   178, 181–3, 185–6
audience   14, 18, 19, 59, 61–4, 66, 67, 102–6
austerity   18, 21, 45, 63, 67, 196

Bateman, Benjamin   11, 13–14
Berlant, Lauren   4, 6, 8, 16, 31, 32, 37, 66, 76, 94, 95, 99, 105, 114–16, 120, 122 n.13, 160–2, 166, 169
Bernes, Jasper   132, 133, 140 n.6
Blackness   7, 75–8, 83–5, 115, 177, 186 n.1
bodily vulnerability   6, 7, 18, 19, 92
Boltanski, Luc   4, 20
Bourdieu, Pierre   3, 5, 6, 58, 59, 66, 160, 162, 174
Brecht, Bertolt   18, 59, 61, 62
Butler, Judith   1, 6–8, 10, 12, 18, 21, 52, 57, 62, 76–9, 83–5, 91, 92, 95, 97, 105, 110, 143, 191, 192, 199

Cameron, Sharon   179, 181
capital   6, 9, 16, 132, 134, 135, 139, 145, 147, 154, 155, 194, 196
Capital   39 n.6
capitalism   17, 20, 27, 28, 30, 38, 42, 43
  industrial capitalism   5, 10, 20, 21, 34, 53 n.1, 129–36, 139, 141 n.6, 153–6, 160, 193
capitalist exploitation   144–6
card system   46–9
Casas-Cortés, Maribel   1, 2, 4, 5
casualization   3, 160, 163, 174
Chiapello, Eve   4, 20
climate change   178, 194, 196, 198, 199
Cobb, Jonathan   44, 45, 48, 49
Commons   189–99
compensation   67, 68, 119
connectedness   91, 94, 99, 100, 102, 103, 106
Connell, Liam   3, 14, 17, 28, 39, 200 n.3
cosmological time   168, 169
Cruel Optimism   31, 66, 68, 93, 94, 115, 116, 118, 119, 122 n.13, 200 n.6
cultural capital   56, 57
cultural forms   11, 15, 163, 164
cultural translation   101, 103, 104
cultures of precarity   11–15
Currie, Mark   160, 167, 168, 177

debt   31–3, 46, 64, 177, 178, 189
de-industrialization   6, 20, 127–41, 146, 149
democracy   109, 111, 112, 119
de/precarization   91–3
'The Details'   178, 183–6
dignity   43–5, 48, 49, 51–3
disappointment   111–12
Driskill, Qwo-Li   80, 86 n.5
Dunkley, Chris   57, 60, 66, 68

economic precarity   151, 153–6
Eight Minutes Idle   32–9
emotions   16, 17, 42, 43, 150, 180
EuroMayDay   1, 4, 5, 94, 177
European Union   4, 91, 95

Fast   179–83
first-person narratives   152, 153
Fisher, Mark   160, 163, 164, 166, 169, 171, 172, 174
Fordism   8, 10, 20, 53 n.1, 92, 109, 128–34, 136, 139, 140 nn.2–3, 141 n.12, 162, 169
Fortress Europe   4, 183, 185
Foucault, Michel   8, 10, 80, 143
fragility   10, 11, 12, 165, 177, 178
Fragkou, Marissa   58, 62
Frames of War: When Is Life Grievable?   8, 77

gambling   43, 49–53
GB84   21, 146, 151–7
'Ghost Strain N'   110–11, 116–21
governmentality   8–10, 19
Graham, Jorie   176–86
grievability   77, 79, 84, 85, 143
Grundrisse   144, 145

Halberstam, Judith/Jack   76, 80
HIV   112–16, 118
Hochschild, Arlie Russell   9, 43, 53 n.4
hummus
    consuming, cultural translation   101–5
    interreligious communion of   98–101

ideology   5, 8, 20, 36, 39 n.7
illness   109–22
imagined sovereignty   18, 75–87
immortality   178, 181, 185, 186
inhabitable now   198–9
insecurity   1–3, 8, 10–12, 14–17, 21, 28, 32, 33, 35, 45, 47, 82, 93, 110, 116, 136, 139, 143, 161, 163, 185, 186 n.6, 190–4, 198, 199
Institute for Precarious Consciousness   17, 42, 53 n.2
intertidal zone   195, 196, 199

Iphigenia in Splott   18, 62–70

Jameson, Frederic   35, 36, 38, 39

Kelman, James   6, 18, 42–54
Keynesianism   8, 28, 38

labour   8, 9, 19, 20, 30, 31, 127, 131–5, 138, 139, 198
    immaterial labour   5, 6, 14, 53 n.5, 129, 131, 132, 139, 140 n.5, 141 n.7
    markets   9, 10, 127, 135–7, 139, 178
La La Land   2, 20, 127–33, 139–40
Lévinas, Emmanuel   14, 78, 91, 92, 105, 143
'Limited Dreamers'   161, 164–6, 174
Lorey, Isabell   4, 8–10, 19, 53, 143, 177, 181, 186, 191, 192, 199

Mackintosh, Anneliese   160–74
Marx, Karl   129, 135, 144–6, 158
Marxism   30, 31, 36, 37, 53 n.3, 53 n.5, 151, 155, 157, 191
Mashigo, Mohale   109–22
Massumi, Brian   16, 30
Maxim Gorki Theatre   98–100, 102, 103
May Day   4, 21, 146, 148–51, 154–7
Mbembe, Achille   78, 81, 84
metonym   19, 110, 111, 116–18, 120
migration   2, 4, 12, 19, 46–7, 57, 91–108, 172, 183, 190
Misplaced Women?   18, 94–8, 105–6
modernism   36, 147–51
Munck, Ronaldo   5, 16, 109, 110, 121

narrative fiction   14, 36, 160, 167
narrative time   160–74
Native Americans   75–85
neoliberalism   8–10, 15–17, 52
    neoliberal economic ideology   8
    neoliberal flexibility   4
New York 2140   21, 189–91, 194–9
Nostalgia   4, 6, 8, 63, 65, 129–31, 136, 139, 140 n.3, 146, 155, 164, 166, 171, 192
Ntshanga, Masande   109–22

Of Precariousness 58, 62
Ostojić, Tanja 19, 94–8, 105
othering 8, 9
Owen, Gary 18, 56–70

Peace, David 21, 146, 148, 149, 151–7
periodization 127–41
Pewny, Katharina 3, 14, 57
poetic time 177, 178, 185, 186
poetry 176–86
political theatre 59–62
post-Fordism 9, 10, 53 n.5, 92, 140 n.3, 163
post-transitional literature 110–12, 115, 121
precariat 189–200
  defining 3–11
The Precariat: The New Dangerous Class 5, 60
precarious aesthetics 94, 105
precarious bodies 91–107, 183
  under attack 105–6
precarious consciousness 17, 42
precarious labour 14, 20, 127–41, 189, 191
Precarious Labour and the Contemporary Novel 14, 28
precarious life 12, 15, 21, 177, 183, 190, 194
Precarious Life 77, 78, 83
precariousness 2, 3, 6–8, 10, 18, 27, 28, 30–2, 34, 35, 91–3, 110, 178, 191, 194
  defining 3–11
  of life 85, 177
  ontological precariousness 21, 143, 144, 148, 151
precarious time 161–4, 166, 169, 170, 173, 174, 178, 191–4
  and culture 163–4
precarious work 19, 31, 92, 94, 97, 178
precarious workers 31, 161, 189
precarity novel 27–40
precarity trap 190, 198, 199
precarization 2, 8, 10–11, 15, 43, 77, 143, 147, 156, 163, 189, 194, 195, 198, 199

production process 130, 131, 144, 145
proletarianization 2, 143–58
  fictions of 146–9
proletarian modernism 21, 144, 146–51, 157
  and *GB84* 151–6

queer 7, 11, 75–6, 79–80, 86 n.3, 101

race 5–7, 9, 16, 18, 47, 81–4, 95, 119, 129–30, 134–7, 140 n.1, 169, 186, 191
Rancière, Jacques 61, 62, 69, 94, 181
The Reactive 110–16, 119–21
reader-response theory 29, 30
realism 14, 28, 34–6, 138, 151, 152
refugees 60, 97, 102, 106, 177, 178, 183, 184, 189, 195
retrospection 160–74
Ricoeur, Paul 166–70
Riley, Boots 129, 135
Robinson, Kim Stanley 21, 189–200
Ronen, Yael 98–101
Rourke, Lee 160–74

Savage, Mike 27–8, 56–9, 67
science fiction 2, 127, 128, 190, 195
security 1, 4, 5, 7–9, 11, 21, 28, 31, 43, 45–7, 53, 68, 77, 92, 110, 118, 128, 130, 133, 137, 156, 162, 169, 176–86, 190, 192
Sennett, Richard 20, 44, 45, 48, 49, 92
The Situation 19, 98–106
social relations 36, 39, 149, 150, 155
society 28, 58, 192
solidarity 5, 6, 21, 29, 31, 32, 34–6, 39, 44, 48, 50, 52, 53, 53 nn.3–4, 54 n.10, 59, 65, 68, 91, 93, 94, 105, 106, 135, 139, 153, 173, 189–94, 196–9
Sommerfield, John 21, 146, 149–51
Sorry to Bother You 127–9, 135–40
South Africa 109, 110, 112–14, 116, 117, 120, 121
sovereignty 78, 79, 82, 84, 85
speculative fiction 46, 53, 84, 85, 189–200
standard employment relationship 1

Standing, Guy   1, 4, 5, 6, 16, 19, 21, 31, 42, 46, 53 n.6, 57–9, 66, 69, 70, 77, 94, 135, 156, 158 n.9, 161, 190–3, 196, 198, 199, 200 n.10
status anxiety   43–5, 48
strike   21, 133, 138, 146, 149, 151–6
substanceless subjectivity   2, 143–58

theatre   60, 69, 91, 102
theatre makers   93, 104
theatre of the precariat   59–62
theatrical performance labour   14
Thorne, Matt   32, 34, 35, 38
Tsing, Anna   160, 162, 164, 166, 169
Tyler, Imogen   58, 63, 66, 69

United Kingdom   8, 61, 62
United States   8, 12, 46, 75, 77, 78, 82–4, 130, 131, 134
utopia   193, 196, 198, 199

violence   65, 76, 77, 79–82, 84, 85, 143, 195
Vulgar Things   161, 169–74
vulnerability   1, 2, 6, 7, 8, 10–12, 14–15, 18, 19, 22, 27–9, 32–3, 35, 45, 52, 57, 60, 62, 68–9, 77, 83, 91–3, 95, 97, 105–6, 110, 113, 121, 143, 150, 157, 189, 191, 193, 195, 198, 199

Weeks, Kathi   9, 132
whiteness   7, 10, 21, 59, 76, 82–3, 93, 115, 122 n.11, 130, 133, 136–8, 141 n.12, 185
Williams, Raymond   147–9, 150, 191, 192, 194
women   6, 7, 9, 10, 75, 76, 80, 97, 98, 164, 165, 172, 173
Woolf, Virginia   58, 148–51
workers   3, 5, 8, 19, 43, 131–3, 136, 138, 139, 146, 150, 153, 161, 173, 177
working class   6, 44, 52, 58, 59, 61, 156, 157
working-class life   42, 49, 50
working-class speculative fiction   18, 45–7
Woven Account   18, 75–6, 79–85

You Have to be Careful in the Land of the Free   6, 18, 43, 45–53

Žižek, Slavoj   144–5

www.ingramcontent.com/pod-product-compliance
Lightning Source LLC
Chambersburg PA
CBHW072235290426
44111CB00012B/2104